CW01306792

FRENCH COMPLETE COURSE

THIS BOOK INCLUDES:

VOCABULARY AND GRAMMAR, COMMON PHRASES AND SHORT STORIES

THE BEST GUIDE FOR BEGINNERS TO LEARN AND SPEAK FRENCH LANGUAGE FAST AND EASY

PAUL BONNET

Table of Contents

FRENCH VOCABULARY AND GRAMMAR

FRENCH COMMON PHRASES

FRENCH SHORT STORIES

FRENCH VOCABULARY AND GRAMMAR

LEARN THE BASICS OF THE FRENCH LANGUAGE AND DISCOVER HOW TO BUILD COMMON PHRASES WITH PRINCIPAL VERBS AND BASIC RULES

PAUL BONNET

Introduction

The French language is one of the most widespread languages in terms of its presence around the world. It is the only language that can be found to be used commonly in every single continent. You may or may not be aware of the fact that French is derived from Latin, along with many other languages that it is similar to such as Spanish and Italian. If you already have some knowledge of Spanish or Italian, then learning French could be quite a breeze for you.

Many languages change over time as different dialects and forms come into practice simply because of time passing and people changing. The interesting thing about the French language though is that there is a governing body whose main mission is to keep and protect the French language as close to its origin as possible in terms of word additions and changes to things like grammar or sentence structure. There are many changes proposed and rejected by this governing body in an effort to maintain its integrity to the past. This is different from the English language as many new words are being added to the dictionary all the time as societies grow, change and develop.

The French language and its prominence are growing rapidly as many of the countries where French is a primary language are developing countries and thus they are growing and changing. What this means for the French language is that it is also growing and becoming more widespread as these countries develop.

Why Should You Learn the French Language?

Employment

Learning any additional language is beneficial when it comes to employment. You can earn more money for being able to speak multiple languages, as it will be beneficial for companies to have employees that are able to speak multiple languages. If you are able to help customers or clients or even other coworkers by using your second language skills, this makes you a huge asset for employers!

The French language is also quite a prominent language when it comes to business relations around the world. As you may be aware, English is the number one language for international business, mandarin is the second and third is French! What this means is that whether or not you are a business worker, you will be very likely to come across the French language in your workplace at one time or another and knowing the language will be very beneficial for you in your career and for your status within your company.

If you own your own business, knowing other languages is extremely beneficial when it comes to sales and marketing. You want to reach as large an audience as possible and if you have the skills to speak in more than one language this will be much easier. With the advent of technology and the wealth of online sales marketplaces, being able to write product descriptions, emails or have telephone conversations in French will benefit you immensely.

People all over the world are beginning to see the value in learning the French language and its education is being added to many curriculums all over the world. Getting ahead of this now and making yourself a valuable asset internationally will allow you to make your mark in society. You will be able to combine travel with work in order to have a greater wealth of job options and with that, a greater wealth of options for places to live. This brings me to our next topic which is travel.

Knowing another language will make you able to make more money in the workplace since you will be a valuable asset to whatever company you work for. You will be able to make yourself worth more in terms of income in addition to being wanted by more companies and for more job positions than ever before.

Travel

French is the only language that is used in every continent, it is such a beneficial language to learn. When you are travelling the chances that you will come across French speaking people who may be working, travelling or needing assistance of some sort are very high.

If you are specifically interested in French speaking places such as France, Canada, Switzerland or any others then coming across French people will be a daily occurrence. Being able to communicate with people in their native language, especially when you are a guest of their country will make them feel happy and in turn, they will be much more likely to welcome you with open arms. Not to mention that ordering food, understanding a menu, asking for directions, checking into hotels, trying to take transit and many more things will be made easier if you have knowledge of the native language of the country you are visiting. It will make for much less headache and will erase the need for a clunky translation app on your phone that may have spotty service.

Travelling Confidence is another key benefit. Knowing another language, no matter where you are travelling to will give you added confidence while you are on the road. Even if you are not travelling to a country where the primary or secondary language is French, you will likely come across French speakers just because of the widespread nature of the language. Also because of the widespread nature of the language, it is likely that other travelers you will come across will be French speakers and getting to know them or finding travel friends will be much easier and much more likely if you can speak their language. You won't have to rely on other people's ability to speak your language if you have an entire second language in your arsenal.

You will have a much broader choice of travel destinations as you will not have to stick to the main cities where there is more chance of finding English speakers. You will have the freedom to travel to less tourist-filled destinations and even to stay in places with no English at all.

Arts and Culture

When it comes to arts and culture, French is quite prominent in terms of literature, film and visual arts. Many visual artists hail from French speaking countries in Europe. If you are interested in the arts, you may be very interested in French artists specifically. These artists will create their art in their native language and if you are not a French speaker, you will have to turn to the translated works. Just like when books become movies, the original is usually quite a bit better than the adaptation. The relevance here is that by knowing how to understand and read in French, you will be able to watch the original French films and read the original French books. You will be able to experience these things exactly as they were created and intended to be consumed. This will give you the most authentic experience of these artists' work possible, and as an arts and culture connoisseur or even just a fan, that will be quite an amazing experience.

When you are just beginning, you can watch the films with English subtitles or read the book with the translated version on hand as well, but when you become more and more comfortable with your knowledge and comprehension of the language, you will be able to leave those English aids aside and really truly experience these art forms fully in French.

The French language will be very beneficial for anyone looking to add another language to their list of skills and talents. French will improve your life in many more ways than just employment, culture and money it will also expand your world in general. Opening you up to new experiences, new challenges and new views of the world. Languages help you to see the world from new points of view and knowing an additional language will only bring positives to your life.

Anytime Is the Right Time

While you may think that it is too late to learn a new language, or that you may be too old to pick up an entire new vocabulary, this is far from the truth! Anytime is the right time to learn a new language, the important thing is taking the first steps. You have already taken the first steps by beginning to read this book!

While many people learn a second languages as children, our brains are still able to pick up new languages as we age. When we are children, we do not fully realize the importance of the second or even third languages that we are learning, we may find it tedious and boring- but as adults we fully realize the benefits of learning a new language and the expansion that it will bring to our mind and our life. Because of this, as adults we tend to be more dedicated, more eager to learn and more likely to put in the practice it takes to become good at a new language. There is no such thing as too old to learn, ans because you have brought yourself here, you are already clearly motivated to learn!

Teach Your Children

If you can learn a new language, you will be able to teach your children this new language too. The brains of children are like little sponges, ready to learn and take in new information every day. If you develop the French language skills for yourself, you will be able to read to your children in French, speak to them in French, sing to them in French and while you are doing this, their brains won't be able to help but pick up some of the language. This will put them at an advantage when they go to school and may enter a French class, as they will already have developed that foundation in the language.

When you travel with your children, if they know the language, you will have a much more enjoyable trip just by watching them read the menu to you or take in the new accents and words in awe. You will feel rewarded because you will have exposed them to the language early in life and you will then be able to see it pay off before your eyes.

Children who speak multiple languages tend to do better in school, they have better memory and attention and they have more opportunities and a bright future ahead of them. If your child already knows two languages, adding a third will be very easy for them as they already have the skills to be able to switch between languages in their brain and the skills to develop new accents.

Teaching your child a new language will not only open up a world of possibilities for them as they grow, but it will be a bonding experience for the two of you as you take on the journey of language together. That is an experience that not everyone gets to have with their child, and it is an extremely rewarding one.

An Overview of The French Language

Learning the French language would be beneficial to anyone who wants to give themselves an edge in their life in terms of work, travel and interests. With this in mind, we will now look a little bit deeper into the French language and what you can expect from it through the rest of this book and beyond as you enter the world of a new language.

The French language is full of many small changes that make big differences to the words they are put with. We will examine in depth these small differences between the different forms of the same word that you will begin to see as you enter the world of French speaking, reading and writing. There are prefixes and suffixes that are added or changed in order to change a word from present to past to future tense. There are prefixes that you add in order to put two vowels side-by-side without having it all jumbled up in your mouth as you try to speak the words. There are small changes you can make to a sentence to take it from a friendly and casual way of speaking to a formal and respectful one. The way these small changes have big impacts on the words and sentences is what makes the French language so interesting to learn and to use. It can also be what makes it difficult, but as soon as you learn the rules-like with anything else, you will be well-equipped to take on anything French.

When comparing the French language to the English language, a large difference to note is that while the meaning of a sentence in the English language can be gleaned primarily by examining the order of the words, in French understanding the meaning of a sentence is reliant on punctuation, prefixes and suffixes. This is especially true when trying to determine whether a sentence is a question or a statement. In English, you can tell this by the order in which the words are written, while in French, forgetting a question mark will turn a sentence from a question to a regular statement.

Another comparison that can be made is that French and English are quite similar languages in terms of the amount of similar words that can be found. These words are mostly technical in nature such as science and mathematics terms as well as terms relating to politics. This makes the learning process simpler than it would be for some other languages for the native English speaker. This is in large part because you will not have to spend a large amount of time memorizing too many terms that can come into play as you get further into your knowledge of the language. Many terms may be quite similar if not the same between both languages.

There is a specific etiquette that is used when writing formal letters or when speaking on the phone in the French language. This can become confusing for native English speakers as there are not as many nuances in the English language. The benefit though, as mentioned above is that there will be many terms that you will already understand which will make learning the etiquette that much easier.

You may not know this but there are places in the United States where French is spoken and is actually a first language of some people. Though, you may not be able to recognize it as French because it sounds quite different-there are different dialects of French spoken all over the world. This is like English where people from Australia, England and the southern states in the United States all have very different accents and many different words that are used between them. Even as a native English speaker, going from one part of the world to another you may hear things that you do not recognize. This is the same way in the united states where French is spoken. In Louisiana, North Dakota, Vermont Maine, Missouri, Massachusetts and Michigan there are regions where French is spoken. This may come as a surprise to you, but it is true! Even all over France you can find different accents and dialects, so from region to region you will notice differences.

If you travel the world as you are learning French or after you learn French, you may have trouble understanding accents and expressions in some places. Try to approach this with an open mind and get ready to learn more than you ever thought possible about the French language. Even as you travel, you may be in some parts of the world where you would never have expected to encounter the French language, but you may actually hear it used. As you travel, keep your ears open and your eyes open for the French language. You may just surprise some people who thought they would not find French speaking tourists!

Chapter 1 - Pronunciation

We are going to explore the alphabet and how to pronounce it, as well as some common pairings of letters that you will come across quite often and their pronunciations. This chapter will get you set up nicely for the rest of this book, where you will learn useful phrases and words.

The Alphabet

The first topic of discussion is the alphabet. The French alphabet is the same as the English language alphabet. If you are a native English speaker, it will be easier to learn French than it would be to learn a language like Russian or Mandarin Chinese, as these use symbols that you would have to learn from scratch. Because of this, you are already beginning part of the way through by knowing the alphabet!

This alphabet used in French, English and a variety of other languages, comes from the Latin alphabet. There are 26 letters in total, each with an uppercase and a lowercase form.

Though the alphabet used in French is the same as that used in English, the pronunciation of some of the letters is quite different. The twenty-six letters are below, with the accompanying pronunciation in brackets beside them;

A (ah)

B (bay)

C (say)

D (day)

E (euh)

F (ef)

G (jh-ay)

H (ash)

I (ee)

J (jh-ee)

K (kah)

L (el)

M (em)

N (en)

O (oh)

P (pay)

Q (koo)

R (err(roll the r))

S (ess)

T (tay)

U (ooh)

V (vay)

W (doo-bl-uh-vey)

X (ee-ks)

Y (ee-greck(roll the r))

Z (zed).

As you can see, here are a few letters whose pronunciations remain the same, like the following letters: f,l,m,n,o, and s. All of the other letters, however, will have new pronunciations.

Common Letter Pairings And Their Pronunciations

As you know from speaking English, the pronunciation of the letters of the alphabet will change when placed together with other letters. We will look at the most common cases, the ones that you will come across most commonly. Practice pronouncing these sounds aloud, just like you did for the letters of the alphabet above.

Ai [eh]

Au [oh]

Eau [oh]

Eu [uh]

Ei [eh]

In [eh]

Ien [yeh]

O [oh]

Ou [oo]

On [aw]

Om [aw]

Oi [wah]

Un [eh]

Ch [sh]

As you can see, sometimes different sets of letter combinations will produce the same sounds as each other, such as *on* and *om*, but you will see both just as often as each other in words. Further, some of these letter combinations and the sounds they produce are different from how they would sound in English, and some of them may not even exist in the English language.

Examples In Words

An example of the above combinations at work in a word is the word *Chaud* (*hot*). This word may seem like it would be pronounced like [sh-ah-ooh-day], according to the sounds of the letters themselves, but when the letters *a* and *u* are placed together in French, it is actually pronounced as [oh], as you can see in the list above. Therefore, the word *chaud* is pronounced *chaud [sh-o-d]*.

Voiture (car) may seem like it would be pronounced as [v-oh-ee-t-uh-r], but in fact, due to the letters *oi* being placed next to each other in this word, they are pronounced as a [wah] sound. Therefore, *voiture* is pronounced [v-wah-t-oo-r]

The Letter *S*

In French, the sound that an *s* makes will often change when it is placed beside a vowel. The example below demonstrates this.

Nous Avons

This phrase means *We have*.

Separately, these two words would be *nous* [new] and *avons* [ah-voh], but when they are together in a phrase, the combination of the *s* at the end of *nous* with the *a* at the beginning of *avons*, changes their pronunciation. This combination of the *s* and *a* makes them come together to form the *z* sound. So now, we would actually say it like this, *nous avons* [new-z-ah-voh]. The *s* that was silent in the word *nous* now comes out but in a different sound.

Keep this rule in mind whenever you see an *s* next to a vowel. It is less important when you are speaking slowly and saying only a few words at a time, but it is helpful to know when you are listening to someone else speak French, especially if it is a fluent and native French speaker. You will likely often hear the *z* sound and be wondering what word they said that had this letter in it. Knowing this rule, you will be able to determine that they were actually saying two words together and that the first one likely ended with the letter *s*, and the second began with a vowel. Understanding words like this will help you to understand native speakers and things like French films, and it will also help you to develop a good French accent of your own.

Another case where we can see this is in the following sets of words;

Vous Avez and *Vous Êtes*

These mean "you guys have" and "you guys are." The verb *Avez* means "to have," and the verb *Etre* means "you guys are."

How Pronunciation Affects Sentence Meaning

In some cases, the emphasis of the pronunciation differences that combinations of letters produce is very important to the meaning of your sentence. Below are two different statements that mean different things, and if we did not change our pronunciation of the words in the first example, (the one with an *s* and a vowel next to each other) like explained above, then we would be confusing people with what we were trying to say. You can see how this is the case below;

Ils Ont they have*[eel-z-oh]*

Vs.

Ils Sont they are *[eel][s-oh]*

The first example, *ils ont* means "they have," while the second example, *ils sont* means "they are." The pronunciations of these two are below;

Ils Ont [eel-z-oh]

Vs.

Ils Sont [eel][s-oh]

Notice how the first example would normally be pronounced as *ils ont [eel][oh],* but since we have the letter s next to a vowel, we would actually say *ils ont [eel-z-oh].* Without making this difference in sound that is caused by the s and the *o,* the person you are speaking to could have trouble determining which of these two statements you are saying. This could confuse the entire meaning of your sentence. Without the *z* sound, these two statements sound very similar to each other.

French Accents

We will look at the different types of accents that you will see above or below letters in French. You have likely seen this before when looking at French words, such as two dots over the letter *e*. We are going to look at all of the different types of accents and how they change the pronunciation of the letters that they are placed on.

The letter *e* is the most commonly used character in the entire French language. You will come across the letter *e* more than any other letter in the entire language. When it comes to the letter *e*, can be pronounced a lot of different ways. When you see an *e* with no accent, you sometimes wonder how it is pronounced, and you can look to the letters before and after it to get some clues. There is one way to find out exactly how to pronounce the letter *e*. If you see an accent over top of it, this will tell you exactly how to pronounce it, and there will be no more wondering. You can also find accents under or over top of the letters c, a, i, u, and o. These accents will change the sound of the letter in specific ways.

The Cédille (Ç)

The cédille is an accent that you see below the letter *c*. This accent will change the way the letter is pronounced. This makes it sound more like an *s*. You will only find the cedille with the letter c but not with any other letter. This will only be seen before a vowel, as this will make the s sound right before a vowel like, sa, so, su. For example,

Garçon [g-ah-r-son]

The Accent Aigu (é)

An accent aigu (é) is placed on top of the letter e. This accent will change the way the letter e sounds. It will make it pronounced more nasally. To say this sound, hold your tongue at the bottom of your mouth and keep it still while pronouncing the e sound nasally, and there you have it.

The accent aigu looks like this;

é

For example, the word écrire [ay-k-ree-r], which is a verb that means *to write*.

The Accent Circonflexe (Ê)

This accent is like a hat on top of a letter and can be found on all vowels (except y). It looks like the following;

â

Ê

î

ô

û

This accent doesn't quite change the way the letter sounds, but it changes the speed at which it is said. It makes it so that the letter is pronounced quicker and with more force. For example,

Poîntu [p-wa-n-too], which means pointy

Août [oo-t], which means August

The Accent Grave (È)

This accent can be found on top of an a, an e or an u. It is similar to the accent aigu, but it is in the reverse direction. You can see this below;

À

È

Ù

This accent changes the meaning of two words which are spelled the exact same way. For example,

Ou vs. Où

[oo] vs [oo]

The former means *or* and the latter means *where*.

La vs. Là

[lah] vs. [lah]

The former means *the* and the latter means *there.*

A vs. À

[ah] vs [ah]

The former means *have,* and the latter means *at* or *to.*

The Accent Tréma (Ë)

This accent is two small dots above the letter e, i, or u. This accent is used to show that the letter is on top of, and the letter immediately after it in a word is to be pronounced separately. Think of the word Noël [noh-el], which means Christmas. This separates the o sound from the e sound. Below you can see the accent on the three letters it can be found with;

Ë

Ï

Ü

The name Chloë is an example of this

As well as the word Jamaïque [jah-mah-ee-k] which is the French way of saying Jamaica.

Chapter 2 - Genders, Plurals, And Their Articles

Genders

Lesson Reminder:

Here we will be taking a look at feminine and masculine nouns. There are nouns that can be switched from one gender to another. But in this lesson, we will only be reviewing the nouns that take on one specific gender only.

Masculine: you can tell that a noun is masculine if it has one of the following endings:

- **"-ment"**: for example: un bâtiment (a building). Be careful not to confuse these words with adverbs as they almost always end with "-ment", you will get used to them with practice.
- **"-isme"**: for example: un séisme (an earthquake).
- **"-al"**: for example: le journal (the newspaper).
- **"-ier"**: for example: le calendrier (the calendar).
- **"-oir"**: for example: le couloir (the corridor).
- **"-age"**: for example: le fromage (the cheese). Exceptions: la page (the page), la plage (the sea), l'image (the image), la rage (the rage).

Feminine: you can tell that a noun is in feminine if it has one of the following endings:

- **"-ure":** for example: une voiture (a car).
- **"-té"**: for example: la fidélité (the loyalty).
- **"-ion"**: for example: une option (an option). Exceptions: un lion (a lion).
- **"-ie"** : for example: la pluie (the rain).

• **"-eur"**: for example: la valeur (the value). Exceptions: le bonheur (happiness), le malheur (the misfortune).

• **"-ée"**: for example: une épée (a sword). Exceptions: le lycée (high school), le musée (the museum).

• **"-ance" or "-ence"**: for example: la tendance (the trend), une urgence (an emergency). Exception: le silence (the silence).

PS: Those aren't definite rules for the genders in French. There may be a few more exceptions to each category.

Exercise: Precise the gender of the following nouns: Male (M) or Female (F).

1. Sortie ((the or an exit): ____

2. Carnaval (carnival): ____

3. Quartier (neighborhood): ____

4. Agence (agency): ____

5. Voyage (trip): ____

6. Soir (evening): ____

7. Fumée (smoke): ____

8. Chevelure (hair, or a lock of hair): ____

Plurals

Lesson Reminder:

Here we will be taking a look at how to transform a noun from its singular form to its plural form.

In general, a lot of words take an "S" at the end to make them plural just like in English. For example: un cahier (a notebook): des cahiers; une porte (a door): des portes.

Words that end with an S, Z, or X in their singular form don't change at all when in plural forms. For example: un tapis (a carpet): des tapis; un quiz (a quiz): des quiz; une croix (a cross): des croix.

Words that end in "-ou" also take an "S" when turned into their plural form. For example: un cou (a neck): des cous; un bisou (a kiss): des bisous.

There are exceptions to this that take an "X" instead of an "S":

- un bijou (a jewel): des bijoux
- un caillou (a pebble): des cailloux
- un chou (cabbage): des choux
- un genou (a knee): des genoux
- un hibou (an owl): des hiboux
- un pou (a louse): des poux (lice)

Words that end in "-ail" also take "S" when turned into their plural form. For example: un détail (a detail): des details; un épouvantail (a scarecrow): des épouvantails.

Exceptions to this take the ending "-aux":

- le corail (coral): les coraux
- le travail (the job): les travaux
- l'émail (enamel): les émaux
- le vitrail (stained glass): les vitraux
- un soupirail (a basement window): des soupiraux

Words that end in "-al" take on the ending "-aux" when turned into their plural form. For example: spécial (special: spéciaux; natal (native or natal): nataux.

Exceptions to this get an "S" added to the word at the end: bal (a dance ball), cal (callus), carnaval (carnival), festival (festival), récital (recital), régal (delight).

Words that end with "-eu", "-au", and "-eau" all take an "X" at the end. For example:

- le milieu (the middle or the environment): les milieux
- le noyau (the core): les noyaux
- un couteau (a knife): des couteaux

Exceptions to this get an "S" added at the end: pneu (tire), bleu (blue), landau (pram), and sarrau (smock).

PS: There are words that are irregular and don't follow any rules. For example: un œil (an eye): des yeux; le ciel (the sky): les cieux.

Exercise 1: Turn the following words to their plural form.

1. Oral (oral): ____________
2. Joyau (jewel): ____________
3. Portail (gate or portal): ____________
4. Oiseau (bird): ____________
5. Flou (blurred, blurry): ____________
6. Nez (nose): ____________
7. Canal (channel): ____________
8. Concours (contest): ____________

Exercise 2: Turn the following words to a singular form.

1. Eaux (waters): ____________
2. Rails (tracks, rails): ____________
3. Stylos (pens): ____________
4. Neveux (nephews): ____________
5. Chandails (sweaters): ____________
6. Clous (nails, pins): ____________

7. Feuilles (papers): ___________

8. Manteaux (coats): ___________

Articles

Lesson Reminder:

“Un” And “Une”:

• **Un**: the masculine version of the English “a” or “an”, it is placed before non-specific nouns or objects. For example: un atelier (a workshop); un mouchoir (tissue or a handkerchief).

• **Une**: the feminine version of the English “a” or “an”, also placed before non-specific nouns and objects. For example: une nuance (a shade); une idée (an idea).

“Le”, “La” And “L’...”:

• **Le**: the masculine version of the English “the”, placed before specific objects and nouns. For example: le cheval (the horse); le lancement (the launching, the start [of a project], or the initiation).

• **La**: the feminine version of the English “the”, also place before specific objects and nouns. For example: la gestion (the management); la fierté (the pride).

• **L’...**: This article is also placed before specific objects and nouns, just like “le” and “la”. The only difference is that it is gender-neutral, and it is placed before nouns that start with a vowel or an “H”. For example: l’allure (the look); l’héroïsme ([the] heroism); l‘énergie (the energy); l’usage (the use).

“Les”: It is pronounced “lé”, it is gender-neutral and is the plural version of “le”, “la” and “l’...”. It is used before defined objects and nouns just like “the”.

“Des”: It is pronounced “dé”, it is gender-neutral and is the plural version of “un” and “une”. It is used before undefined objects and nouns.

Exercise 1: Use the correct gender article before these nouns:

1.________ cruauté (the cruelty).

2.________ avancement (an advancement).

3.________ opinion (the opinion)

4.________ miroir (the mirror).

5.________ lueur (a glow).

6.________ journalisme ((the) journalism).

7.________ acier ((the) steel).

8.________ vengeance (a revenge).

Exercise 2: Transform the following nouns into their plural form then put "les" or "des" before each one of them:

1. Un mal (a pain): ________

2. Le pinceau (the paint brush): ________

3. L'épieu (the spear): ________

4. La souris (the mouse): ________

5. Un iglou (an igloo): ________

6. Le camail (the hackle): ________

7. Une voix (a voice): ________

8. L'os (the bone): ________

Switching Genders

Lesson Reminder:

In all of the following points, the ending mentioned at first will be replaced with the one following it.

Words that end with "-ier" or "-er" take on the endings "-iére" or "-ère": for example: fier (proud): fière; boulanger (baker): boulangère.

Words that end with "-eur" take on the ending "-euse": for example: fumeur (someone who smokes): fumeuse.

Words that end with "-teur" take on the ending "-trice": for example: acteur (actor): actrice (actress).

PS: Be careful not to confuse the previous three categories with the previously learned invariable words that are only masculine or feminine.

Words that end with "-ien" take on the ending "-ienne": for example: quotidien (daily): quotidienne.

Words that end with "-if" take on the ending "-ive": for example: pensif (thoughtful): pensive.

Words that end with "-on" take on the ending "-onne": for example: bouffon (jester): bouffonne.

Words that end with "-x" take on the ending "-se": for example: époux (husband): épouse (wife). Except: doux (soft): douce. Be careful not to confuse this category of words with the plural forms of others.

PS: There are words that are irregular and don't follow any rules. For example: un fou (a crazy person): une folle; sec (dry): sèche; un vieux (an old person): une vielle. You will get used to them with practice.

Exercise 1: Transform the following nouns and adjectives from their masculine form to their feminine form.

1. Un prisonnier (a prisoner): Une ____________

2. Une jaloux (a jealous person): Une ____________

3. Un dépressif (a depressed person): Une __________

4. Un végétarien (a vegetarian person): Une _______

5. Un frimeur (a person who shows off): Une _______

6. Un lion (a lion): Une ____________

7. Un passager (a passenger): Une ___________

8. Un conducteur (a driver): Une ___________

Exercise 2: Transform the following nouns and adjectives from their feminine form to their masculine form.

1. Une politicienne (a politician): Un ___________

2. Une rêveuse (a dreamer): Un ___________

3. Une sorcière (a witch): Un _________ (a wizard)

4. Une bouchère (a butcher): Une ___________

5. Elle est audacieuse (she is bold): Il est __________

6. Une animatrice (a host): Un ___________

7. Une sportive (an athletic person): Un __________

8. Une chatonne (a kitten): Un___________

Exercise 3: Indicate the gender of the following words using M or F then transform them into the opposite one.

1. Policier (police officer): _____: ___________

2. Spectatrice (spectator): _____: ___________

3. Facultatif (optional): _____: ___________

4. Chanceux (lucky): _____: ___________

5. Espionne (spy): _____: ___________

6. Menteur (liar): __________: ___________

7. Chère (expensive or dear): _____: ___________

8. Logisticienne (logistician): _____: ___________

Chapter 3 - Adjectives And Prepositions

Adjectives

Lesson Reminder:

The general rule of adjectives: When using adjectives in French, they have to have the same form as the nouns they are related to. Unlike in English, where the adjective stays the same every time, they change according to the gender of the noun and its quantity (singular or plural).

Examples:

Masculine singular: un petit garçon (a little boy).

Feminine singular: une petit**e** fille (a little girl).

Masculine plural: des petit**s** garçons (little boys).

Feminine plural: des petit**es** filles (little girls).

Types of adjectives: In French, there are two types of adjectives:

The first type is called "**adjectif épithète**". It is placed right before or after the noun it qualifies with nothing separating them. For example: un grand mur (a big wall); une feuille blanche (a white paper).

The second type is called "**adjectif attribut**". It is linked to the noun with the use of a descriptive verb. The verbs that come before "un adjectif attribut" usually are: être (to be), sembler (to seem), paraître (to appear), devenir (to become), rester (to stay), demeurer (to remain), avoir l'air (to look or to look like), passer pour (to pass for).

For example:

- Ses yeux **sont** bleus (his/her eyes **are** blue)

- la chaise **semble** vieille (the chair **seems** old)
- la valise **a l'air** lourde (the suitcase **looks** heavy)

Exercise 1: Mention the gender "M or F" and the quantity "S or P" of the following adjectives.

1. La soupe est chaude. (The soup is hot.): ____ / ____
2. Le film est trop long. (The movie is too long.): ____ / ____
3. Des stylos verts (green pencils): ____ / ____
4. Ces robes sont chères. (These dresses are expensive.): ____ / ____
5. Une belle écriture (beautiful writing): ____ / ____
6. Des rues lumineuses (bright streets): ____ / ____
7. Le restaurant est ouvert. (The restaurant is open.): ____ / ____
8. Je suis heureux. (I am happy.): ____ / ____

Exercise 2: Transform the following adjectives into the mentioned forms.

1. Gentille (kind) F/S: ____________ F/P
2. Douloureux (painful) M/P: ____________ F/P
3. Protectrices (protective) F/P:____________ M/S
4. Mauvais (bad) M/S: ____________F/P
5. Craintifs (fearful) M/P: ____________F/S
6. Dernière (last) F/S: ____________M/P
7. Pluvieux (rainy) M/P: ____________F/S
8. Légères (light) F/P: ____________M/S

Exercise 3: Put "A" for "adjectif attribut" or "E" for "adjectif épithète".

1. Il est adorable. (He is adorable.): ____

2. Un endroit <u>mystérieux</u> (a mysterious place): ____

3. La pièce semble <u>spacieuse</u>. (The room seems spacious.): ____

4. Des réunions <u>importantes</u> (important meetings): ____

5. Tu as l'air <u>anxieuse</u>. (You look anxious.): ____

6. Une réponse <u>fausse</u> (a wrong answer): ____

7. Un voyage <u>fatigant</u> (a tiring trip): ____

8. Les dégâts restent <u>considérables</u>. (The damage stays significant.): ____

Prepositions Related To Time 1

Lesson Reminder:

"à" or "au": their literal translation is "at". They're used to indicate the exact hour of an event, before centuries or before the spring season. For example: On se voit **à** 10h. (We'll meet **at** 10 am.); **au** vingtième siècle (**in** the 20th century); **au** printemps (**in** spring).

"de... à..." or "du... au...": their literal translation is "from... to ...". It is used the same way as in English. For example: La réunion est **de** 9h **à** 10h. (The meeting is **from** 9 am **to** 10 am.); L'événement dure **du** Samedi **au** Mercredi. (The event lasts **from** Saturday **to** Wednesday.)

"quand": its literal translation is "when". It is used like in English, to ask questions about time and to indicate an event happening after another. For example: **Quand** est-ce qu'on part ? (**When** are we leaving?); Je t'aiderai **quand** je rentre. (I'll help you **when**I'm back home.)

"après": its literal translation is "after". It is used the same way as in English. For example: Il rentre **après** 20h. (He returns **after** 8 pm.); Le film commence **après** les cours. (The movie starts **after** school.)

"avant": its literal translation is "before". It is used the same way as in English. For example: Il rentre **avant** 20h. (He returns

before 8 pm.); Je prends une douche **avant** de sortir. (I take a shower **before** going out.)

"dans": its literal translation is "in". It is used the same way as in English. For example: Elle arrive **dans** une heure. (She arrives **in** one hour.)

Exercise: Use the right preposition to fill in the blanks.

1)Ranger ta chambre _______ tu finis.

(Clean up your room when you're done.)

2)Mon vol est _______ 1h 30.

(My flight is at 1:30 am.)

3)Tu dois être présent 30 minutes _______ le début.

(You have to be present 30 minutes before the start.)

4)Va voir ta tante _______ le dîner.

(Go see your aunt after dinner.)

5)Les heures de visite sont _______ 11h _______ 15h.

(Visiting hours are from 11 am to 3 pm.)

6)Le train arrive _______ 15 minutes.

(The train will arrive in 15 minutes.)

7)J'adore faire des randonnées _______ printemps.

(I love hiking in spring.)

8)Elles seront occupées _______ Dimanche _______ Jeudi.

(They will be busy from Sunday to Thursday.)

Prepositions Related To Time 2

Lesson Reminder:

"depuis": its literal translation is "since". It is used the same way as in English but also in another form. For example:

depuis 1996 (**since** 1996)

Ils sont là **depuis** 3 heures. (They've been here **for** 3 hours.)

Il pleut **depuis** que nous sommes sortis. (It's been raining **ever since** we went out.)

"dès" or "dès que..." and "à partir de...": their literal translation is "from", but they're used to say "starting from". For example:

Tu seras parti **dès** Lundi. (You will be gone **from** Monday **on**.)

Je serai au bureau **à partir de** 8h. (I'll be at the office **starting from** 8 am.)

"Dès que" is mostly used when something needs to happen, or that has happened immediately after the time frame given, a bit like "as soon as". For example: Appelle moi **dès que** tu arrives. (Call me **as soon as** you get there.) It's one of those expressions that sound more natural in French than when translated.

"en": its literal translation is "in". It is used like in English with months, years and seasons except for spring. For example:

Le criminel a été arrêté **en** Février. (The criminal was arrested **in** February.)

Ce bâtiment a été abandonné **en** 1985. (This building was abandoned **in** 1985.)

La forêt est plus belle **en** automne. (the forest is prettier **in** fall.)

"jusqu'à" or "jusqu'en": their literal translation is "until". It is used the same way as in English, but "jusqu'en" is used before months and years. For example:

La cérémonie continuera **jusqu'à** 19h. (The ceremony will continue **until** 7 pm.)

Mon colis n'arrivera que **jusqu'en** Juin. (my package won't arrive **until** June.)

"pendant": its literal translation is "during". It is used to indicate an event happening for a period of time. For example:

Je serai là **pendant** les vacances. (I'll be here **during** the holidays.)

Je serai là **pendant** 3 mois. (I'll be here **for** 3 months.)

Je cuisinerai **pendant** que tu finisses. (I'll cook **while** you finish.)

Exercise: Use the right preposition to fill in the blanks.

1)Le magasin est ouvert ___________ 20h.

(The store is open until 8 pm.)

2)Tu peux me passer ton cahier ___________ la récréation s'il te plaît ? (Could you pass me your notebook during recess, please?)

3)On part à Tokyo ___________ été.

(We're going to Tokyo in summer.)

4)Ils sont mariés ___________ 5 ans.

(They've been married for 5 years.)

5)Je commence à travailler ___________ Lundi prochain.

(I start working starting from next Monday.)

6)La pièce est devenue silencieuse ___________ le film a commencé.

(The room went silent as soon as the movie started.)

7)Il reste à l'hôpital ___________ Décembre.

(He'll stay at the hospital until December.)

Prepositions Related To Space 1

Lesson Reminder:

"à": its literal translation is "in" or "at". It is used before cities and specific buildings. For example:

Nous nous sommes rencontrés **à** Paris. (We met **in** Paris.)

Je révise **à** la bibliothèque. (I'm studying **at** the library.)

"au" or "aux": their literal translation is "in" or "at". Just like the previous one, but they're used before countries that have masculine names. For example:

Je suis **au** Maroc. (I'm **in** Morocco.)

Il est **aux** États Unis. (He's **in** the United States.)

"à droite" and "sur la droite de": their literal translations are "right" and "on the right side of". They're used just like in English. For example:

Tourner **à droite** (turn **right**)

Sur la droite de mon miroir (**on the right side of** my mirror)

Sometimes "à droite de" is used instead of "sur la droite de", but it's less frequent.

"à gauche" and "sur la gauche de": their literal translations are "left" and "on the left side of". They're used just like in English. For example:

Tourner **à gauche** (turn **left**)

Sur la gauche de mon miroir (**on the left side of** my mirror)

Sometimes "à gauche de" is used instead of "sur la gauche de", but it's less frequent.

"à côté de" or "à côté du": their literal translation is "next to", used just like in English. For example:

Mes clefs sont **à côté de** mon portefeuille. (My keys are **next to** my wallet.)

La table est **à côté du** canapé. (The table is **next to** the sofa.)

"au-dessus de" and "au-dessous de": their literal translations are "above" and "underneath", respectively. They are used just like in English. For example:

Nous vivons **au-dessus d'**un restaurant. (We live **above** a restaurant.)

Mon chat se cache **au-dessous de** la table. (My cat hides **underneath** the table.)

"sur" and "sous": their literal translations are "on" and "under". They're used just like in English. For example:

Le livre est **sur** mon bureau. (The book is **on** my desk.)

Mon oreiller est tombé **sous** le lit. (My pillow fell **under** the bed.)

"loin de" and "près de": their literal translations are "near" and "far from". They're used just like in English. For example:

Mon ami vit **loin de** chez nous. (My friend lives **far from** us.)

Mon ami vit **près de** chez nous. (My friend lives **near from** us.)

Exercise: Fill in the blanks using the right preposition.

1)Mon hamster était ____________ le chapeau.

(My hamster was under the hat.)

2)La Statue de la Liberté se trouve ____________ New York.

(The Statue of Liberty is located in New York.)

3)Le parc est ____________ la plage.

(The park is close to the beach.)

4)Mon sac est ____________ tes affaires.

(My purse is next to your stuff.)

5)J'ai une belle veilleuse ___________ ma table de nuit.

(I have a pretty nightlight above my bedside table.)

6)Il y'a une librairie non ___________ De notre école.

(There is a library not far from our school.)

7)Il a mis tes clefs ___________ le bar.

(He put your keys on the bar.)

8)En entrant dans le magasin, tu trouveras le riz ___________ la section des pâtes.

(When entering the store, you'll find the rice on the left side of the pasta section.)

9)Mon chien aime rester ___________ du chauffage durant les journées froides.

(My dog likes to stay underneath the heater during cold days.)

Prepositions Related To Space 2

Lesson Reminder:

"au-delà de" and "à travers" or "par": their literal translations are "beyond" and "through" or "across" respectively. They're used just like in English. For example: **au-delà des** montagnes (**beyond** the mountains); **à travers** l'océan (**through** the ocean); Je regarde **par** la fenêtre. (I look **through** the window.) When translating, "across" is used to say "par" with roads.

"devant" and "derrière": their literal translations are "in front of" and "behind", respectively. They're used just like in English. For example:

Il y'a un jardin **devant** notre maison. (There's a garden **in front of** our house.)

Il y'a un jardin **derrière** notre maison. (There's a garden **behind** our house.)

“dans” and “en”: their literal translation is “in”, but they’re used in different contexts. “Dans” is used before rooms, means of transport, or before books and newspapers. For example:

Je suis **dans** la salle de bain. (I’m **in** the bathroom.)

Je suis **dans** le métro. (I’m **in** the metro.)

J’ai lu ça **dans** le journal. (I read that **in** the newspaper.)

“En” is used before countries that have a feminine name. For example: Je suis **en** France. (I’m **in** France.)

“chez”: its literal translation is “at”. It is used the same way as in English. For example:

Je suis **chez** le dentiste. (I’m **at** the dentist’s clinic.)

Je suis **chez** ma copine. (I’m **at** my friend’s house.)

“de” or “du”: their literal translation is “from”. They are used the same way as in English. For example:

Il rentre **de** France. (He’s returning **from** France.)

Il rentre **du** centre-ville. (He’s returning **from** downtown.)

“vers”: its literal translation is “towards”. It is used the same way as in English. Example: Je marche **vers** les arbres. (I’m walking **towards** the trees.)

“en dehors de” and “dehors”: their translations are “outside of” and “outside”, respectively. They’re used just like in English. For example:

Je suis **en dehors de** l’école. (I’m **outside of** the school.)

Attends moi **dehors**. (Wait for me **outside.**)

“en face de” or “en face du”: their literal translation is “facing”. It is used the same way as in English. For example: La banque se trouve **en face du** centre commercial. (The bank is located **facing** the mall.)

Exercise: Fill in the blanks using the right preposition.

1)Elle est ___________ la coiffeuse.

(She's at the hairdresser's salon.)

2)Tu dois passer ___________ cette ruelle.

(You have to go across this alley.)

3)Nous allons ___________ la plage.

(We're going towards the beach.)

4)Il y'a une petite boutique de vêtements ___________ ce marché.

(There's a little clothing shop behind this market.)

5)L'Afrique se trouve ___________ la Mer Méditerranée.

(Africa is located beyond the Mediterranean Sea.)

6)Il s'est installé ___________ Chine.

(He settled down in China.)

7)Il y'a une petite exposition d'arts ___________ la grande villa.

(There is a small art expo facing the big villa.)

8)Les ingrédients sont ___________ le troisième tiroir.

(The ingredients are in the third drawer.)

9)Ils sont tous ___________ la salle de cinéma.

(They're all outside of the movie theater.)

10)Le petit garçon marche ___________ ses parents.

(The little boy is walking in front of his parents.)

11)Nous regardons le film ___________ ces lunettes 3D.

(We are watching the movie through these 3D glasses.)

Important Prepositions

Lesson Reminder:

Important abbreviations to remember:

à + le = au: used before masculine nouns; for example: café au lait (coffee with milk).

à + les = aux: used before plural nouns; for example: une tarte aux fraises (a strawberry pie).

de + le = du: used before masculine nouns; for example: loin du marché (far from the market).

de + les = des: used before plural nouns; for example: à côté des maisons (next to the houses).

It is **very** important to remember these as they are used all the time in the French language. Not just with prepositions, but they also sometimes replace the articles that come before nouns.

"avec" and "sans": their literal translations are "with" and "without". They're used the same way as in English. For example: viens **avec** moi (come **with** me); **avec** plaisir (**with** pleasure); vas y **sans** moi (go **without** me); **sans** regrets (**without** regrets).

"en": its literal translation is "by" when used before means of transportation, but it is also used to describe the material of something, and that doesn't have a translation in English. For example: Je pars **en** voiture. (I'm leaving **by** car.); un pull **en** laine (a wool sweater).

"à" or "au": just like "en", its literal translation is "by" when used before means of transportation, but it is also used to describe an ingredient in a dish or certain machines. For example: Je pars **à** pieds. (I'm leaving **by** foot.); une tarte **au** citron (a lemon pie); une machine **à** café (a coffee machine).

"malgré" and "grâce à": their literal translations are "despite" and "thanks to". They are used the same way as in English. For example: Je sors **malgré** la chaleur. (I'm going out **despite** the heat.); C'est **grâce à** toi. (It's all **thanks to** you.)

"entre": its literal translation is "between". It is used like in English. For example: Ça doit rester **entre** nous. (This has to stay **between** us.)

Exercise: Fill in the blanks with the right preposition.

1)Ils ont besoin de plus de pailles ___________ acier.

(They need more steel straws.)

2)J'ai mis mon t-shirt dans la machine ___________ laver.

(I put my shirt in the washing machine.)

3)Le gâteau ___________ fruits de ma tante est délicieux.

(My aunt's fruit cake is delicious.)

4)Le vieux est sauvé ___________ docteur qui était dans les environs.

(The old man is saved thanks to the doctor that was around the area.)

5)J'ai vu un petit renard ___________ les buissons.

(I saw a little fox between the bushes.)

6)Emmenez ton petit frère ___________ toi au parc.

(Take your little brother with you to the park.)

7)Il fait chaud, ne sortez pas ___________ bouteilles d'eau.

(It's hot outside, don't go out without water bottles.)

8)___________ ce que tout le monde dit, tu dois continuer à te battre pour tes rêves.

(Despite what everyone says, you should keep fighting for your dreams.)

Chapter 4 - Object Complements And Circumstantial Complements

COD And COS

Lesson Reminder:

Object complements point out the person or the thing on which the action is done. Let's see the different types of object complements.

Compléments d'Objets Directes: It translates to Direct Object Complements and they are referred to as "COD". They are directly linked to the verb without any preposition separating them, and they answer the questions, "Qui ?" (who?) and "Quoi ?" (what?). For example:

J'appelle **ma mère.** (I'm calling **my mom.**) -> J'appelle **qui** ? (**Who** am I calling?) -> **Ma mère** (**My mother**).

Je bois **du thé**. (I'm drinking **some tea**.) -> Je bois **quoi** ? (**What** am I drinking?) -> **Du thé** (**some tea**).

PS: The verbs that introduce CODs are called "verbes transitifs directes" (direct transitional verbs), they are all the verbs that **need** a COD to be able to understand the meaning of the sentence. For example, the verb "marcher" (to walk) doesn't need a COD. It is simply put in a sentence "Je marche." (I am walking.) Verbs like these are called "verbes intransitifs" (non-transitional verbs).

Compléments d'Objets Seconds: It translates to Secondary Object Complements, and they are referred to as "COS". They are introduced after a COD with the use of a preposition. They are not necessary to the meaning of the sentence and can be eliminated. They are linked to the same verb as the COD that precedes them. If another verb is introduced, then it can't be considered a COS. For example:

Je bois du café <u>pour</u> *bien me réveiller*. (I drink coffee <u>to</u> *wake up*.)

PS: The verbs that introduce COSs are also “verbes transitifs directes”, just like CODs.

Exercise: Underline the Object Complements in the following sentences and precise their nature (COD/COS).

1)On a fait un cours intéressant aujourd'hui.

(We had an interesting class today.): ____________

2)J'ai perdu mon chapeau de Noël.

(I lost my Christmas hat.): ____________

3)Mon père a fait un gâteau pour mon anniversaire.

(My father baked a cake for my birthday.): ____________

4)Mon cousin a perdu ses lunettes.

(My cousin lost his glasses.): ____________

5)Je mange mon diner.

(I'm having my dinner.): ____________

6)Elle entend son chien courir en ouvrant la porte de son appartement.

(She hears her dog running while opening her apartment's door.):

____

COI

Lesson Reminder:

Compléments d'Objets Indirectes: It translates to Indirect Object Complements, and they are referred to as “COI”. They are indirectly linked to the verb via a preposition separating them. They answer the questions “À qui ?/À quoi ?” (Whose?/To or for what?) and “De qui ?/De quoi ?” (From or of who?/From or of what?). For example:

Cette robe appartient à **Aileen**. (This dress belongs to **Aileen**.) **À qui** appartient cette robe ? (**Whose** dress is this?) -> À **Aileen** (to **Aileen**).

Il a peur de **tomber**. (He's afraid of **falling**.) -> Il a peur **de quoi** ? (He's afraid **of what**?) -> De **tomber** (of **falling**).

Be careful; the meaning can sometimes be lost in the translation when asking the question. For example:

Fais confiance à **ton père**. (Trust **your father**.) -> Fais confiance **à qui** ? (Trust **who**?) -> **À ton père (your father)**.

See how we didn't use the question form given in the translation above? For this reason, it's better not to count on them to know if it's a COI or a COD, the best option would be to learn your prepositions to be able to differentiate them from articles.

PS: The verbs that introduce COIs are called "verbes transitifs indirectes" (indirect transitional verbs). They **need** a COI to be able to understand the meaning of the sentence. One sentence could also contain both a COD and a COI.

Be careful, if the prepositions "à" or "de" come after a verb and introduce a **place** or a **time**, what comes after them is **not a COI**, that verb is still considered "verbe intransitif" or "verbe transitif directe" if it has a COD.

Exercise 1: Underline the Object Complements in the following sentences and precise their nature (COD/COI).

1)Prends soin de ton petit frère.

(Take care of your little brother.): ____________

2)Ma mère a adoré le cadeau de papa !

(My mom loved dad's gift!): ____________

3)Tu t'intéresses vraiment aux arts.

(You're very interested in arts.): ____________

4)Elle a besoin du médicament prescript.

(She needs the prescribed medicine.): ___________

5)Faites attentions aux voitures en traversant la route.

(Be careful of the cars when crossing the road.): ___________

6)Nous tenons beaucoup à nos chats.

(We are really attached to our cats.): ___________

Exercise 2: Determine the nature of the verbs in the following sentences, write "VTD" for "verbe transitif directe", "VTI" for "verbe transitif indirecte" or "VI" for "verbe intransitif".

1)Nous allons à la plage.

(We're going to the beach.): ___________

2)Passe moi le couteau.

(Pass me the knife.): ___________

3)Ça dépend du temps.

(It depends on the weather.): ___________

4)Ramenez vos serviettes avec vous.

(Bring your towels with you.): ___________

5)Elle est rentrée de son voyage.

(She came back from her trip.): ___________

7)Ils habitent à Toronto.

(They live in Toronto.): ___________

8)Mettez les chaises au fond.

(Put the chairs in the back.): ___________

9)Mon père se réveille à 6h.

(My father wakes up at 6 am.): ___________

10)Tu joues à quoi ?

(What are you playing?): ___________

Circumstantial Complements

Lesson Reminder:

Circumstantial complements add more meaning and preciseness to the sentence. They can be placed at the beginning or at the end of the sentence. They can usually even be moved around or even deleted, but it's not always the case.

Let's take a look at their different types:

Complément Circonstanciel de Temps: It translates to Circumstantial Complement of Time. They are referred to as CCT. Much like their name suggests, they are an indication of the time in which the verb takes action in. They usually come after a preposition related to time but not all the time. For example: Je reviens à **minuit**. (I'll be back at **midnight**.); **Ce soir**, je reviens un peu tard. (**Tonight** I'll be back a bit late.) They answer the question, "Quand ?" (When?).

Complément Circonstanciel de Lieu: It translates to Circumstantial Complement of Place/Space. They are referred to as CCL. They are an indication of the place in which the verb is taking action. They usually come after a preposition related to space but not all the time. For example: Le chat se cache dans **la boîte**. (The cat hides in **the box**.); Ils sont tous **dehors**. (They're all **outside**.) They answer the question, "Où ?" (Where?).

Complément Circonstanciel de Manière: It translates to Circumstantial Complement of Way/Manner. They are referred to as CCM. They indicate how an action is done. They are sometimes introduced by a preposition and other times. They are an adverb. For example: Elle sourit avec **gentilesse**. (She smiles with **kindness**.); Elle sourit **gentiment**. (She smiles **kindly**.). They answer the question, "Comment ?" (How?).

Exercise: Identify the Circumstantial Complements by underlining them in the following sentences then precise their nature (CCL/CCT/CCM).

1)La maison était très calme ce matin.

(The house was so calm this morning.): ______

2)Les enfants jouent bruyamment.

(The kids are playing loudly.): ______

3)Nous dînons à table.

(We are dining on the table.): ______

4)Elle a géré l'événement avec confiance hier.

(She managed the event with confidence yesterday.): ______ / ______

5)Mon mari et moi partons à Las Vegas en été.

(My husband and I are going to Las Vegas in the summer.): ______ / ______

6)Il marche devant moi en toute timidité.

(He's walking in front of me timidly.): ______ / ______

7)L'autre jour au restaurant, ton frère parlait avec tristesse.

(The other day at the restaurant, your brother was talking with sadness.): ______ / ______ / ______

Chapter 5 - What Is The Present Perfect Tense In English?

So, let's start with this, my favourite tense, the present perfect.

Now, let me start by talking about this tense in English. If you understand how the tense works in English, you can easily convert it to French. In English, the present perfect is made up of two parts: **an auxiliary verb** and **a past participle**.

The auxiliary verb in English is "**have**" and it comes in seven different forms:

I have

you have

he has

she has

one has

we have

they have

So, you use one of those and then you chuck a past participle onto the end of it. In English, to make a past participle, you choose a verb and then put **–ed** on the end. For example:

jump – jump**ed**

talk – talk**ed**

phone – phon**ed**

call – call**ed**

finish – finish**ed**

So, you take an **auxiliary verb** and then you put a **past participle** on the end.

E.g.

I have finished

you have jumped

he has called

she has phoned Pierre

we have worked very hard today

they have painted a picture for their friend

he has delivered the news to the family

Sometimes, in English, you can't make the past participle by adding the letters **–ed**; sometimes you have to add **–en** instead. For example:

eat – eat**en**

speak – spok**en**

take – tak**en**

give – giv**en**

write – writt**en**

see – se**en**

You can do the same thing again, just get an auxiliary verb and chuck one of these past participles on the end.

E.g.

we have spoken to the teacher about John

they have eaten a lot today

I have given Marie the message

he has taken everything with him

she has written a letter for Simon

you have seen the film already

So, in English, most of the time the past participle ends in **–ed** or **–en**, but we also have lots of "*exceptions to the rule*" in English. For example:

do – **done**

read – **read**

sing – **sung**

go – **gone**

make – **made**

put – **put**

fly – **flown**

You can still chuck these on the end of an auxiliary verb, though.

E.g.

I have made a cake for Julia

We have put the keys on the table

They have flown to Rome

He has sung non-stop all day

They have gone to Barcelona without Steve

So, that's what the present perfect tense is in English. Now, in French, it's pretty much the same.

How do you form the present perfect tense in French?

Remember how you need an auxiliary verb and then a past participle. In English, the auxiliary verb was “**have**” and here it is again in its different forms:

I have

you have

he has

she has

one has

we have

they have

In French, the auxiliary verb is “**avoir**”.

Here is the verb “**avoir**” in its many different conjugations:

j’ai

tu as

il a

elle a

on a

nous avons

vous avez

ils ont

elles ont

Now, you may have noticed that English had seven forms, whereas French had nine forms. Well, let’s look at what the French forms mean:

j'ai – I have

tu as – you have

il a – he has

elle a – she has

on a – one has

nous avons – we have

vous avez – you have

ils ont – they have

elles ont – they have

So, firstly, there are two ways to say "**you have**" in French, and secondly, there are two ways to say "**they have**"

<u>"tu as" vs. "vous avez"</u>

The "**tu as**" form is used to mean "**you have**" when you know the person you're speaking to quite well. It can be used with friends, family, or anyone who's younger than you.

The "**vous avez**" form is used to mean "**you have**" when either you don't really know the person you're speaking to. It can be used with anyone who's older than you, or with strangers. I tend to use this form more often because I don't have any friends. I'm joking. I do use it a lot more though, just to be on the safe side. I really do have friends, honestly.

You can also use "**vous avez**" if you're talking to more than one person, regardless of whether you know them or not. Therefore, "**tu as**" is often referred to as informal and singular, whereas "**vous avez**" is referred to as formal or plural.

<u>"ils ont" vs. "elles ont"</u>

These both mean "**they are**" but the difference is quite easy to understand. "**ils ont**" is used if you're talking about a group of men or a group of men and women. "**elles ont**" is used if you're talking about a group of women. So, "**ils ont**" is often referred to as masculine, and "**elles ont**" is referred to as feminine.

So, that's the auxiliary verb and that goes first. You have to pick one form of "**avoir**" and then you can chuck a past participle on the end.

Remember how in English, to form the past participle, you can take a verb and put **–ed** on the end, or sometimes you put **–en** on the end, or sometimes it was just completely irregular. Well, in French, there are three types of verb: those that end in the letters **–er**, those that end in the letters **–ir**, and those that end in the letters **–re**.

To form the past participle in French, if the verb ends in **–er**, you change the **–er** to **–é**. So, for example:

parl**er** – parl**é** (speak – spoken)

regard**er** – regard**é** (watch – watched)

mang**er** – mang**é** (eat – eaten)

pay**er** – pay**é** (pay – paid)

envoy**er** – envoy**é** (send – sent)

appel**er** – appel**é** (call – called)

commenc**er** – commenc**é** (start – started)

copi**er** – copi**é** (copy – copied)

So, you can take any form of the auxiliary verb and chuck a past participle on the end:

j'ai parlé (I've spoken)

il a commencé (he has started)

nous avons appelé Marie (we have called Marie)

ils ont payé (they have paid)

tu as regardé le film (you have watched the film)

elle a mangé la pizza (she has eaten the pizza)

j'ai envoyé la lettre à Jeanne (I have sent the letter to Jeanne)

Easy peasy, lemon squeezy!

So, that's with –**er** verbs, you just change it to –**é**.

If you have a verb that ends in –**ir**, you change the –**ir** on the end to just the letter –**i**. For example:

fin**ir** – fin**i** (finish – finished)

chois**ir** – chois**i** (choose – chosen)

réuss**ir** – réuss**i** (succeed – succeeded)

rempl**ir** – rempl**i** (fill – filled)

maigr**ir** – maigr**i** (lose weight – lost weight)

gross**ir** – gross**i** (gain weight – gained weight)

And then, you simply chuck these after any of the auxiliary verb forms.

E.g.

j'ai fini (I have finished)

nous avons réussi (we have succeeded)

elle a maigri (she has lost weight)

ils ont grossi (they have gained weight)

tu as rempli la bouteille (you have filled the bottle)

il a choisi le vin (he has chosen the wine)

So, if a verb ends in –**er**, you change the –**er** to –**é**, if the verb ends in –**ir**, you change the –**ir** to –**i**, and finally, if the verb ends in –**re**, you change this to –**u**.

So, for example:

vend**re** – vend**u** (sell – sold)

attend**re** – attend**u** (wait – waited)

perd**re** – perd**u** (lose – lost)

rend**re** – rend**u** (give back – given back)

répond**re** – répond**u** (answer – answered)

And again, you can just chuck these onto the end of any of the auxiliary verb forms.

E.g.

j'ai perdu Pierre (I have lost Pierre)

nous avons rendu la voiture (we have given back the car)

ils ont répondu au téléphone (they have answered the telephone)

elle a attendu (she has waited)

tu as vendu la maison (you have sold the house)

OK, so that's how you do it in French, you pick a form of the auxiliary verb "**avoir**" and then you chuck a past participle on the end. To form the past participle, you just have to look at what the verb ends in and change it appropriately:

er – é

ir – i

re – u

Let's practise forming the past participle

Now, here's a list of useful verbs that I've split up into three groups: **er**, **ir** and **re**. Grab a piece of paper and see if you can turn them into their past participles. I've done the first one for you as an example and I've put the answers at the end of each group for you to check:

Group 1 – **er verbs**

1. **travailler** *(to work)* – travaillé (*worked*)

2. **parler** *(to speak)*

3. **chercher** *(to look for)*

4. **donner** *(to give)*

5. **demander** *(to ask)*

6. **jouer** *(to play)*

7. ***montrer*** (to show)

8. ***regarder*** (to watch)

9. ***trouver*** (to find)

10. **visiter** *(to visit)*

11. **réserver** *(to reserve)*

12. **apporter** *(to bring)*

13. **oublier** *(to forget)*

Answers:

1. travaillé (worked)

2. parlé (spoken)

3. cherché (looked for)

4. donné (given)

5. demandé (asked)

6. joué (played)

7. montré (shown)

8. regardé (watched)

9. trouvé (found)

10. visité (visited)

11. réservé (reserved)

12. apporté (brought)

13. oublié (forgotten)

<u>Group 2</u> – ir verbs

1. **finir** *(to finish)*

2. **choisir** *(to choose)*

3. **établir** *(to establish)*

4. **grandir** *(to grow up)*

5. **grossir** *(to gain weight)*

6. ***maigrir*** *(to lose weight)*

7. **remplir** *(to fill up)*

8. **réfléchir** *(to think about)*

9. ***réussir*** *(to succeed)*

10. **vieillir** *(to grow old)*

Answers:

1. fini (finished)

2. choisi (chosen)

3. établi (established)

4. grandi (grown up)

5. grossi (gained weight)

6. maigri (lost weight)

7. rempli (filled up)

8. réfléchi (thought about)

9. réussi (succeeded)

10. vieilli (grown old)

<u>Group 3</u> – re verbs

1. **attendre** *(to wait)*

2. ***entendre*** *(to hear)*

3. **perdre** *(to lose)*

4. ***rendre*** *(to give back)*

5. ***répondre*** *(to answer / to respond)*

6. **vendre** *(to sell)*

Answers:

1. attendu (waited)

2. entendu (heard)

3. perdu (lost)

4. rendu (gave back)

5. répondu (answered / responded)

6. vendu (sold)

Chapter 6 - Complex Sentences

The complex sentence is composed of several conjugated verbs. It contains a main proposal, followed or accompanied by one or more subordinate proposals. It is often related to the subordinate proposition by a relative pronoun.

Relative pronouns

Relative pronouns replace the subject or object that precedes it. It varies in kind and in number; however, most of them are invariable.

Invariable relative pronouns

qui - que - quoi - dont - où

Qui: (That, Who)

"Qui" has a double meaning. "Qui" replaces an object (table, chair etc.) and also a person or an animal. In English, it has several variants, depending on the circumstances (that,who) and the subject, but not in French.

Ex.:

L'homme qui est venu me chercher est mon père. (People)

(The man who came to fetch me is my father.*)*

Le chien qui aboie *fait peur (Animals)*

*(*The dog who's barking is scary.*)*

Le bus qui doit me prendre est en retard (Things, not alive)

*(*The bus that has to take me is late.*)*

<u>Que: (That)</u>

The relative pronoun "Qui" has a subject function; that is, it replaces the preceding subject. The relative pronoun "Que" has a complement function; it replaces the complement that precedes it.

Ex.:

la fille **qui** est à côté de moi est très jolie

« **Qui** » replaces la fille . la fille est jolie (The girl is pretty.)

Le livre **que** tu me donnes semble trop vieux

"Que" replaces the word "livre," which is a complement. (You give me the book which is too old.*)*

Let's take the example we used above.

" Le bus qui doit me prendre est en retard" *(*The bus that has to take me is late*)* would become, "Le bus que je dois prendre est en retard" *(*The bus I have to take is late*)*.

Subject: Le bu, because the bus is late.

In two sentences it would be:

Le bus est en retard. Je dois prendre ce bus.

The bus is late. I have to take this bus.

<u>Quoi : (What)</u>

This is only used when you talk about things or objects. It is just a complement in a sentence.

Ex.:

Je ne sais pas quoi penser de cette société

I do not know what to think of this society.

<u>Dont: (Of which)</u>

The relative pronoun "Dont" may have different functions. It replaces people, animals or things.

Cette belle maison dont je t'ai parlé est à vendre. *(*This beautiful house of which I spoke to you is for sale.*)*

Here is "complement of direct object" indirect object. (I told you about this pretty house.)

Voici le professeur dont les cours sont captivants. (Les cours de ce professeur sont captivants)

Here is the teacher whose courses are captivating. (This teacher's courses are captivating.)

Où: (Where)

The relative pronoun "Où" is also called a circumstantial complement of place or time.

Place : Cette ville est l'endroit où j'ai grandi

J'ai grandi dans cette ville

This city is where I grew up

I grew up in this city

Time : Je me souviens de l'époque où je passais mes vacances chez mes grands parents

Je passais mes vacances chez mes grands parents à l'époque

I remember the time when I spent my holidays with my grandparents.

I spent my holidays with my grandparents at the time.

The different forms of phrases

The affirmative sentence
We have already seen quite a number of affirmative sentences in previous courses. The affirmative sentence affirms something.

Ex.:

Je cherche mon train

I'm looking for my train.

Ils sont là

They are there.

Nous te cherchions

We were looking for you.

Les chiens aboient

Dogs bark.

The negative sentence
To mark the negation, the French language uses this formula:

Subject + **ne** + verb + **pas** + complement.

Ex.:

Affirmative*:* Je cherche mon train

Negative*:* Je ne cherche pas mon train

Nous te cherchions

Nous ne te cherchions pas

Les chiens aboient

Les chiens n'aboient pas

Ne...pas mark the negation.

Another word that marks the negation is "Jamais."

"Jamais" marks the negation on an uncontrollable scale because it is used for a wish that will not change, or an action without appeal. Do not add "Pas" when using "Jamais."

Affirmative*:* Les chiens aboient

Negative*:* Les chiens n'aboient pas

Negative using Jamais*:* Les chiens n'aboient jamais

The exclamatory sentence
The exclamatory sentence is marked by the presence of an exclamation mark at the end. It expresses surprise, astonishment, anger.

Ex.:

Quel temps horrible !

Quelle petite peste cette fille !Quelle audace il a eu de me répondre en classe Quelle belle journée !

What a horrible timeWhat a small plague this girl!

What daring he had to answer me in class!

Such a good day!

The interrogative sentence
The interrogative sentence is used to ask a question. It is marked by a "?" at the end of the sentence.

Unlike other types of sentence, what characterizes the interrogative sentence is the disposition of the elements in it.

Declarative sentence	**Interrogative sentence**	**Formula**
Tu cherches ton chemin (Your search your way)	Cherches-tu ton chemin? Est-ce-que tu cherches ton chemin?	Verb+ Personal pronoun subject +Complement+ ? Est-ce-que+Personal pronoun subject +complement+ ?
Vous connaissez le chemin pour aller à l'école (You know the way to go to school.)	Connaissez-vous le chemin pour aller à l'école? Est-ce-que vous connaissez le chemin pour aller à l'école ?	Verb+ Personal pronoun subject +Complements+ ? Est-ce-que+ Personal pronoun subject +complement+ ?

It is also possible to ask a question by putting an adverb or an interrogative pronoun at the beginning of the sentence.

The formula Verb + Subject + Complement +? does not change.

Inversion Questions in French

One of the easiest sorts of questions to ask in French is called an inversion question. It is named so because of the way in which the question is formed, by inverting the subject and the verb of the sentence and just adding a "?" at the end.

As-tu un chat ?

Do you have a cat?

If you want to ask an even wider variety of questions, you can use French question words alongside the *est-ce que* structure. French question words include **qui** (who), **quand** (when), **où** (where), **pourquoi** (why) and **comment** (how). These words are simply tacked on to the beginning of an **est-ce que** question in order to have the desired meaning.

Qui est-ce que tu cherches ?

Who are you searching?

Quand est-ce qu'on atterit?

When are we landing?

Où est-ce qu'on va ?

Where are we going?

Pourquoi est-ce que tu cries?

Why are you screaming?

Comment est-ce que ça marche ?

How does it work?

<u>Que :</u>

Que fais-tu ? (What do you do ?)

Que vas-tu faire? (What are you going to do ?)

Qui: ”Qui” is used to ask a question about a person.

Ex.:

Qui est là ? (Who’s there?)

Qui va venir à ma fête demain ? (Who’s coming to my party tomorrow?)

Qui veux-tu que j’appelle aussi tard ? (Who do you want me to call this late?)

Quand:

"Quand" is used to know the time.

Ex.:

Quand est-ce-que tu arrive à Paris ?

Quand pourrais-je passer chez toi ?

When do you come to Paris?

When can I go to you?

Quoi / De quoi / À quoi :

These are used in a question to know the details, and to talk about a thing or a situation.

Ex.:

A quoi penses-tu ?

De quoi as-tu peur ?

Maintenant, je fais quoi ?

What are you thinking about?

What are you afraid of?

Now what do I do?

<u>Où:</u>

"Où" is used to ask about a place.

Ex.:

Où est-ce-que tu habites?

Où allons-nous dormir ?

Où se trouve ma serviette ?

Where do you live?

Where are we going to sleep?

Where is my towel?

That being said, there are two types of questions:

The total query:

The total query is a question whose answers are either "Oui" or "Non."

Ex.:

As-tu faim ? (*Are you hungry*?)

-Non (*No*)

Or

-Non, je n'ai pas faim. (*No, I'm not*)

Veux-tu que je t'aide ? (*Do you want me to help you* ?)

-Oui (*Yes*)

Question Tags in French: *Est-ce que* (and *Qu'est-ce que*)

The basic question tag in French is "*Est-ce que*." It marks the beginning of a yes/no question, much in the same way that inversion does. ***The difference here is that the sentence that follows will retain the basic French sentence structure.***

Est-ce que tu veux partir ? — Do you want to leave?

Qu'est-ce que is a variation on this question tag. By putting que or "what" at the beginning, you can ask a question requiring a more elaborate answer (The Partial query).

Qu'est-ce que tu veux manger ? — What do you want to eat?

The partial query

The partial query concerns one of the elements of the sentence; it can not be answered with "Oui" or "Non."

The answers are often explanations for the answer given.

Ex.:

Pourquoi ne veux-tu pas répondre ?

-Parce que je n'en ai pas envie.

Où est-ce-que tu habite ?

-J'habite aux alentours de Marseille.

Why don't you want to answer?

-Because I do not feel like it.

Where do you live?

-I live in the neighborhoods of Marseille.

Chapter 7 - General Greetings

When you meet someone for the first time, you usually greet with a handshake. This may be someone who you have been introduced to or someone that you meet and begin a dialogue. Let's say you run into someone that you have previously met and know a little bit. You would then greet them and give a small kiss on either cheek. These are simple niceties that are always practiced by the French. If you know someone really well, then the usual greeting is four kisses, but this is typically reserved for people like family.

The following phrases will help you introduce yourself to someone and to say hello, no matter what time of day it is. The written French in the middle of the page is correct French and to the right, you will find the phonetic pronunciation of the words so that you can say them easily:

Good Morning	**Bonjour**	Bon Joor

(This can be used as hello as well)

Hi!	**Salut!**	Saloo

(As a general rule, you do not pronounce the last letter of a word unless it is followed by a word that begins with a vowel.)

Check out these additional greetings. Say them aloud.

I am pleased to meet you.	**Enchanté**	*Onshontay*
What's up?	**Quoi de neuf?**	*Kwah de nuff?*

Goodbye	**Au Revoir**	*Orh revwa*
See you later!	**À tout à l'heure!**	*Ah toot ah lhur*
I am sorry I am late.	**Je suis désolé d'être en retard.**	*Juh swee dezolay detra on retar*

Note: This is a perfect example of how **être (to be)** is used in a sentence. In this case it means literally, "I am sorry to be late", but it's the same way you would say, " I am sorry I am late."

This is a useful phrase that you can use when you need to ask someone on an adjoining seat to let you through or if you bump into someone by accident and wish to say that you are sorry.

Excuse me!	**Excuser Moi!**	Excusay mwa!

Quiz Time!

Easy right? In the span of 5 minutes, you have learned to say eight phrases. Learning French is nothing without repetition. Can you pass this brief quiz?

*Try to work from your memory only by using a voice recorder on your phone or handheld device, then check what you said against the phrases previously provided. How did you do? Ready to move on?

Let's look at some more niceties of introduction. Perhaps you want to introduce your friend or family member to someone and in this case you would use the following phrase:

This is my husband	**Voici! Mon mari**	*Vwassee mon maree*
This is my wife	**Voici! Ma Femme**	*Vwassee ma famm*
This is my daughter	**Voici! Ma Fille**	*Vwassee ma fee*
This is my son	**Voici! Mon Fils**	*Vwassee mon feece*

Of course if you are introducing your whole family, you would not need to say Voici! Each time but could shorten it by saying:

Voici! Mon mari, ma femma et mon fils

Or change the sentence according to who you are introducing. The word ET means AND and is pronounced as "AY". Voici! Mes Amis! These are my friends. This is the easiest way to break the ice and to get to know everyone without having to break into the formality of the French language. People today recognize these greetings and introductions and they can be used so easily.

Now, it's time to put some words together to make sentences. There is not much use in saying "hello" if you can't follow it up with asking how someone is, or asking a question. When you are on holiday, you may want to get somewhere and the "hello" will allow you to approach someone, but you will need to go further by putting words together in such a way that whoever you approach will understand what you want. If you are on the plane to France and want to practice your French on the stewardess, here are some phrases that you can try just to see how your accent is understood.

The verb that I will introduce you to is VOULOIR or "to want to". However, merely saying that you want something in English is considered a bit rude. It's the same in French. You would never use the equivalent of I WANT which would be je veux. The polite way of saying this in French is to use the equivalent of "I would like". Remember niceties go a long way in any language.

I would like a coffee	**Je voudrais un café**	*Juh voodray un cafay*

It is usual in France to be served coffee that is black unless you ask for milk. Thus, when the stewardess asks you if you would like a drink and you tell her that you would like a coffee, you will also need to specify that you want milk or cream.

With milk please	**Avec du lait s'il vous plaît**	*Ahvec du lay sih voo play*

Having learned that it is polite to say I would like rather than I want, you also need to know another nicety. One would never use the expression "What?" when you do not hear something that has been said. It's a very bad reflection of upbringing and the better option is to say "Comment?" (pronounced comm on?) or to even ask the person you are speaking to, to repeat that which was said, using the phrase.

Can you repeat that please?	**Répétez cela s'il vous plait**	*Reppettay sella see voo play*

Perhaps your fellow passenger is French and you would like to practice your pronunciations. Introduce yourself using the salutations shown above and then try some phrases if the person in the neighboring seat seems friendly.

May I practice my French with you?	**Puis-je pratiquer mon français avec vous?**	*Pwee juh pratikay mon froncay aveck vous?*

Do you know what time it is?	**Quelle heure est-il?**	*Kell urr ett eel?*

General conversation that may follow on the plane could involve phrases that use French, but also explains a little bit about yourself. You will need to listen to the replies and be aware of how to ask a French person to slow down so that you can understand a little better.

Can you speak slower please?	**Pouvez-vous parler plus lentement s'il vous plaît**	*Poovay voo parlay ploo lontimon sih voo play*

Now that you have a general understanding of French greetings, why not try these common phrases out!

Hello! / Good Day/ Good Morning/ Good Afternoon	**Bonjour!**	*Boh-joor!*
Good Evening!	**Bonsoir!**	*Boh-swahr*
Hello (answering phone)	**Allô**	*ah-lo*
Hello Sir	**Bonjour Monsieur**	*Boh-joor Moh-syuh*

Hello Ma'am	**Bonjour Madame**	*Boh-joor Mah-dahm*
Nice to meet you!	**Enchanté**	*On-shawn-tay!*
How are you?	**Comment vas tu?** **ça va?** **comment allez-vous?**	*Koh-mahn vah-too?* *sah-vah?* *koh-mahn allay-voo?*
I'm fine, I'm fine, thanks!	**ç ava bien.** **Bien, merci!**	*sah-vah bee-yen.* *Bee-yen, mayr-see*
And You?	**Et toi?** **Et vous?**	*Ay twah* *Ay voo*
What's up?	**Quoi de neuf?**	*Kwah de nuff?*
Welcome!	**Bienvenue!**	*Bee-yen-vuh-nyu!*
I'm happy to see you!	**Je suis ravi de te revoir.**	*Jzay-swee rah-vee deh the euh-vwar.*
Have a good holiday!	**Bonnes vacances!**	*Bohn vah-kahns!*
Safe trip!	**Bonne route!**	*Bohn root!*
See you later!	**á plus tard!**	*ah ploo tahr!*
See you soon!	**á bientôt**	*ah bee-yen toh!*
Goodbye!	**Au revoir!**	*Oh ruh-vwar!*
Good night!	**Bonne nuit!**	*Bohn-nwee!*

See you tomorrow!	**á demain!**	*Ah de-mahn*
Enjoy your weekend!	**Bon weekend!**	*Bohn week-end!*
Have a good week!	**Bonne semaine!**	*Bohn seh-mane!*
Yes	**Oui**	*Wee*
No	**Non**	*Nohn*
Please	**S'il vous plait**	*Seel voo play*
Thanks!	**Merci**	*Mair-see*
No thank you.	**Non merci.**	*Nohn mair-see*
Sorry	**Pardon**	*Pahr-dohn*
Sorry to disturb you	**Je suis désolé de vous avoir derange.**	*Jzay-swee day-zoh-lay de voo-zah-vwar day-rahn.*
Good luck!	**Bonne chance!**	*Bohn-shawns!*
Have fun!	**Amuses-toi bien!**	*Ah-muze-twa bee-yen!*
Cheers!	**Santé**	*Sahn-tay!*
All the best!	**Bonne continuation!**	*Bohn kohn-tee-nwah-see-ohn!*

Learning these words by heart will help you when you speak French because you will be able to catch snatches of words in replies you get. Thus, the more words you know, the more likely you are to be able to understand the conversation. The problem with conjugating French is that all of the verbs change when you associate them with different genders, so it's best to keep things simple at this time. In sentences throughout the book, however, you will see that verbs are used differently when referring to different people. If you want to learn more about how this works, it may be a good idea to invest in a verb conjugation book, although as a tourist, you really don't need to dig that deeply into the language to make yourself heard and understood.

I know we have touched on this before, but I feel it bears repeating. The biggest problem many people have with the French language is that every object is either masculine or feminine and that, quite often, the sex of the object doesn't really make much sense. If you ask a French man why a certain word is masculine or why it's feminine, they will usually answer you with a shrug. It's a very old language and is well established and even French people make mistakes with the prefixes used to describe the sex of something. *Le, la and les* are used to describe the word that we use in our language that is "the". However, *le* is masculine and thus refers to masculine objects, *la* is feminine and *les* is plural. You can't make a mistake when talking about a person as the sex is obvious but when you start to speak and listen to French, you will find that things such as a table, a bedroom, a bookcase and even a car, all have a masculine or feminine prefix because in the French language that's the way that the words are ordered.

You are fairly safe using the salutations that we have used because they don't really refer much to the sex of someone. Bonjour is universal, as is Salut! It is only when you start to construct sentences to try and explain something to a French person that the sexes come into play.

Quiz Time!

Here we are at the end of the first lesson. I know it seems like we have gone over a lot of information, but let's make sure you are actually retaining some of this info. Take this short quiz to find out!

1)How do you say hello?

2)How do pardon yourself after bumping into someone?

3)How would you introduce your friends?

4)How would you request a coffee?

5)How do you say “Good Night”?

Answers :

1)Salut! / Bonjour!

2)Excuser Moi!

3)Voici! Mes Amis!

4)Je voudrais un café

5)Bonne nuit!

Chapter 8 -Knowing People/Nationality/Job

Connaître les gens, la nationalité et l'emploi

The focus of this chapter will be on people and the titles we can use to describe them. Remember, I outlined the fact that everything in French has an assigned gender in the introduction of this book? This will be evident in this chapter as the words will be preceded by an article, such as *le, la, des,* and *de la,* which are different ways of saying *the* or *a* but which have associated genders. Along with this will be either an (e) or an (s), which means that if it is someone female you are talking about, you will add the *e*, and if it is plural, like a group of people, you will add the *s*.

Knowing People

This will focus on people you know in your life and what you would call them in French.

The first example will be a friend. While in English, we don't say the word "friend" any differently, whether we are talking about a man or a woman. In French, there is a difference when writing the word, and therefore, a slight difference in pronunciation can be noticed. First, if you are talking about a male friend, you would call them *Un Ami* [uhn][ah-mee]. If you are talking about a female friend, you would say *Une Amie* [oo-nuh][ah-mee-uh]. Notice how the words are a little more drawn out to demonstrate the added *e's*.

If you want to talk about your partner, you would say *mon petit ami* if you are talking about your boyfriend and *ma petite amie* if you are talking about your girlfriend. These translate to "my boyfriend" and "my girlfriend," respectively.

If you are talking about your teacher or your professor, you could say a few different things. The options are explained below:

Une/Un/La / Le Professeur(e)

Une/Un / L' Enseignant(e)

With these two options, either one can mean a teacher, and if you are talking about a university professor, you can use the first option. Both of these would be preceded by *Le* or *Un*, depending on if you want to say *a (un)* or *the (le)*. The second example drops the *e* from *le* because the word *enseignant* begins with a vowel. This is done for smooth speaking and to avoid a mouthful of vowels tripping you up. As you now know, adding *e* or *s* to the end is dependent on who you are speaking about. You will add an *e* for a female teacher or professor and an *s* for multiples.

The French word for "group" is very similar to the English word, though you will roll your tongue in the pronunciation, which is noted in the vocabulary list. In French, the word is *groupe*. Notice how, in this example, the word ends with the letter *e*? Since this one is not in brackets, it tells us that the *e* is a part of the word and not a letter that is added according to the gender of the person. The word for a club is also quite similar to the English word, except for the pronunciation. In French, we would say *Une Club* pronounced as, *[oon][k-loo-b]*. If you want to mention a team of some sort, you would say *l'Equipe* [ay-keep], which means the team.

Another person you may need to reference would include a coworker or a colleague, which, in French, is *un collègue*.

If you want to mention someone who is an acquaintance of yours, and you don't want to call them a friend or they are not a colleague, you would say *une connaissance*.

If there is someone who you do not like, you would say *un(e) ennemi(e)* when describing them, which means that they are "an enemy." If you want to say "my enemy," you would say *mon ennemi(e)*.

Now, we will look at a few sentence examples so that you can use these when speaking to someone:

Elle est une de mes ennemies. She is one of my enemies.

Il est sur l'équipe. He is on the team.

Il est mon collègue. He is my colleague.

Elle est ma professeure. She is my teacher/professor.

For any of the examples of people above, you can insert them into a sentence by saying one of the following:

Il/elle est le/la/une __________ de mon ami(e). She/he is the _______ of my friend.

il/elle est mon/ma ___________. She/he is my _________.

With these examples, there are a few things to keep in mind. Notice the (e) at the end of *ami*. It is there because, depending on the gender of the friend about which you are speaking, you will either add the letter *e* to the end or not. Also, you see "le/la/une." Which of these you use will depend on the title you are using. For example, if you were saying, "She is a colleague of my friend," you would say *Elle est un collègue de mon ami*. However, if you were saying, "She is an enemy of my friend," you would say *Elle est une ennemie de mon ami*. Notice how these can vary depending on the word you are inserting to create the sentence, so when you learn a word like *professeur* (teacher), be sure to also learn that *un* or *le* goes with it instead of *une* or *la*. This will make remembering it much easier when you go to form a sentence.

Nationalities

We will now look at the nationalities of the world and how we can say them in French. You can then see how to insert these into sentences at the end of this section. To begin, though, the word continent is *un continent*.

North America

L'Amérique du nord

Nord-Américain

Un Américain, Une Américain(e)(s)

Un Canadien, Une canadien(e)(s)

Le Mexique

Un Mexicain, Une Mexicaine

Europe

L'Europe

Européen(e)(s)

Français(e)(s)

Italien / Italienne

Grec, grecque

Suisse

Belge

Suédois / Suédoise

Polonais

Islandais(e) / Icelandic

One example that is a little tricky is when we describe someone who is English. We would say they are *Anglais(e)*. However, when we speak about England as a country, we call it *L'Angleterre*.

Asia

L'Asie

Asiatique

Japonais(e)

Coréen(e)

Chinois(e)

Taïwanais(e)

South America

L'Amérique du sud

Sud-Américain(e)

Brésilien(ne)

Argentin(e), Argentinian

Africa

L' Afrique

Africain(e)

Sud-Africain

Kényan, Kenyan

Australia

L'Australie

L'Australien(e)

New Zetland

Néo-zélandais(e)

India

L'Inde

Indien(ne)

Antarctica

L'antarctique

Notice how these nationalities have the letter *e* and *s* in brackets at the end of them. What this means is that it depends on who you are speaking about. If you are speaking about a female, you will add the letter *e* to the end of the word. If you are speaking about multiple people, you will add the letter *s*, and if you are speaking about multiple women, you will add both. For example, "those

Americans," if you are speaking about all women, would be *Les Americain**es***. Notice how we have added both an *e* and an *s*. The reason that this is important to note in conversational French is that this will change the pronunciation slightly.

We will now look at some practical examples of how to use these nationalities in a sentence.

Elle habite au continent de L'amérique du nord. Elle est Canadienne.

Il est *Coréen*

Elle est *Coréene*

Occupations

Docteur [dok-t-ur], Doctor

Dentiste [don-tee-s-t], Dentist

Postier [poh-s-tee-ay], Mailman

Promeneur de Chien [p-roh-men-ur][duh][sh-yen], Dog Walker

Avocat [ah-vo-k-ah], Lawyer

Professeur [pro-f-ess-err], Teacher

Comptable [k-om-tah-b-luh], accountant

Conducteur de camion[k-on-doo-k-tur][duh][k-am-ee-on], truck driver

Banquier [bon-k-ee-yay], male banker

Banquière [bon-k-ee-y-air], female banker

Vocabulary

Connaître les gens, la nationalité et l'emploi

Knowing People

Un Ami [uhn][ah-mee], a friend

Une Amie [oo-n][ah-mee], a friend

Mon petit ami [m-oh][puh-tee][ah-mee], my boyfriend

Ma petite amie [m-ah][puh-tee-tuh][ah-mee], my girlfriend

Le Professeur(e) [luh][p-roh-f-ess-urr], the teacher

L' Enseignant(e) [l-on-sen-y-ohn-t], the teacher

Un Groupe [uhn][g-roo-puh], a group

Club [k-loo-b], club

Equipe [ay-keep], team

Un collègue [uhn][k-aw-l-egg], a colleague

Une connaissance [oo-n][k-on-ess-on-s], an acquaintance

Un ennemi [uhn][eh-n-eh-m-ee], an enemy

Une ennemie [oo-n][eh-n-eh-m-ee], an enemy

Mon ennemi [m-oh][eh-n-eh-m-ee], my enemy

Elle est une de mes ennemies [el][ay][oo-n][duh][m-eh][eh-n-eh-m-ee] She is one of my enemies.

Il est sur l'équipe [eel][ay][s-oo-r][l-eh-k-ee-puh]. He is on the team

Il est mon collègue [eel][ay][m-oh][k-aw-l-egg]. He is my colleague

Elle est ma professeure [el][ay][mah][pr-aw-f-ess-urr]. She is my teacher/professor.

Elle est un collègue de mon ami. [el][ay][uhn][k-aw-l-egg][duh][m-oh][ah-mee]. She is a colleague of my friend.

Elle est une ennemie de mon ami [el][ay][uhn][eh-n-eh-m-ee][duh][m-oh][ah-mee]. She is an enemy of my friend.

Nationalities

Un Continent [uhn][k-on-tee-n-on-t], a continent

L' Amérique du nord, [l-ah-meh-r-ee-k][doo][n-or], North America

Un American, [uhn][ah-meh-ree-k-ah-n], an American

Une Américaine [oo-n][ah-meh-ree-k-ah-nuh], an American

Un Canadian [uhn][k-ah-nah-d-ee-yeh-n], a Canadian

Une canadienne [oo-n][k-ah-nah-d-ee-yeh-nuh], a Canadian

Le Mexique [luh][m-eh-k-see-k], Mexico

Un Mexicain [uhn][m-eh-k-see-k-ah-n], a Mexican

Une Mexicaine [oo-n][m-eh-k-see-k-ah-n] , a Mexican

L'Europe [l-oo-roh-puh], Europe

Européen [eu-roh-peh-en], European

Français [f-ron-s-ay], French

Italien [eh-tah-l-ee-en], Italian

Italienne [eh-tah-l-ee-en-uh], Italian

Grec [g-reh-k], Greek

Suisse [s-wee-suh], Swiss

Belge [b-el-j], Belgian

Suédois [s-weh-d-wah], Swedish

Suédoise [s-weh-d-wah-suh], Swedish

Polonais [poh-loh-nay], Polish

Anglais, [on-g-lay], English

L'Angleterre [l-on-g-let-air], England

Islandais [ee-lon-day], Icelandic

L'Asie [l-as-ee], Asia

Japonais [jah-poh-nay], Japanese

Coréen [k-oh-ray-en], Korean

Chinois [sh-ee-n-wah], Chinese

Taïwanais [t-eye-wah-n-ay], Taiwanese

L'Amérique du sud [l-ah-meh-ree-k][d-oo][s-oo-d], South America

Sud-Américain [s-oo-d][ah-meh-ree-k-an], South American

Brésilien [b-reh-see-lee-en], Brazilian

Brésilienne [b-reh-see-lee-en-nuh], Brazilian

Argentin [ar-j-on-t-eh-n], Argentinian

Argentine [ar-j-on-tee-nuh], Argentinian

L' Afrique [l-ah-f-ree-k], Africa

Africain [ah-f-ree-k-ah-n], African

Sud-Africain [s-oo-d][ah-f-ree-k-ah-n], South African

Kényan, [k-eh-n-yeh-n], Kenyan

L'Australie [l-aw-s-t-rah-lee], Australia

L'Australien [aw-s-t-rah-lee-en], Australian

Néo-zélandais [n-eh-oh][z-ay-lon-day], New Zealander

Néo-zélandaise [n-eh-oh][z-ay-lon-day-suh], New Zealander

L'Inde [l-eh-n-duh], India

Indien [l-eh-n-dee-en], Indian

Indienne [l-eh-n-dee-en-uh], Indian

L'antarctique [l-an-tar-k-tee-k], Antarctica

Islandais(e) [ee-l-on-day], Icelandic

Occupations

Docteur *[dok-t-ur], doctor*

Dentiste *[don-tee-s-t], dentist*

Postier *[poh-s-tee-ay], mailman*

Promeneur de Chien [p-roh-men-ur][duh][sh-yen], dog walker

Avocat [ah-vo-k-ah], lawyer

Professeur [pro-f-ess-err], teacher

Comptable [k-om-tah-b-luh], accountant

Conducteur de camion [k-on-doo-k-tur][duh][k-am-ee-on], truck driver

Banquier [bon-k-ee-yay], male banker

Banquière [bon-k-ee-y-air], female banker

Chapter 9 - What Day Is It?

Learn how to measure and tell the time is hugely important. In many cultures, punctuality is extremely important and viewed as a form of respect, and I personally think it is a great sign of courtesy. Of course, you will also learn the days of the week and months, so you can make plans. Another thing you may want to know when traveling abroad is what season is it, to know how to dress accordingly.

Second	Seconde
One minute has sixty **seconds**.	Une minute équivaut à soixante **secondes**.

Seh-gon-duh

Minute	Minute
One hour has sixty **minutes**.	Une heure équivaut à soixante **minutes**.

Mee-nu-tuh

Hour	Heure
There are twenty-four **hours** in a day.	Il y a vingt-quatre **heures** dans une journée.

Eu-ruh

Great, let's carry on.

Day	Jour
January has thirty-one **days**.	Il y a trente-et-un **jours** en Janvier.

Joor

Week	Semaine
We have one **week** to finish.	Nous avons une **semaine** pour terminer.

Suh-main-uh

Month	Mois
We will be there next **month**.	Nous serons là le **mois** prochain.

Mwah

Year	Année
One more birthday, one more **year**.	Un anniversaire de plus, une **année** de plus.

Ah-neh

Decade	Décennie
This **decade** is going to end soon.	Cette **décennie** va bientôt se terminer.

Deh-seh-nee

Century	Siècle
This is the discovery of the **century**.	C'est la découverte du **siècle**.

See-eh-kluh

Morning	Matin
The meeting was this **morning**.	La réunion était ce **matin**.

Mah-ten

Afternoon	Après-midi

Will you be there in the **afternoon**?	Tu seras là cet **après-midi**?

Ah-preh-mee-dee

Night	Nuit
The Moon comes out at **night**.	La lune sort la **nuit.**

Nu-ee

Spring	Printemps
Everything flowers in **spring**.	Tout fleurit au **printemps**.

Pren-tam

Summer	Eté
We had a fun **summer**.	Nous avons eu un **été** divertissent.

Eh-teh

Autumn	Automne
Look at the first **autumn** leaf.	Regardes la première feuille d'**automne**.

Oh-to-nuh

Winter	Hiver
Winter is here.	l'**hiver** est arrivé.

Ee-ver

January	Janvier
January is the first month of the year.	**Janvier** est le premier mois de l'année.

Jan-vee-eh

February	Février
That tree flowers in **February**.	Cet arbre fleurit en **Février**.

Feh-vree-eh

March	Mars
March is a good month for harvesting.	**Mars** est un bon mois pour la récolte.

Mars

April	Avril
We stop activities in **April**.	Nous arrêtons les activités en **Avril**.

Ah-vreel

Have you noticed how most of the names of the months are similar between English and French? That's a relief, isn't it?

May	Mai
May is going to be a great month.	**Mai** va être un mois super.

Meh

June	Juin
The break starts in **June**.	Les vacances commencent en **Juin**.

Ju-ein

July	Juillet
July is a hot month in France.	**Juillet** est un mois chaud en France.

Ju-ee-yeh

August	Août
This **August** will be rainy.	Ce mois d'**Août** sera pluvieux.

Ah-oo-t

September	Septembre
Next semester starts in **September**.	Le prochain semestre commence en **Septembre**.

Sep-ten-bruh

October	Octobre
My birthday is in **October**.	Mon anniversaire est en **Octobre**.

Ok-to-bruh

November	Novembre
We celebrated Halloween all **November**.	Nous avons célébré Halloween tout le mois de **Novembre**.

Noh-vem-bruh

December	Décembre
Year ends in **December**.	L'année se termine en **Décembre**.

Deh-cem-bruh

Monday	Lundi
Today is **Monday**.	Aujourdhui, c'est **Lundì**.

Leun-dee

Tuesday	Mardi
I have an appointment for next **Tuesday**.	J'ai un rendez-vous pour **Mardì** prochain.

Mar-dee

Wednesday	Mercredi
Wednesday is not a good day for me.	**Mercredi** n'est pas un bon jour pour moi.

Mer-kruh-dee

Thursday	Jeudi
I'll see you next **Thursday**.	Je vous verrai **jeudi** prochain.

Juh-dee

Friday	Vendredi
The party is next **Friday**.	La fête est **Vendredi** prochain.

Ven-druh-dee

Saturday	Samedi
I play every **Saturday**.	Je joue tous les **Samedis**.

Sah-muh-dee

Sunday	Dimanche
We can have lunch this **Sunday**.	Nous pouvons déjeuner ensemble ce **Dimanche**.

dDee-man-shuh

How is it going? Are you ready for a short dialogue?

Ally: *So, what are your plans for next year?*

Alors, quels sont tes plans pour l'année prochaine?

Juan: *I honestly don't know what will happen after winter.*

Sincèrement, je ne sais pas ce qui va se passer après l'hiver.

Ally: *Will you at least come back in February? The spring is lovely here.*

Tu pourras au moins revenir en Février? Le printemps est superbe ici.

Juan: *If I don't, I promise I will be back to celebrate summer, in July.*

Si je ne reviens pas, je promets que je serais là en Juillet, pour célébrer l'été.

Ally: *Everyone loves summer. I love autumn.*

Tout le monde adore l'été. Moi j'adore l'automne.

Juan: *Why?*

Pourquoi?

Ally: *Leaves change colors and I love the weather between September and November.*

Les feuilles changent de couleur et j'adore le climat entre Septembre et Novembre.

Juan: Two weeks ago you didn't love in it that much.

Il y a deux semaines tu n'aimais pas tellement ça.

Ally: Are you talking of that rainy Wednesday? I hated that.

Tu parles de ce mercredi pluvieux? J'ai détésté.

Juan: Yeah. As if it was not enough with those boring Mondays.

Oui. Comme si ces lundi ennuyants n'étaient pas assez.

Ally: Oh, sure. I don't like Mondays. I love Fridays.

C'est sur. Je n'aime pas les lundis. J'adore les vendredis.

Juan: Like everyone. But I like Saturdays better.

Comme tout le monde. Mais je préfère les samedis.

Ally: Yes. Especially the ones in Spring, when you take your boat for a ride.

Oui. Surtout au printemps. Quand tu peux prendre ton bâteau pour faire un tour.

Juan: You remember it. Good.

Tu t'en souviens. Super.

It is not as hard as you thought, right? There is a lot to remember, but sometimes it's easier if you find the similarities between English and French, as some in the names of the months. And let us repeat, practice makes perfect.

Now has come the time to learn some important verbs and how to conjugate them.

Chapter 10 - There Is No Gift Like The Present

Just as in any other language, in French, verbs are an important part of everyday speaking. When studying a foreign language, the present is the first tense you learn as this allows you to form simple sentences. It is used to describe something that is happening right now or a state of being. Using the present tense, you will be able to speak about your desires, interests and plans.

First of all, in French, verb conjugation is done by changing the ending of the verb. Verbs are divided into 3 different categories of verbs, called "conjugations" – as in English. Each one is characterized by a specific ending in its infinitive form:

- First conjugation: Verbs ending in -ER (like aimer)

- Second conjugation: Verbs ending in -IR (like dormir)

- Third conjugation: Verbs ending in -RE (like croire)

I will teach you how to conjugate the regular verbs.

Hopefully, with a bit of practice, you will realize that French verb conjugation is actually much easier than it seems.

So, let's get started. There is no time like the present!

<table>
<tr><th>To love</th><th>Aimer</th><th>Root</th><th>Termination</th></tr>
<tr><td>I love</td><td>J'aime</td><td rowspan="2">Aim-</td><td>ER changes for "e"</td></tr>
<tr><td>You love</td><td>Tu aimes</td><td>ER changes for "es"</td></tr>
</table>

He/She loves	Il/Elle aime
We love	Nous aimons
You love	Vous aimez
They love	Ils/Elles aiment

ER changes for "e"
ER changes for "ons"
ER changes for "ez"
ER changes for "ent"

The root of all regular verbs never changes. As you can see, the root is the part preceding the infinitive ending. So, for example, in "Aimer" the root is "Aim-". As we said, the root always remains the same and different endings are added to denote the person, number or tense. Let's look at some examples.

I love the rain.	J'aime la pluie.
She loves the music.	Elle aime la musique.
You love movies.	Tu aimes les films.
They love to play music.	Ils aiment jouer de la musique.

Great! Here is a tip: using the above table you will be able to conjugate every other regular verb that ends in "-ER", all you will have to do is add to the root the relevant ending, as we just did. Clearly, the same logic applies to verb of the second and third conjugation (-IR and -RE). That's good to know, right?

Here are a few more examples. For the verb "to sing" - "chanter", you can separate the root "Chant-", and all you will need to do is to add the correct ending, as previously explained. The root of the verb "to sleep" – "dormir" is "dor-", and of the verb "to sell" - "vendre", the root is "Vend-".

Let's exercise with a fundamental verb: finir. In this case, the root is "Fin-".

To finish	**Finir**	**Root**	**Termination**
I finish	Je finis	Fini-	Ir changes for "s"
You finish	Tu finis		Ir changes for "s"
He/She finishes	Il/Elle finit		Ir changes for "t"
We finish	Nous finissons		Ir changes for "ons"
You finish	Vous finissez		Ir changes for "ez"
They finish	Ils/Elles finissent		Ir changes for "ent"

I finish work at 5pm.	Je finis de travailler à 17h.
She finishes school early today.	Elle finit l'école tôt aujourd'hui.
He finishes building his house.	Il finit de construire sa maison.
They finish their meal.	Ils finissent leur repas.

So, anyhow, what do you like to do in your free time? What are your interests? What are you passionate about? Come on, think about this for a moment. Verbs are important to discuss all of these things.

To believe	**Croire**	**Root**	**Termination**
I believe	Je crois		RE changes for "is"
You believe	Tu crois		RE changes for "is"
He/She believes	Il/Elle croit	Cro-	RE changes for "it"
We believe	Nous croyons		RE changes for "yons"
You believe	Vous croyez		RE changes for "yez"
They believe	Ils croient		RE changes for "ient"

Note that even though they are written differently, the 1st, 2nd, 3rd singular person, as well as the 3rd plural person, are pronounced the same. This applies to all French verbs. Isn't that amazing?

You believe in loyalty.	Tu crois en la loyauté.
He believes in what he can touch.	Il croit en ce qu'il peut toucher.
You believe in yourselves.	Vous croyez en vous-même.
They believe in you.	Ils croient en toi.

The root of the verb "Croire" is "Cro-".

So, what have you learned, and what do you have faith in? Repeat with me: “Je crois....”. Eventually, you will be able to better express yourself in French, but –in the meantime- “Je crois” is good enough.

Now let’s look at the present of the auxiliary verb “to be” – “être”. This verb is one of the most versatile and you will use it a lot in French, to introduce yourself, find out more about something or someone, describe places and things, etc. It is an auxiliary verb and its purpose is to help other verbs conjugate in compound tenses. In other words, it helps to create more complex sentences and tenses.

To be	**Être**
I am	Je suis
You are	Tu es
He/She/It is	Il/Elle est
We are	Nous sommes
You are	Vous êtes
They are	Ils sont

Alongside the verb “to be”, “to have” – “avoir” – is the second most important verb in the French language. It is an auxiliary and irregular verb. It allows you to express numerous things: possessing something (literally or in a figurative way), communicate, express your needs and desires, etc.

To have	**Avoir**
I have	J’ai
You have	Tu as
He/She has	Il/Elle a

We have	Nous avons
You have	Vous avez
They have	Ils ont

I have a meeting at nine.	J'ai une reunion à neuf heures.
He has a television at home.	Il a une television à la maison.
We have a plan.	Nous avons un plan.
They have a place by the lake.	Ils ont une propriété près du lac.

Now let's see how the « présent progressif » - the present progressive – can help us.

The « présent progressif » could be compared to the present continuous in English. It forms with the verb to be in the present and the expression « en train de » + verb to infinitive.

The expression *être en train de* + infinitive verb is used to emphasize actions in progress, similar to the present progressive tense in English. These constructions take a conjugated form of the verb *être* (in the present) + *en train de* + inifinitive verb.

Unlike the simple present tense, which is sometimes used for actions in progress, *être en train de* never describes a regular or habitual action.

Examples:

What are you doing ? I'm working.	Tu fais quoi ? Je suis en train de travailler.
Have you finished writing the letter ? We are finishing.	Tu as fini d'écrire la lettre ? Nous sommes en train de finir.

Did he go to the grocery store? He is shopping right now.	Est-il allé au supermarché? Il fait les courses maintenant.
They are taking a test in classroom A.	Ils sont entrain de passer une évaluation dans la salle A.

Are you looking forward to putting this into practice?

Emma: *Hi. I am Emma.*

Salut. Je suis Emma.

David: *Nice to meet you. I am David.*

Enchanté. Je suis David.

Emma: *Tell me, David. What do you like to do?*

Dis moi, David. Qu'est-ce que tu aimes faire?

David: *I enjoy sailing on weekends.*

J'aime faire de la voile les weekends.

Emma: *Do you have a boat?*

Tu as un bâteau?

David: *Yes, I do. And what do you like to do?*

Oui, j'en ai un. Et qu'est-ce que tu aimes faire?

Emma: *I have a dancing academy. I love to teach.*

J'ai un club de dance. J'adore enseigner.

David: *Really? I have a niece. She loves to dance.*

Vraiment? J'ai une niece qui adore danser.

Emma: *Great! How old is she?*

Super! Elle a quel âge?

David: *She is 6 years old. Turns 7 in two weeks.*

Elle a 6 ans. Elle aura 7 ans dans deux semaines.

Emma: *I teach from 7. Maybe you could bring her. I am currently working on a ballet choreography.*

J'enseigne à partir de 7 ans. Peut-être que tu pourrais l'amener. Je suis en train de travailler sur une chorégraphie de ballet.

David: *Awesome. I am sure she will love it.*

Génial. Je suis sûr qu'elle va adorer.

As you can see, is very important to know how to conjugate the Present simple. Carry on with the practice until you achieve a better understanding.

Chapter 11 - Family

La famille

We will look at the members of your family and how you can refer to them in French. Most of the time, when you are using these words, it will be when talking about someone to someone else, so we will also look at how to say this in a sentence and what words will need to come before and after them. To begin, below are the names for the different members of your family.

Père [p-air], Father

Mère [m-air], Mother

Soeur [s-urr], Sister

Frère [f-r-air], Brother

Cousine [k-oo-zee-n], Female Cousin

Cousin [k-oo-z-in], Male cousin

Tante [t-on-t], Aunt

Oncle [on-k-leh], Uncle

Grandmère [g-ron-d-m-air], Grandmother

Grandpère [g-ron-d-p-air], Grandfather

Grandparents, Grandparents

Demi-Soeur [duh-mee][s-urr], stepsister

Demi-Frère [duh-mee][f-r-air], stepbrother

Belle Frère [b-el][f-r-air], brother in law

Belle Soeur [b-el][s-urr], sister in law

Belle Mère [b-el][m-air], mother in law

We will now look at how to use these words in a sentence. These words will come in handy when you are talking to someone about someone else who is related to you, or if you are speaking within a family setting about other family members. Keep in mind that according to the gender of the person you are speaking about, you will need to change the word you use to describe them. In French, we have different ways of saying "my" according to gender. We will use *ma* if we are speaking about a female, like *my mother* or *my aunt*, and *mon* if we are speaking about a male, like *my father* or *my male cousin.* If you are using the plural, like *my cousins* or *my grandparents*, you will say *mes,* regardless of gender. Below are examples of this and how you can use them practically in a sentence.

Ma belle-soeur

Mon oncle

Ma tante

Mon cousin

Ma cousine

Some common sentences where you would use these words are to follow.

Le frère de ma mère est mon oncle. The brother of my mother is my uncle.

Le Petit Ami de ma soeur s'appelle Jean. My sister's boyfriend is named Jean.

Ma cousine est mon meilleur ami. My (female) cousin is my best friend.

Mon frère joue au baseball. My brother plays baseball.

Ma grand-mère est très belle. My grandmother is very pretty.

Je suis allez chez mes grand parents. I went to my grandparents' house.

J'ai mangé le petit déjeuner avec ma mère. I ate breakfast with my mother.

Mon père m'a conduit à l'école ce matin. My father drove me to school this morning.

As you learn more about the French language, you will be able to substitute any of these sentence examples with different nouns of your choice. For example, you could switch "school" to "hockey practice" or something of the sort. You can also switch out the person you are talking about. For example, instead of saying, "I went to my grandparent's house," you could say, "I went to my cousin's house." Knowing the basics of these types of sentences will allow you to create any type of sentence you want.

The above sentences concerned the family that you were born into, but now, we will look at other members of the family.

Ma femme, my wife

Mon mari, my husband

Une épouse, a spouse

Mes enfants, my kids

Mon fils, my son

Ma fille, my daughter

Un bébé, a baby

Un Bambin, a toddler

Les jumelles, twins

Now, we will use these in sentence examples for you to see how to use them practically.

J'adore ma femme. I love/adore my wife.

Avez-vous entendu que Jacques a maintenant une épouse? Have you heard that Jacques now has a spouse?

Les jumelles sont très enjouées! The twins are very playful!

Mes enfants sont âgés maintenant. My kids are grown now.

Vocabulary List

When reading through this list, practice the pronunciation of these words, especially the first five, as you will see them over and over again in the example sentences further down the list. In the example sentences, the words that have not yet been spelled out for you to practice their pronunciation will be written between the brackets below the sentence itself and the words that you have practiced the pronunciation of can be found in the list. Be sure to read aloud for the best results!

La famille

Ma [mah], my

Mon [m-oh], my

De [duh], of

La [l-ah], the

Le [luh], the

Père [p-air], father,

Mère [m-air], mother

Soeur [s-urr], sister

Frère [f-r-air], brother

Cousine [k-oo-zee-n], female cousin

Cousin [k-oo-z-in], male cousin

Tante [t-on-t], aunt

Oncle [on-k-leh], uncle

Grand-mère [g-ron-d-m-air], grandmother

Grand-père [g-ron-d-p-air], grandfather

Demi-Soeur [duh-mee][s-urr], stepsister

Demi-Frère [duh-mee][f-r-air], stepbrother

Belle Frère [b-el][f-r-air], brother in law

Belle Soeur [b-el][s-urr], sister in law

Belle Mère [b-el][m-air], mother in law

Le frère de ma mère est mon oncle. My mother's brother is my uncle.

Est [eh]

Le Petit Ami de ma soeur s'appelle Jean. My sister's boyfriend is named Jean.

S'appelle [s-ah-peh-luh]

Ma cousine est mon meilleur ami. My (female) cousin is my best friend.

Meilleur [may-ur]

Mon frère joue au baseball. My brother plays baseball.

Joue [j-oo]

Au [oh]

Baseball [bay-suh-bah-l]

Ma grand-mère est très belle. My grandmother is very pretty.

Très [t-r-ay](rolled r)

Belle [b-el]

Je suis allez chez mes grand parents. I went to my grandparents' house.

Suis [s-wee]

Allez [ah-lay]

Chez [sh-ay]

Mes [m-ay]

J'ai mangé le petit déjeuner avec ma mère. I ate breakfast with my mother.

Mangé [m-on-j-ay]

Petit déjeuner [puh-t-ee][day-j-uh-nay]

Avec [ah-veh-k]

Mon père m'a conduit à l'école ce matin. My father drove me to school this morning.

M'a [m-ah]

Conduit [k-on-d-wee]

L'école [l-eh-k-oh-l]

Ce [s-uh]

Matin [mah-t-ah-n]

Ma femme [f-emm], my wife

Mon mari [mah-ree], my husband

Une épouse [ay-poo-suh], a spouse

Mes enfants [on-f-on-t-s], my kids

Mon fils [f-ee-suh], my son

Ma fille [fee], my daughter

Un bébé [bay-bay], a baby

Un Bambin [bah-m-b-ah-n], a toddler

Les jumelles [j-oo-m-el], twins

J'adore ma femme. I love/adore my wife.

J'adore [j-ah-d-oh-r]

Avez-vous entendu que Jacques a maintenant une épouse? Have you heard that Jacques now has a spouse?

Avez-vous [ah-vay-v-oo]

Entendu [on-ton-doo]

Que [k-uh]

Jacques [j-ah-k]

Maintenant [meh-n-tuh-nah-n-t]

Les jumelles sont très enjouées! The twins are very playful!

Sont [soh-n]

Enjoués [on-j-oo-ay]

Mes enfants sont âgés maintenant. My kids are grown now.

Ages [ah-j-ay]

Chapter 12 - Looking for a Ride?

Welcome to the holiday you always dreamed about! There's just one more thing you will have to worry about before you can enjoy a refreshing drink next to the Eiffel Tower: how to get to your hotel. And so, the time has come to test your knowledge. Now that you arrived at your destination, your super-intensive-Italian immersion is about to start. How exciting is that?

First, let's begin with some basic words.

Taxi	Taxi
I need a **taxi**.	J'ai besoin d'un **taxi**.

Same word? 1 point for globalization!

Shuttle	Navette
Where can I get a **shuttle** to the Hilton Paris Opera?	Ou est-ce que je peux prendre la **navette** pour le Hilton Opera Paris?

Nav-veh-tuh

Bus	Bus
Where can I take a **bus** downtown?	Ou est-ce que je peux prendre un **bus** dans le centre?

Remember, the sound for the French "u" doesn't exist in English. The closest sound we have in English is OU as in "soup".

If you are traveling with family, you are possibly thinking about driving around. We should take you to a car rental.

Rent a car	Louer une voiture
I want to **rent a car**.	Je veux **louer une voiture**.

Vwa-tuu-ruh

Driver's license	Permis de conduire
I will need a **driver's license**.	J'aurai besoin d'un **permis de conduire**.

Per-mi duh con-dwi-ruh

You finally made it to your hotel. The panorama is wonderful and your room has a nice view all over Paris. Can you imagine it? Great! Me too! You will be able to get some rest soon. But, first, you have to check-in.

Check-in	Check in
I would like to **check into** my room.	J'aimerais faire le **check in** de ma chambre.

As you can see, check-in is used in French as well, and it's pronounced in the same way.

Reservation	Réservation
Under what name is the reservation?	Sous quel nom est la **réservation?**

Reh-zer-vah-ssion

Key	Clef
Here is your **key**.	Voici votre **clef**.

Klé (Here, you don't pronounce the "f".)

This is going to depend on what type of hotel you stay in. They now have keycards (clefs magnétiques), or you can even access by pin code (code). In any case, you can use the general word "clef", and everyone will understand.

Elevator	Ascenseur
The **elevator** is down the hall.	L' **ascenseur** se trouve au bout du couloir.

ah-sen-seur

Floor	Etage
Our room is on the 7th **floor.**	Notre chambre se trouve au 7ème **étage**.

This one sounds like "é-ta-guh".

Hey! I know you are eager to get into your room, so let's go in.

Hey! I know you can't wait to see your room, so come on, open the door!

Look around your room. I am sure there is a nice comfy bed, maybe a flat-screen, and a closet. You stop a minute to admire the sunset from your window. But now it's time to learn the name of the things around you.

Bed	Lit
Honey! Our **bed** is huge!	Chéri! Notre **lit** est énorme!

Once again, the "t" doesn't pronounce itself. "lee"

TV	Télévision/ TV
Is it a smart **TV**?	Est-ce-qu'il s'agit d'une smart **TV**?

Closet	Armoire
I'll put the suitcases in the **closet**.	Je vais mettre les valises dans l'**armoire**.

Ar-mwah-ruh.

Go inside your bathroom. Given that bathrooms go with water, and water leaks, you want to pay attention to the following words and phrases in case you have to report any problems with the pipes.

Shower	Douche
We have a massage **shower**.	Nous avons une **douche** hydromassante.

Doo-shuh. I know what you are thinking, this sounds like another word I know. Keep in mind that in French, the "ch" sound is similar to the "sh" one.

Toilet	Toilettes
Two bathrooms! We have a **toilet** each.	Deux salles-de-bains! Nous avons chacun nos **toilettes**.

Twa-let

Sink	Lavabo
I will put some things by the **sink.**	Je vais mettre des affaires à côté du **lavabo**.

La-va-boh

Towels	Serviettes
Hello! I need more **towels**.	Bonjour! J'aurais besoin de plus de **serviettes**.

Ser-vee-et

Pillows	Coussins
I also need 2 more **pillows**.	J'aurais aussi besoin de deux **coussins** de plus.

Koo-sen

It turns out my girlfriend uses four pillows, and I always use extra towels. These two are basic survival for us.

Also, some hotels don't put mini-fridges inside the bedrooms anymore. In case you have any requests, follow me to the next phrase.

Mini fridge	Mini-réfrigirateur
I would like a **mini-fridge** in my bedroom.	J'aimerais avoir un **mini-réfrigérateur** dans ma chambre.

You know the word for "mini". Let's practice the hard one:

Ré-fri-ge-ra-tuhr

Mini-réfrigérateur

You have a nice bedroom in there! So, how about some practice?

Concierge: *Hello! How can I help you?*

Bonjour! Comment puis-je vous aider?

Dan: *Hello! I think my sink is leaking.*

Bonjour! Je pense que mon lavabo coule.

Concierge: *I will send someone right away!*

Je vais vous envoyer quelqu'un tout de suite!

Dan: *Thanks. I appreciate your help.*

Merci pour votre aide.

Concierge: *I am sorry for the inconvenience. Is there anything I can do to make your stay more pleasant?*

Je suis désolé pour le désagrément. Est-ce que je peux faire quelque chose pour rendre votre séjour plus agréable?

Dan: *Now that you mention it, I notice my room does not have a mini-fridge.*

	Maintenant que vous le mentionnez, je vois qu'il n'y a pas de mini-réfrigérateur dans ma chambre.
Concierge:	*Of course! Anything else?*
	Bien-sûr, je m'en occupe. Autre chose?
Dan:	*I'd like a couple more towels, and one extra pillow, please.*
	J'aimerais avoir deux serviettes supplémentaires, et un coussin, s'il vous plait.
Concierge:	*Sure! Just in case you need more pillows, you have an extra inside the closet.*
	Bien-sûr! Juste au cas ou, si vous avez besoin de coussins supplémentaires, vous en avez un dans l'armoire.
Dan:	*Good to know! Thanks!*
	C'est bon à savoir! Merci!
Concierge:	*Is there anything else I can do for you today?*
	Est-ce que je peux faire autre chose pour vous?
Dan:	*I am okay. Thank you very much.*
	Non tout vas bien. Merci beaucoup.
Concierge:	*I will send all that right away. Again, sorry for the inconvenience.*
	Je vous envoie tout ça immédiatement. Encore une fois, navré pour le désagrément.
Dan:	*It is all good. Thanks for your help.*
	C'est tout bon. Merci pour votre aide.
Concierge:	*Thank you for being our guest!*
	Merci à vous, d'être notre client!

Good! I think we are all set! Ready to go work on your tan?

Chapter 13 - Exploring the City

When you are in the city, you will find that large roads usually have a pelican crossing and you are permitted to cross the road when the light is green. You may take the metro to travel from one place to another, or in some cities may take the tram. There are special prices available for people who are going to be in the city for a set number of days and buying these tickets can be advantageous to you when wishing to discover as much as you can within the limits of your stay. A Carte Orange is one such special priced ticket for the Paris Metro and it will save you a lot of money on having to pay individual fares each time you catch the metro. Look on the bulletin boards and then you can ask for the specific promotional ticket. For example, if you choose to buy the Carte Orange you would say:

One Carte Orange please	**Une carte orange s'il vous plait**	*Oon cart oronge see vous play*

You will always be able to get a tourist map from the Tourist Information Office in any large city in France. You will first need to find the tourist information office.

Where is the tourist information offices please?	**Où est l'office de Tourisme ?**	*Ooh aye loffiss duh tourisme?*

As you are going to a town that you don't know, it is quite possible that you will need to ask for a lot of directions. It is wise to have your map with you because someone can easily show you on the map how to get somewhere, whereas their explanation in French may be difficult to understand. The basics of directions include these phrases:

where is ...?	**Où est**	*Ooh ess*
straight on	**Tout droit**	*Too dwat*
to the right	**à droite**	*Ah dwaht*
to the left	**à gauche**	*Ah goash*

You may be told to take the second turn on the right. Let's look at the words that denote first (premier), second (Deuxième) or third (Troisième). As you can see these are fairly easy words to memorize. If you already know the French numbers, this helps too.

Let's take a moment to review these useful phrases for exploring the city.

Do you know where the metro is?	**Est-ce que vous savez comment aller au metro?**	*S kay voo sah-vay koh-mahn ah-lay oh meh-tro?*
the park	**le parc**	*luh pahrk*
the train station	**ál a gare**	*ah lah-gahr*
the travel agency	**l'agence de voyage**	*lah zahn duh vwah-yaj*
the grocery store	**l'épicerie**	*lay pee-suh-ree*
the shopping center	**le centre commercial**	*luh sahntr koh-mehr-shal*
the town hall	**la mairie**	*lah mar-ree*
the town center	**la centre-ville**	*luh- sahntr-veel*
the public bathrooms	**les toilettes publiques**	*lay twa-let puh-bleek*

the bar	**le bar**	*luh bahr*
Where can I park my car?	**Où puis-je garer ma voiture?**	*Ooh pweez gah-ray mah vwah-tyur?*
Where is the nearest restaurant?	**Où est le restaurant le plus proche?**	*Ooh eh luh rehs-toh-rahn lun plyu prosh?*
Is there a bank nearby?	**Est-ce qu'il y a une banque prés d'ici?**	*S-keel-ya oon bahnk preh dee-see?*
Is it very far?	**Est-ce que c'est loin d'ici?**	*S-kuh seh lwehn dee-see?*
It's far.	**C'est loin.**	*Seh lwehn.*
Is it close by?	**Est-ce que c'est prés d'ici?**	*S-kuh seh preh dee-see?*
It's close by.	**C'est prés d'ici.**	*Seh preh dee-see.*
Can I go on foot?	**Est-ce que je peux y aller á pied?**	*S kuh zay puh ee yah-lay ah piay?*
Take the next left.	**Prends la prochaine á gauche**	*Prahn lah proh-shain ah gosh.*
Take the next right	**Prends la prochaine á droite.**	*Prahn lah proh-shain ah dwaht.*
cross the...	**traverse le...**	*trah-vehrs luh...*
follow the...	**suis les...**	*swee lay*
until you reach the...	**jusqu'au...**	*zhyus-koh...*

It's on the left.	**C'est à gauche.**	*Seh tah gosh.*
It's on the right.	**C'est tout droite.**	*Seh too dwat.*
It's next to ...	**C'est à côté...**	*Seh tah koh-tay*
It's in front of...	**C'est devant**	*Seh duh-vahn*
It's behind...	**C'est derrière**	*Seh deh-riair*
It's to the North	**C'est au nord.**	*Seh toh nor*
It's to the South	**C'est au sud.**	*Seh toh syud.*
It's to the East	**C'est à l'est.**	*Seh tah lest.*
It's to the West	**C'est à l'ouest**	*Seh tahl-west.*

Now let's look at some of the things that you are likely to want to find in the city. This includes museums and places of interest to tourists.

The Museum - **le musée** – Pronounced: Luh Muzay

It's a good idea to know which particular museum and to have the name of the museum at hand so that you can ask the directions specificially for that museum. Paris is so filled with Museums that you can use your map to point to the exact museum that you are looking for and get help to get there.

The Eiffel tower	**la tour Eiffel**	*Lah toor eefelle*

Simply by adding the name of the place that you are looking for to the question, where is (**Où est**) you will be able to find your way around. This is pronounsed as *oow ay.*

Where is the Eiffel tower?	**Où est la tour Eiffel**	*Oow ay lah toor eefelle*

Looking for somewhere for a coffee and a break? You can ask people locally if they can recommend a good coffee shop. If you stop someone on the street to ask something, it is polite to say excuse me before you ask them what it is that you want to know.

Excuse me

Excusez-moi

You would then qualify this by saying Madam (to a lady), Monsieur (to a man), mademoiselle (to a young lady).

Excuse me, please but can you tell me where I can get a good coffee?

Excusez-moi, Madame, Connaissez-vous un bon café ici ?

One of the best verbs that you can learn in French when you are hitting the town is the verb CHERCHER which means to look for. You can use this in the street when you are looking for a particular shop, to pinpoint a tourist spot or to even ask when you are in a shop or a pharmacy for a particular product.

I am looking for the Eiffel Tower	**Je cherche le tour Eiffel**	*Jzuh Share sh luh toor eefell*
I am looking for the station	**Je cherche la gare**	*Jzuh Share sh la garr*
I am looking for a gift for my mother	**Je cherche un cadeau pour ma mère –**	*Ju share sh un cadow pour ma mare*

Quiz Time!

Here we are at the end of the third lesson!. Are you ready for quiz number three? Let's see!

1)How would you ask, "Where is the Eiffel Tower"?

2)How would you say, "It's on the right" ?

3)What is the shopping center called?

4)What is the discounted travel pass called?

5)How would you ask if something is close by?

Answers :

1)Où est la tour Eiffel?

2)C'est tout droite

3)Le centre commercial

4)Une carte orange

5)Est-ce que c'est prés d'ici?

Chapter 14 - So Many Roads and So Many Places

I personally love to walk. When I was younger and single, I would put my earphones in and walk through any new city I got the chance to visit. Now, with my girlfriend, I put the headphones away and we enjoy long chats while walking and looking around. Sometimes she takes pictures, and they are mostly of me taking pictures of her or the landscape. But I enjoy watching her under all the different shades and lights. Have you ever noticed how every city has different colors and vibes?

Back to business. Tell me, what do you typically want to visit first when exploring a new city? Wherever you want to go, I am here to help you. Why don't we start with a few basics?

Museum	Musée
Where is the Louvres **Museum**?	Où se trouve le **musée** du Louvres?

Mu-zé

Square	Place
How can I get to Saint-Georges **Square**?	Comment puis-je me rendre à la **place** Saint-Georges?

Pla-ssuh

Avenue	Avenue
What can I find on the main **avenue?**	Que puis-je trouver sur l'**avenue** principale?

Ah-veh-nuh

This one should not be a problem. The pronunciation is very similar to the English "avenue".

Monuments	Monuments
Paris is rich in history and **monuments.**	Paris est riche en histoire et **monuments.**

Moh-nuh-men

Park	Parc
Park Buttes-Chaumont is in Paris.	Le **Parc** Buttes-Chaumont se situe à Paris.

Par-k

Church	Eglise
They gave me this **church** as a reference.	Ils m'ont donné cette **église** comme référence.

Ee-glee-zuh

Not to be disrespectful, but travelling is not just about history and monuments. It is also about having fun and experiencing the true local culture, as well as going to bars and clubs.

Bar	Bar
Where is this **bar**?	Où se trouve ce **bar**?

See? Globalization scores again!

Now that you have learned the name of some places, let's go there together.

Across	En face
You can find them **across** the avenue.	Vous pouvez les trouver **en face** de l'avenue.

En fah-suh

In front of	Devant
He is waiting **in front of** the statue.	Il attends **devant** la statue.

Deh-van

Opposite	Opposé
We were walking in the **opposite** direction.	Nous étions en train de marcher du côté **opposé.**

Oh-poo-zé

Street	Rue
You can find it down the **street.**	Vous pouvez trouver ça en bas de la **rue.**

ruh

Subway	Métro
We can get there by **subway.**	Nous pouvons nous y rendre en **métro.**

Meh-troh – This word comes from "Metropolitain" which as you can guess, means "Metropolitan".

Mall	Centre commercial
What kind of **mall** would you like to visit?	Quel type de **centre commercial** souhaiteriez-vous visiter?

Cen-truh ko-mer-sial

Recommend	Recommander
What can you **recommend?**	Qu'est-ce que vous **recommandez?**

Re-co-men-déh

"Recommander" is a general word for "suggestions". So, whenever you are out of ideas, just remember this one.

In terms of tourism, you should already be an expert at getting around. You learned how to request a cab, rent a car, and ask for directions and recommendations. You are almost done with this section, so why don't we practice a little more?

Front desk (Recepción):	*Hello! How can I help you?* Bonjour! Comment puis-je vous aider?
Allen:	*I would like some recommendations for places to visit.* J'aimerais avoir des recommandations d'endroits à visiter.
Front desk:	*Very well. What type of place did you have in mind? A club, a museum?* Très bien. Quel type d'endroit aviez-vous en tête? Un club, un musée?
Allen:	*I heard that you have beautiful squares and monuments in this city.* J'ai entendu que vous avez des places et des monuments magnifiques dans la ville.
Front desk:	*That is true. Sadly, most cultural attractions are across town.* C'est vrai. Malheureusement, la plupart des attractions touristiques sont de l'autre côté de la ville.
Philip:	*Oh, I see. Could you give me some directions, please?*

	Oh, je vois. Pouvez-vous m'indiquer comment m'y rendre, s'il-vous-plaît?
Front desk:	*Sure! Would you like to travel by car or take the subway?*
	Bien-sûr! Vous préferez vous y rendre en voiture ou plutôt prendre le métro?
Philip:	*I would rather take a subway and walk.*
	Je préfèrerais prendre le métro et marcher.
Front desk:	*Very well. The subway is only 300m away.*
	Très bien. Le métro se trouve à seulement 300m d'ici.
Philip:	*Perfect! How do I get there?*
	Parfait! Comment puis-je m'y rendre?
Front desk:	*You only have to go down this street, take a right, and walk straight for 200m.*
	Vous avez seulement à descendre la rue, prendre à droite puis marcher tout droit pendant 200m.
Philip:	*That sounds easy. Thank you very much!*
	Ça à l'air facile. Merci beaucoup!
Front desk:	*All right, then. After you get to the subway, go to the mainline and take a train to étoile station.*
	D'accord, alors, en arrivant au métro, allez à la ligne principale et prenez le métro jusqu'à la station étoile.
Philip:	*Very good. I appreciate your help.*
	Très bien. Merci pour votre aide.

Front desk: *My pleasure. Have a nice day.*

Avec Plaisir. Bonne journée.

Allen: *Likewise. Bye.*

Egalement. Au revoir.

Ready to walk around the city and get lost in its little streets? I'm sure you can't wait. Then you'd better get ready. Go out and have fun. Who knows how many funny stories you will be able to tell once back from your trip!

Although now I am getting a bit hungry. Sorry, what did you say? Should we go and grab a bite to eat?

Chapter 15 - Eat, Travel, Love

Food is one of my favorite parts of traveling. Eating is an awesome way to learn a bit more about the culture and history of each place. Your nose and tongue become guides that can lead you through unknown passages, allowing you to enjoy the aromas of France in a glass of Cabernet; or to experience the culinary revolution in Paris, in the shape of a sweet and crusty croissant. Flavors are unique everywhere you go, and that is what makes them a huge part of traveling.

For this reason, I want to be sure I am giving you the opportunity to have the best experience. Plus, ordering food is a recurrent activity, which means you will have many chances to practice. I can also assure you something: some of the best typical food places will not have a translator.

Restaurant	Restaurant
Let's go into that **restaurant.**	Rentrons dans ce **restaurant.**

Rehs-to-ran

It is very similar to the English word, except for the intonation (Also, French people don't pronounce the "t" at the end.)

Table	Table
Table for four, please.	Une **table** pour quatre, s'il-vous-plaît.

Once again, the word is the same but the pronunciation is not. The French way to pronounce is: Tah-bluh".

Suggestions	Suggestions
Do you want to hear today's **suggestions?**	Vous voulez voir les **suggestions** du jour?

Suh-gest-eeon

Portion	Portion
I want a **portion** of fries.	J'aimerais avoir une **portion** de frites.

Pors-eeon

Quite easy, huh?

Fork	Fourchette
I dropped my **fork.**	J'ai fait tomber ma **fourchette.**

Foor-chett

Spoon	Cuillère
Can I get a **spoon**?	Puis-je avoir une **cuillère**?

Cu-ee-eh-ruh

Knife	Couteau
I will need a meat **knife.**	J'aurais besoin d'un **couteau** à viande.

Koo-toh

Plate	Assiette
Can you bring an extra **plate**?	Pouvez-vous apporter une **assiette** en plus?

Ass-ee-et

Entry	Entrée
Do you want an **entry**?	Voulez-vous une **entrée**?

An-tré

Main dish	Plat principal
For the **main dish**, I want the chicken.	En **plat principal**, j'aimerais le poulet.

Pla-prehn-si-pal

Well-cooked	Bien cuit
I want my steak **well-cooked.**	J'aimerais mon steak **bien cuit.**

Bee-n koo-ee

"Bien" (Bee-n) means "good".

Medium	A point
Medium is fine for me.	**A point,** ça me convient.

Ah poo-ehn

Dessert	Dessert
Of course, I want a **dessert.**	Bien-sûr que j'aimerais avoir un **dessert.**

Deh-ssehr (The "s" is pronounced as "s", not as a "z", like the English way.)

Vegan	Végétalien
Do you have a vegan menu?	Est-ce que vous avez un menu **végétalien**?

Veh-geh-tal-ee-ehn (Note that French people also say "vegan" sometimes, so they will probably understand this word, especially in restaurants.)

Check	Addition
I want the **check**, please.	J'aimerais avoir l'**addition**, s'il-vous-plaît.

Ah-dee-ssion

Are you excited to order your first dish? Why don't we go practice a bit more first...

Waiter (serveur): *Good afternoon! Welcome to our restaurant. My name is Shawn. How many are you?*

Bonjour! Bienvenue dans notre restaurant. Mon nom est Shawn. Vous êtes combien?

Mike: *Hello! We have a reservation under Paulson. Table for four.*

Bonjour! Nous avons une réservation sous le nom de Paulson, table pour quatre.

Waiter: *Yes, here you are. Come with me, please.*

Oui, je vois. Venez avec moi, s'il-vous-plaît.

Mike: *I would like to order right away. We are starving.*

J'aimerais commander maintenant. Nous sommes morts de faim.

Waiter: *Perfect. What would you like to order?*

Parfait. Que voulez-vous commander?

Mike: *What are your suggestions?*

Quelles sont vos suggestions?

Waiter: *The lobster ceviche as an appetizer. For the main dish, we have a beef tartare which is excellent.*

Le ceviche de homard en entrée. En plat principal, nous avons un excellent tartare de boeuf.

Mike: *Sounds great! I want one of each. Also, a salad and two beef dishes.*

Ça a l'air fabuleux! Je voudrais un de chaque. Aussi, une salade et deux plats à base de boeuf.

Waiter: *Do you want extra plates to share?*

Vous voulez des assiettes pour partager?

Mike: Yes, please.

Oui, s'il-vous-plaît.

Waiter: *Perfect. I will be back in a second with your plates, forks, and meat knives.*

Parfait. Je reviens dans une seconde avec vos assiettes, fourchettes et couteaux à viande.

Mike: *Thank you very much.*

Merci beaucoup.

Waiter: *I'll be right back.*

Je reviens tout de suite.

How did you feel after repeating that last dialogue? Look... I do not want to freak you out, but you are about to feel a bit under the weather.

Exercises

See how well you remembered your new French words from this lesson:

1. The English words for Rentrons dans ce restaurant are ____________________.

2. The English words for Une table pour quatre, s'il-vous-plaît are ____________________.

3. The English words for Lo encuentro realmente increíble are ____________________.

4. The English words for Vous voulez voir les suggestions du jour are ____________________.

5. The English words for J'aimerais is ____________________.

6. The English words for fourchette is ____________________.

7. The English words for cuillère is ____________________.

8. The English words for couteau is ____________________.

9. The English words for plat principal are ____________________.

10. The English words for bien cuit are ____________________.

Chapter 16 - Dining Out

-Bonjour. J'ai une réservation pour deux sous le nom de ... / Hello. I have a reservation for two under the name of ...

-Avez vous une table pour ... / Do you have a table for ...

-La carte, s'il vous plaît. / The menu, please.

-Qu'est-ce que vous recommandez? / What do you recommend?

-Quelle est las spécialité de la maison? / What's the house specialty?

-Je voudrais ... / I would like ...

What You May Hear

-Qu'est-ce que vous voulez commander? / What would you like to order?

-Vous avez choisi? / Have you decided?

-Qu'est-ce que je vous sers? / What can I get you?

Table Setting

bowl	le bol	*luh-bohl*
cup	la tasse	*lah-tahs*
dinner plate	l'assiette *f.*	*lah-syeht*
fork	la fourchette	*lah-foor-sheht*
glass	le verre	*luh-vehr*
knife	le couteau	*luh-koo-to*

menu	la carte	*lah-kahrt*
napkin	la serviette	*lah-sehr-vyeht*
pepper shaker	la poivrière	*lah-pwah-vree-yehr*
salt shaker	la salière	*lah-sahl-yehr*
saucer	la soucoupe	*lah-soo-koop*
soup dish	l'assiette à soupe	*lah-syeht-ah-soop*
soup spoon	la cuiller à soupe	*lah-kwee-yeah-ah-soop*
tablecloth	la nappe	*lah-nahp*
teaspoon	la cuiller	*lah-kwee-yehr*
wine glass	le verre à vin	*luh-vehr-ah-vaN*

Food and Drink

aioli	*ah-yoh-lee*	garlic-flavored mayonnaise
bercy	*behr-see*	a fish or meat sauce
crécy	*kray-see*	carrots
daube	*dohb*	a stew, usually beef
Florentine	*floh-rahN-teen*	spinach
forestière	*foh-rehs-tyehr*	wild mushrooms
parmentier	*pahr-mahN-tyay*	potatoes
périgourdine	*pay-ree-goor-deen*	truffles

Provençale	*proh-vahN-sahl*	a vegetable garnish
une salade	*ewn-sah-lahd*	salad, lettuce
les hors-d'œuvres	*lay ohr-duhvr*	appetizers
escargots à la bourguignonne	*ehs-kahr-go-ah-lah-boor-gee-nyohn*	snails in garlic-herb butter
pâté	*pah-tay*	pureed liver served in a loaf
foie gras	*fwah-grah*	fresh goose or duck liver
les soups	*lay-soop*	soups
la bouillabaisse	*lah-boo-yah-behs*	seafood stew
le consommé	*luh-kohN-soh-may*	clear broth
la soupe à l'oignon	*lah-soop-ah loh-nyohN*	onion soup
le velouté	*luh-vuh-loo-tay*	creamy soup
les viandes	*lay-vyahnd*	meats
le bifteck	*luh-beef-tehk*	steak
le chateaubriand	*luh-shah-to-bree-yahN*	a porterhouse steak
la côte de boeœuf	*lah-kot-duh-buhf*	prime rib
le rosbif	*luh-rohs-beef*	roast beef
le dessert	*luh-dee-sehr*	dessert

une bavaroise	*ewn-bah-vahr-wahz*	Bavarian cream
une bombe	*ewn-bohNb*	ice cream with different flavors
une glace	*ewn-glahs*	ice cream
un yaourt	*uhN-yah-oort*	yogurt
le vin	*luh-vaN*	wine
le vin rouge	*luh-vaN-roozh*	red wine
le vin blanc	*luh-vaN-blahN*	white wine
le champagne	*luh-shahN-pah-nyuh*	champagne

Drinking

Je voudrais … / I'd like …

une bière (pression) – a (draught) beer

une bière anglaise – an ale

une bouteille de vin – a bottle of wine

un cognac – a brandy

un martini – a martini

une vodka – a vodka

-*Sans glaçons s'il vous plaît.* – No ice, please.

-*Cul sec!* – Bottoms up!

-*Santé!* – Cheers!

-*Une autre tournée, s'il vous plaît.* – Another round, please.

-On va prendre des shooters. / We're going to take shots.

-Je suis saoul(e). – I'm drunk.

Health and Emergency

Calling for Help

-Aidez-moi! / Help me!

-Ja besoin d'un docteur qui parle Anglais. / I need a doctor who can speak English.

-J'ai eu un accident. Je besoin d'une ambulance. / I've had an accident. I need an ambulance.

-C'est une urgence. / It's an emergency.

-Appelez un docteur! / Call a doctor!

Visiting a Doctor

-Où est l'hôpital le plus proche? / Where's the nearest hospital?

-Je ne me sens pas bien. / I'm not feeling well.

-Je suis malade. / I'm sick.

-Ça fait mal ici. / It hurts here.

-J'ai fais mes rappels. / I have had vaccinations.

-Je fais une allergie. / I have an allergy.

Parts of the Body

arm	le bras	*luh-brah*
back	le dos	*luh-do*
chest	la poitrine	*lah-pwah-treen*
ear	l'oreille *f.*	*loh-reh-y*

elbow	le coude	*luh-kood*
eye	l'œil *m.*	*luhy*
eyes	les yeux	*lay-zyuh*
face	la figure	*lah-fee-gewr*
finger	le doigt	*luh-dwah*
foot	le pied	*luh-pyay*
hand	la main	*lah-maN*
head	la tête	*lah-teht*
heart	le cœur	*luh-kuhr*
hip	la hanche	*lah-ahNsh*
kidney	le rein	*luh-raN*
knee	le genou	*luh-zhuh-nou*
leg	la jambe	*lah-zhahNb*
lip	la lèvre	*lah-lehvr*
lung	le poumon	*luh-poo-mohN*
mouth	la bouche	*lah-boosh*
neck	le cou	*luh-koo*
nose	le nez	*luh-nay*
shoulder	l'épaule	*lay-pohl*
stomach	l'estomac	*leh-stoh-mah*
throat	la gorge	*lah-gohrzh*
toe	l'orteil *m.*	*lohr-they*
tongue	la langue	*lah-lahNg*

tooth	la dent	*lah-dahN*
wrist	le poignet	*luh-pwah-nyeh*

-*J'ai mal à la poitrine.* / My chest hurts.

-*J'ai mal à la gorge.* / I have a sore throat.

-*J'ai mal de tête terrible.* / I have a terrible headache.

Drugstore Items

absorbent cotton	du coton	*dew-koh-tohN*
alcohol	de l'alcool	*duh-lahl-kohl*
antacid	un anti-acide	*uhN-nahN-tee-ah-seed*
antihistamine	un antihistaminique	*uhN-nahN-tee-ees-tah-mee-neek*
antiseptic	un antiseptique	*uhN-nahN-tee-sehp-teek*
anti-dandruff shampoo	du shampooing anti-pellicules	*dew-shahN-pwaN-ahN-tee-peh-lee-kewl*
aspirins	des aspirines	*day-zah-spee-reen*
Band-aid	un pansement adhésif	*uhN-pahNs-mahN-ahd-ay-zeef*
bottle	un biberon	*uhN-beeb-rohN*
brush	une brosse	*ewn-brohs*
comb	un peigne	*uhN-peh-nyuh*

cough drops	des pastilles contre la toux *f.*	*day-pah-stee-y-kohNtr-lah-too*
cough syrup	le sirop contre la toux	*luh-see-roh-kohNtr-lah-too*
deodorant	du déodorant	*dew-day-oh-doh-rahN*
diapers	des couches	*day-koosh*
eye drops	du collyre	*dew-koh-leer*
gauze pads	des bandes de gaze *f.*	*day-bahnd-duh-gahz*
ice pack	une vessie de glace	*ewn-veh-see-duh-glahs*
laxative	un laxatif	*uhN-lahk-sah-teef*
mouthwash	de l'eau dentifrice *f.*	*duh-lo-dahN-tee-frees*
nail clippers	un coupe-ongles	*uhN-koop-ohNgl*
pacifier	une sucette	*ewn-sew-seht*
safety pins	des épingles de sûreté *f.*	*day-zay-paNgl-duh-sewr-tay*
sanitary napkins	des serviettes hygiéniques *f.*	*day-sehr-vyeht-ee-zhyay-neek*
shaving cream	de la crème à raser	*duh-lah-krehm-ah-rah-zay*
sleeping pills	des somnifères *m.*	*day-sohm-nee-fehr*
soap bar	une savonnette	*ewn-sah-voh-neht*
suntan lotion	de la lotion solaire	*dew-lah-loh-syohN-soh-lehr*

tampons	des tampons périodiques	*day-tahN-pohN-pay-ree-oh-deek*
thermometer	un thermomètre	*uhN-tehr-moh-mehtr*
tissues	des mouchoirs en papier *m.*	*day-moosh-wahr-ahN-pah-pyay*
toothbrush	une brosse à dents	*ewn-brohs-ah-dahN*
toothpaste	de la pâte dentifrice	*duh-lah-paht-dahN-tee-frees*
vitamins	des vitamines *f.*	*day-vee-tah-meen*
wound bandages	des pansements *m.*	*day-pahNs-mahN*

Exercises – Translate in French

A. At the Airport

1) airport

2)check-in counter

3) flight

4) gate

5) baggage claim area

6) cart

7) aisle

8) I'd like to have a window seat.

9) I'll stay here for a month.

10) Where can I exchange my money?

Answers :

1) l'aéroport

2) le guichet d'embarquement

3) le vol

4) la porte

5) les bagages

6) le chariot

7) le couloir

8) Je voudrais avoir un siège du côté hublot.

9) Je vais rester ici un mois.

10) Où puis-je échanger mon argent?

B. Getting Where You're Going

1) one-way ticket

2) subway

3) Slow Down

4) No Parking

5) How much is the fare?

6) I'd like to reserve a seat.

7) What's the next stastion?

8) Wait for me.

9) I'd like to rent a car.

10) Does it include insurance?

Answers :

1) un billet simple

2) le métro

3) Ralentir

4) Défense de Stationner / Stationnement Interdet

5) Combien coûte un billet?

6) Je voudrais réserver une place.

7) Quelle est la prochaine station?

8) Attendez-moi.

9) Je voudrais louer une voiture.

10) Est-ce que ça inclut une assurance?

C. At the Hotel

1) elevator

2) swimming pool

3) single room

4) safe

5) key

6) I have a reservation.

7) What time is the check-out?

8) Do you have a room for tonight?

9) Is there en-suite bathroom?

10) Is breakfast included?

Answers :

1) l'ascenseur

2) la piscine

3) une chambre à un lit

4) un coffre

5) une clé

6) J'ai une réservation.

7) À quelle heure est le check-out?

8) Avez-vous une chambre libre pour ce soir?

9) Y a-t-il une salle de bain?

10) Le petit déjeuner est-il inclus?

D. Seeing the Sights

1) to the castle

2) to the lake

3) to the cathedral

4) to the tower

5) to the ruins

6) What's there to see?

7) Do you know where the museum is?

8) How do I get there?

9) Are there guided tours?

10) At what time does it close?

Answers :

1) au château

2) au lac

3) à la cathédrale

4) à la tour

5) aux ruines

6) Qu'est-ce qu'il y a à voir?

7) Est-ce que vous savez où se trouve le musée?

8) Comment y aller?

9) Y a-t-il des visites guidées?

10) À quelle heure ferme-t-il?

E. Dining Out

1) dinner plate

2) wine glass

3) steak

4) an ice cream

5) appetizers

6) The menu, please.

7) I'd like some seafood stew.

8) Do you have a table for three?

9) Cheers!

10) I'd like a bottle of wine.

Answers :

1) l'assiette

2) le verre à vin

3) le bifteck

4) une glace

5) les hors-d'œuvres

6) La carte, s'il vous plaît.

7) Je voudrais des bouillabaisse.

8) Avez-vous une table pour trois?

9) Santé!

10) Je voudrais une bouteille de vin.

F. Health and Emergency.

1) my stomach

2) my ears

3) my hands

4) aspirins

5) antihistamine

6) Help me!

7) It's an emergency.

8) I'm not feeling well.

9) I have an allergy.

10) My chest hurts.

Answers :

1) mon estomac

2) mes oreilles

3) mes mains

4) des aspirines

5) un antihistaminique

6) Aidez-moi.

7) C'est une urgence.

8) Je ne me sens pas bien.

9) Je fais une allergie.

10) J'ai mal à la poitrine.

Chapter 17 - Beginner's Phrases

Common Question Answers

Here is a list of the most common answers to questions that we could come up with. You will be using these a lot so be sure to pay attention.

Mon nom est... – My name is...

Je suis.... J'ai ans. – I am ... years old.

Je viens de... – I'm from...

Oui – Yes

non – No

Peut être – Maybe

Je fais – I do

toujours – Always

jamais – Never

Parfois – Sometimes

effectivement – Indeed

correct - Correct

Bien sûr – Of course

Oui, je parle un peu français – Yes, I speak a little French

Je comprends – I understand

Je ne comprends pas – I don't understand

Je le pense – I think so

Je ne pense pas – I don't think so

Quiz

Question #1: What is the *French* translation for "My name is..."

Answer: Mon nom est...

Question #2: What is the *French* translation for "Maybe?"

Answer: Peut être

Question #3: What is the *French* translation for "Of course"?

Answer: Bien sûr

Question #4: What is the French translation for "I don't think so"?

Answer: Je ne pense pas

Greetings and Expressions

Here's an essential list of greetings and expressions for when you first meet someone or are introduced to them.

bonjour – Hello

bienvenu – Welcome

bonjour – Good Morning

Bonne après midi – Good Afternoon

bonsoir – Good Evening

salutations - Greetings

ma maison est votre maison – My house is your house

Au revoir – Goodbye

Bienvenue chez moi – Welcome to our home

Bonne nuit – Good night

À plus tard – See you later

Ravi de vous rencontrer – Nice to meet you

À bientôt – See you soon

À demain – See you tomorrow

À lundi – See you on Monday

Ravi de vous rencontre – Nice to meet you

Ravi de vous rencontrer– Pleased to meet you

Bonne journée! – Have a nice day!

Quiz

Question #1: What is the *French* translation for "see you later?"

Answer: À plus tard

Question #2: What is the *French* translation for "Have a nice day!"?

Answer: Bonne journée!

Question #3: What is the *French* translation for "Good night"?

Answer: Bonne nuit

Question #4: What is the French translation for "See you on Monday"?

Answer: À lundi

Follow Up Questions

The perfect assortment of follow up questions to hold a conversation when speaking in French.

Comment vas-tu? – How are you? (informal)

Comment ça va?– How's it going?

Comment ça va? – How are things?

Comment vas-tu?– How are you?

Comment avez-vous été?– How have you been?

Quoi de neuf? – What's up?

Et vous?– How about you?

Je vais bien merci. Et vous? – I'm good, thanks. How about you?

Et toi? – What about yourself?

Et toi? – And you?

Que faites-vous? – What are you doing?

Quiz

Question #1: What is the *French* translation for "What's up?"

Answer: Quoi de neuf?

Question #2: What is the *French* translation for "How are you?"?

Answer: Comment vas-tu?

Question #3: What is the *French* translation for "What are you doing?"?

Answer: Que faites-vous?

Question #4: What is the French translation for "and you?"?

Answer: Et toi?

Polite Answers

For use when you are being polite to someone in French.

Oui s'il vous plaît – Yes please

Merci – Thank you

Bien - Good

S'il bous plaît – Please

Merci beaucoup – Thank you very much

pardon – Excuse me

j'apprécie vraiment cela – I really appreciate it

Vous êtes les bienvenus – You're Welcome

Oui, merci – Yes, thank you

Je suis désolé – Sorry

Oui s'il vous plaît – Yes please

Quiz

Question #1: What is the *French* translation for "good"?

Answer: bien

Question #2: What is the *French* translation for "Excuse me"?

Answer: pardon

Question #3: What is the *French* translation for "Sorry?"

Answer: Je suis désolé

Question #4: What is the French translation for "you are welcome"

Answer: Vous êtes les bienvenus

Exclamations

Some exclamations to really emphasize any point you might be trying to make.

sensationnel! – Wow!

Arrêtez! – Stop!

feu! – Fire!

cool! – Cool!

Aidez moi! – Help!

Tais toi! – Shut up!

attendre! – Wait!

Regardez! – Look!

S'amuser! – Have fun!

Bon voyage! – Have a good trip!

laisse nous manger! – let's eat!

Toutes nos félicitations – Congratulations!

Bienvenue ici! – Welcome here!

Bon anniversaire – Happy Birthday!

excellent! – Excellent!

Bien houé – Well done!

Prends soin! – Take care!

à votre santé! – Cheers!

joyeux Noël! – Merry Christmas!

Bonne chance! – Good luck!

Quiz

Question #1: What is the *French* translation for "Have a good trip!"?

Answer: Bon voyage!

Question #2: What is the *French* translation for "Take care!"?

Answer: Prends soin!

Question #3: What is the *French* translation for "Good luck"?

Answer: Bonne chance

Question #4: What is the French translation for "well done"?

Answer: Bien houé

Resolving Problems

Every now and then we run into problems or issues and they need to have resolutions. Now it's now problem if you are in a French speaking area.

Quel est le problème?– What is the problem?

Je ne comprends pas!– I don't understand!

Je ne sais pas– I don't know

Je ne suis pas positif – I'm not positive

Je n'ai aucune idée – I have no idea

Je ne parle pas francais – I don't speak *French*

Appelle la police!– Call the police!

Puis-je vous aider?– Can I help you?

Pouvez-vous m'aider? – Can you help me?

Aucun problème! – No problem!

Peux-tu répéter cela?– Can you say that again?

je suis perdu - I'm lost

Quelle est la prochaine étape? – What's the next step?

Mon français est mauvais – My *French* is bad

Pouvez-vous parler plus lentement? – Can you speak more slowly?

Viens par ici! – Come over here!

Appelle un docteur! – Call a doctor!

Quiz

Question #1: What is the *French* translation for "I have no idea"?

Answer: Je n'ai aucune idée

Question #2: What is the *French* translation for "No problem!"?

Answer: Aucun problème!

Question #3: What is the *French* translation for "I'm lost"?

Answer: je suis perdu

Question #4: What is the French translation for "my French is bad"?

Answer: Mon français est mauvais

Saying Different Ages

Whatever your age might be, here is how to say it in French

j'ai dix ans-I am 10 years old

j'ai vingt deux ans-I am 22 years old

j'ai quatorze ans-I am 14 years old

J'ai huit ans-I am 8 years old

j'ai cinquante cinq ans-I am 55 years old

j'ai quarante ans-I am 40 years old

j'ai trente deux ans-I am 32 years old

Quiz:

Question #1: How do you say "I am 22 years old" in *French!*

Answer: j'ai vingt deux ans

Question #2: How do you say "I am 55 years old" in *French?*

Answer: j'ai cinquante cinq ans

Question #3: How do you say "I am 40 years old" in *French?*

Answer: j'ai quarante ans

Restaurant Conversations

When at a restaurant in any French speaking country, you want to make sure your order is correct. Here are some restaurant questions and statements for when you need them.

Est-ce que je peux voir le menu? – Can I see the menu?

Combien de temps pour la nourriture? – How long for the food?

Qu'est-ce qui est populaire ici?– What is popular here?

Voulez-vous commander? – Would you like to order?

C'est très bien – This is very good

Où se trouve un bon restaurant? – Where is a good restaurant?

Où est le restaurant? – Where is the restaurant?

Que voudriez-vous manger?– What would you like to eat?

Que voudriez-vous boire? – What would you to drink?

Je voudrais réserver une table pour deux. – I'd like to reserve a table for two.

je voudrais commander... - would like to order...

Délicieux - Delicious

Un instant s'il vous plaît.– One moment, please.

Qu'est-ce qui est inclus? – What is included?

Est-ce qu'il vient avec de la salade? – Does it come with salad?

Quelle est la soupe du jour? – What is the soup of the day?

Que recommandez-vous? – What do you recommend?

Peux-tu m'apporter...? – Can you bring me ...?

Pour le plat principal, je voudrais... - For the main course, I would like...

Pour boire je voudrais... - To drink I would like...

Nous sommes prêts à commander – We are ready to order

L'addition s'il vous plait. – The bill, please.

C'était délicieux. – That was delicious.

Pour commencer, je voudrais... - To start, I would like...

Quels plats n'ont pas de viande? – Which dishes have no meat?

Quoi d'autre est dans le plat? – What else is in the dish?

Quiz

Question #1: What is the *French* translation for "To start, I would like..."?

Answer: Pour commencer, je voudrais...

Question #2: What is the *French* translation for "What else is in the dish?"?

Answer: Quoi d'autre est dans le plat?

Question #3: What is the *French* translation for "Can you bring me ...?"?

Answer: Peux-tu m'apporter...?

Question #4: What is the French translation for "the bill, please"?

Answer: L'addition s'il vous plait.

Question #5: What is the French translation for "...would like to order"?

Answer: je voudrais commander...

Question #6: What is the French translation for "can I see the menu?"?

Answer: Est-ce que je peux voir le menu?

Conversation Starters

Here are some great conversation starters in French!

Comment gagnez-vous votre vie? – What do you do for a living?

Qu'est-ce qu'un livre que vous me recommanderiez? – What is a book that you would recommend to me?

Es-tu religieux? – Are you religious?

Savez-vous à quelle heure ferme cet endroit? – Do you know what time this place closes?

Avez-vous des frères et sœurs? – Do you have any siblings?

Avez-vous des enfants? - Do you have children?

Voyez-vous souvent vos grands-parents? – Do you see your grandparents often?

Es-tu proche de tes parents? – Are you close with your parents?

Es-tu proche de tes parents? – How old are they?

Que font tes parents pour le travail? – What do your parents do for work?

Où as tu grandi?– Where did you grow up?

Aimez-vous cuisiner? – Do you like to cook?

Avez-vous des animaux domestiques? – Do you have any pets?

De quelle race est votre animal de compagnie?– What breed is your pet?

A quoi ressemble ta ville natale? – What's your hometown like?

Où travaillez vous? - Where do you work?

Veux tu danser avec moi? – Would you like to dance with me?

J'aime ce que tu portes. Où l'as-tu acheté? – I like what you're wearing. Where did you buy it?

Vous venez souvent ici? – Do you come here often?

Savez-vous quelle heure il est? – Do you know what the time is?

Que signifie ton nom?– What does your name mean?

Aimes-tu faire du sport? – Do you like to play sports?

Quelle est la tradition culturelle de votre pays que vous préférez? – Which of your country's cultural traditions is your favorite?

Pouvez-vous me recommander un bon restaurant près d'ici? – Can you recommend me a good restaurant near here?

Parlez-vous d'autres langues? – Do you speak any other languages?

Qu'aimez-vous faire pour vous amuser?– What do you like to do for fun?

Quel est votre type de musique préféré?– What's your favorite type of music?

Quelle est la chose la plus folle que les gens font ici?– What is the craziest thing that people do here?

Est-ce que cette place est occupée? – Is this seat taken?

Aimes-tu voyager? – Do you like to travel?

Quel est ton endroit préféré? – What's your favorite place you've been to?

Dans quels pays êtes-vous allé? – Which countries have you been to?

Si tu pouvais voyager n'importe où, où irais-tu? – If you could travel anywhere, where would you go?

Quel est ton plat préféré? – What's your favorite food?

Quiz

Question #1: What is the *French* translation for "Do you speak any other languages?"?

Answer: Parlez-vous d'autres langues?

Question #2: What is the *French* translation for “Do you like to cook?”?

Answer: Aimez-vous cuisiner?

Question #3: What is the *French* translation for “What do your parents do for work?”?

Answer: Que font tes parents pour le travail?

Question #4: What is the French translation for “do you like to travel?”?

Answer: Aimes-tu voyager?

Question #5: What is the French translation for “is this seat taken?”?

Answer: Est-ce que cette place est occupée?

Question #6: What is the French translation for “do you have any pets?”?

Answer: Avez-vous des animaux domestiques?

Chapter 18 - Famille Et Professions

Laura accepta volontiers d'accompagner Louis et de participer à sa réunion de famille le weekend suivant. Ils étaient désormais officiellement en couple et ce serait l'occasion idéale pour la présenter à sa mère, son père et ses frères.

L'oncle de Louis, qui s'appelait David, participait également à la réunion familiale. David exerçait la profession d'ingénieur en mécanique et il travaillait avec tout type de machines, notamment les turbines à gaz et à vapeur et les générateurs électriques. C'était un homme extrêmement intelligent qui avait conseillé Louis quand il était plus jeune.

Tout en discutant avec son oncle, il remarqua que ses deux cousins Enzo et Sophie se trouvaient en arrière-plan. Lorsqu'ils étaient petits, ils avaient l'habitude de passer beaucoup de temps ensemble tous les trois et ils avaient partagé de nombreux souvenirs d'enfance. Ils s'étaient malheureusement éloignés en grandissant et ils avaient perdu le contact lorsqu'ils étaient entrés dans la vie active. Enzo avait fini par gravir les échelons pour occuper un poste de responsable au sein d'un commerce de détail. Et Sophie était coiffeuse à temps partiel mais maman à plein temps.

Laura semblait visiblement dépassée parmi tous ces nouveaux visages, mais elle a quand même eu l'occasion de faire plus ample connaissance avec au moins une personne lors de cet évènement. Il s'agissait de Marie, la belle-sœur de Louis. Elles se sont parfaitement entendues dés le départ, et elles ont immédiatement établi de bons rapports. Laura était journaliste de profession et Marie était rédactrice pour une émission télévisée, qui était produite par la société de médias qui les employait toutes les deux. Elles s'étaient déjà croisées au bureau, mais c'était la première fois qu'elles prenaient le temps de discuter.

Finalement, les invités étaient bien trop nombreux pour que Laura fasse la connaissance de tout le monde, et même pour que Louis puisse prendre des nouvelles de chacun d'entre eux. Ils ont rapidement dit bonjour à sa grand-mère et ses tantes, mais ils n'ont pas eu l'occasion de saluer ses nièces et ses neveux. Tous les enfants étaient occupés à s'amuser ensemble dans l'arrière-cour.

La famille a réussi à prendre une photo de groupe avec Laura, après lui avoir proposé de poser avec eux. Chaque année, le père de Louis avait pour mission de créer la plus belle des photos de famille. Il était logique de lui confier cette tâche car il était photographe professionnel.

Le soleil commençait à se coucher et la journée touchait à sa fin. Alors que tout le monde partait, Louis a eu à nouveau l'occasion de discuter avec son oncle David. Il lui a confié ses inquiétudes concernant le surmenage qu'il subissait à son poste actuel au sein de la compagnie d'assurances, et il lui a également dit qu'il réfléchissait aux éventuelles voies qu'il pourrait suivre. Oncle David lui a conseillé de commencer à suivre des cours dès que possible, même s'il n'avait pas encore choisi l'emploi qu'il souhaiter exercer à l'avenir.

English Translation

Laura happily agreed to accompany Louis on his visit to his family gathering the following weekend. They were now officially a couple, and it would be a good time to introduce her to his mother, father, and brothers.

Also at the get-together was Louis's uncle, named David. David was a mechanical engineer, who worked on all kinds of machines, including steam and gas turbines and electric generators. He was an extremely intelligent man, who helped guide Louis in his younger years.

While chatting with his uncle, he noticed his two cousins Enzo and Sophie in the background. The three of them hung out quite frequently as kids and shared a lot of childhood memories. They grew apart as they got older, unfortunately, and lost contact with one another as they entered the workforce. Enzo ended up working his way up to a management position at a retail store. And Sophie was a part-time hairdresser but a full-time mom.

Laura was obviously overwhelmed by all the new faces, but she was able to get to know at least one person at the event. This person was Louis's sister-in-law Marie. From the very get-go, the two hit it off and established an instant rapport. Laura was a journalist by trade, and Marie was a writer for a TV show that was produced by the same media company they both worked for. While they had seen each other around the office, they had never met until now.

In the end, there were just too many people for Laura to meet and even for Louis to catch up with. They briefly said hello to his grandmother and aunts, but they never got the chance to greet his nieces and nephews. All the kids were busy playing together in the backyard.

The family was able to take a group photo, which included Laura, who was invited to join in. Every year, it's Louis's dad who is given the task to create the best family photo possible. Leaving the task to him makes sense, given that he's a professional photographer.

The sun started going down, and the day was growing late. As everyone was leaving, Louis had another opportunity to speak with his Uncle David. He voiced his concerns about burning out at his current job at the insurance company and was considering a few possible paths he could take. Uncle David advised him that, even though he's not sure where he wants to work in the future, he should definitely start taking classes as soon as possible. Waiting to start was the worst thing he could possibly do.

Vocabulary

Famille et professions --- family and occupations

Accompagner --- to accompany

Participer --- to take part, to participate

Officiellement --- officially

Être l’occasion idéale pour --- to be a good time to

Mère --- mother

Père --- father

Frères --- brothers

Oncle --- uncle

Ingénieur en mécanique --- mechanical engineer

Machines --- machines

Turbines à gaz et à vapeur --- gas and steam turbines

Générateurs électriques --- electric generators

Extrêmement intelligent --- extremely intelligent

Cousins --- cousins

Arrière-plan --- background

Souvenirs d’enfance --- childhood memories

S’éloigner --- to grow apart

Grandir --- to get older

Perdre le contact --- to lose contact

La vie active --- the workforce

Poste de responsable --- management position

Commerce de détail --- retail store

Temps partiel --- part-time

Coiffeuse --- hairdresser

Plein temps --- full-time

Maman --- mom

Dépassér --- to overwhelm, to exceed

Nouveaux visages --- new faces

Belle-sœur --- sister-in-law

Établir des rapports --- to establish rapport

Journaliste --- journalist

De profession --- by trade

Rédactrice --- writer

Émission télévisée --- TV show

Être produite par --- to be produced by

Société de médias --- media company

Grand-mère --- grandmother

Tantes --- aunts

Saluer --- to greet

Nièces --- nieces

Neveux --- nephews

Enfants --- kids

S'amuser ensemble --- to have fun together

Arrière-cour --- backyard

Photo de groupe --- group photo

Photos de famille --- family photos

Photographe --- photographer

Surmenage --- overwork

Éventuelles voies --- possible paths

Conseiller --- to advise

Suivre des cours --- to take courses

Dès que possible --- as soon as possible

Comprehension Questions

1. Quelle est la profession de l'oncle de Louis ?

A) Ingénieur en électricité

B) Ingénieur civil

C) Ingénieur chimiste

D) Ingénieur en mécanique

2. Les parents d'Enzo et de Sophie sont... de Louis.

A) le grand-père et la grand-mère

B) le père et la mère

C) l'oncle et la tante

D) le frère et la sœur

3. Qui la belle-sœur de Louis a-t-elle épousé ?

A) Son frère

B) Son père

C) Son cousin

D) Son patron

4. Où les enfants jouaient-ils pendant la réunion de famille ?

A) A l'école

B) Dans la maison

C) Dans l'arrière-cour

D) Dans la salle de jeux

5. Une personne hautement qualifiée pour un poste appartient à la catégorie...

A) des amateurs.

B) de la main-d'œuvre.

C) des employés.

D) des professionnels.

Answers :

1) D

2) C

3) A

4) C

5) D

Chapter 19 - Education

Avec un emploi à temps plein et une petite amie, l'emploi du temps de Louis était plutôt chargé. Mais pour accéder à un avenir meilleur, il s'était inscrit à l'université locale pour suivre un programme de cycle supérieur consacré à l'économie. Louis avait déjà suivi un programme de premier cycle et il avait obtenu une licence en philosophe, cependant ce choix n'était pas le plus approprié pour chercher un emploi et débuter une carrière, comme la plupart des diplômes de sciences humaines.

La situation serait différente cette fois-ci. L'expérience et la sagesse qu'il avait acquises devraient lui permettre de poursuivre ses études en profitant pleinement de cette opportunité. Le programme de cycle supérieur consacré à l'économie s'annonçait comme un défi redoutable, mais s'il parvenait à le relever, ses efforts seraient amplement récompensés. Les cours qu'il avait suivi au collège communautaire constituaient une sinécure en comparaison de ce programme. Ce cursus nécessitera de nombreuses révisions et une grande persévérance.

Les manuels s'avèreront souvent beaucoup plus utiles que les cours eux-mêmes. Certains des professeurs avec qui il avait discuté tenaient des discours tellement interminables qu'il s'avérait extrêmement difficile de rester concentré pendant les cours. Il pouvait passer la moitié du temps à lire les chapitres du manuel pour obtenir deux fois plus d'informations qu'en assistant à un cours dans l'amphithéâtre. Les assistants du professeur s'avéraient toutefois plus utiles, car ils parvenaient à expliquer des concepts complexes en utilisant un langage très simple.

Pour mémoriser parfaitement les informations, les étudiants devaient fournir un travail sérieux en dehors des cours. Les groupes de travail qui étaient organisés par les étudiants ont aidé Louis à préserver sa motivation et sa volonté de bien travailler en classe. Au sein de ces groupes, les étudiants partageaient les notes qu'ils prenaient en classe et ils révisaient les informations qui feraient probablement l'objet d'un examen, selon eux. Ils ne restaient toutefois pas sérieux en permanence, car les bavardages étaient encouragés au cours de leurs fréquentes pauses afin d'évacuer le stress et la frustration qu'ils avaient accumulés.

Les examens de première année approchaient et l'anxiété était palpable dans la salle de classe pendant les derniers cours. L'épreuve inclurait uniquement des questions à développement, et il ne comporterait aucune question à choix multiples.

Le bachotage ne serait d'aucune utilité pour cette épreuve. Il était indispensable d'avoir bien mémorisé les informations requises pour obtenir une bonne note. Louis et tous ses camarades de classe payaient des frais de scolarité très élevés, mais ils ne pourraient pas tous réussir l'épreuve. Les élèves qui obtiendraient les meilleures notes étaient ceux qui avaient assisté aux cours, qui avaient participé aux groupes de travail, et qui avaient lu de manière intensive.

Cela ressemblait beaucoup à l'apprentissage d'une langue étrangère. Les élèves les plus doués sont ceux qui s'immergent totalement dans la langue concernée. Ils lisent autant de textes en langue cible qu'ils le peuvent et lorsqu'ils n'en ont pas l'occasion, ils passent tout leur temps libre à écouter la langue cible. Cette immersion passe avant leurs anciens passe-temps et leurs modes de vie. Cette méthode leur permet d'atteindre une maîtrise parfaite de la langue concernée.

L'important n'est pas de savoir si Louis a réussi l'épreuve finale. L'essentiel est de savoir si vous prendrez les mesures nécessaires pour maîtriser parfaitement la langue que vous étudiez.

Étudiez bien ! Et merci de votre attention !

English Translation

With a full-time job and a girlfriend, Louis's schedule was pretty tightly packed. But for the sake of a better future, he enrolled in a graduate program for economics at his local university. Louis had already completed an undergraduate program and graduated with a bachelor's degree in philosophy, yet like most liberal arts degrees, it was not the greatest choice for seeking employment and starting a career.

This time would be different. With much more experience and wisdom, this opportunity to further his education would not go wasted. A graduate program in economics was going to be a formidable challenge, but if he succeeded, the rewards would be great. The classes he took at community college would be a cakewalk compared to this. Intense study and perseverance would be required.

The textbooks would often prove to be much more useful than the lectures. Some of the professors he had talked with such long-winded delivery that it was incredibly difficult to maintain focus in class. He could spend half the time reading chapters from the book and come away with double the information he got in the lecture hall. The teacher assistants, however, were most helpful, as they could explain complex concepts using very basic language.

To make the information stick, serious work was needed to be done outside the classroom. Study groups organized by students were instrumental in providing Louis the motivation and drive required to do well in the course. In the groups, students shared the notes they took in class and reviewed the information they thought would appear on the exams. Not all this time was serious though, as there were multiple breaks where chit-chat was encouraged as a means to vent built-up stress and frustration.

Finals for the first year were approaching, and anxiety filled the classroom during the last few lectures. On the test would be essay questions only; there would be no multiple choice. Cramming wasn't going to get you anywhere on this test. You had to know the information in order to get a good grade. Louis and all his classmates paid hefty tuition fees, but not all would pass the test. It would be those who attended the lectures, participated in the study groups, and read extensively that would pass with high marks.

It was very much like learning a foreign language. Those who do the best are those who immerse themselves in the foreign language. They read as much as possible in the target language, and when they can no longer read, they spend all their free time listening to the target language. Immersion takes precedence over their old hobbies and lifestyles. That's how they achieve high levels of fluency.

The question is not whether or not Louis passed the final exam. The true question is whether or not you will do what it takes in order to achieve fluency.

Happy studying! And thank you for reading!

Vocabulary

Education --- education

Petite amie --- girlfriend

Programme de cycle supérieur --- graduate program

Économie --- economics

Université --- university

Programme de premier cycle --- undergraduate program

Licence --- bachelor's degree

Philosophie --- philosophy

Diplômes de sciences humaines --- liberal arts degrees

Chercher un emploi --- seeking employment

Débuter une carrière --- starting a career

Expérience ---experience

Sagesse --- wisdom

Poursuivre ses études --- to further one's education

Défi redoutable --- formidable challenge

Collège communautaire --- community college

Sinécure --- cakewalk

De nombreuses révisions --- intense study

Persévérance --- perseverance

Manuels --- textbooks

Professeurs --- professors

Discours interminables --- long-winded delivery

Rester concentré --- to maintain focus

Lire les chapitres --- to read chapters

Amphithéâtre --- lecture hall

Assistants du professeur --- teacher assistants

Concepts complexes --- complex concepts

Langage simple --- basic language

Mémoriser les informations --- to make information stick

Travail sérieux --- serious work

Groupes de travail --- study groups

Motivation et volonté --- motivation and drive

Classe --- course

Notes --- notes

Réviser les informations --- to review information

Examen --- exam

Bavardages --- chit-chat

Évacuer --- to vent

Frustration --- frustration

Accumulé --- built-up

Salle de classe --- classroom

Épreuve --- test

Questions à développement --- essay questions

Choix multiples --- multiple choice

Bachotage --- cramming

Bonne note --- good grade

Frais de scolarité --- tuition fees

Élevé --- high, hefty

Élèves --- students

Réussir l'épreuve --- to pass the test

Lire de manière intensive --- to read extensively

Meilleures notes --- best grades

Langue étrangère --- foreign language

Temps libre --- free time

S'immerger --- to immerse

Passer avant --- to take precedence

Modes de vie --- lifestyles

Atteindre --- to achieve

Maîtrise --- fluency

Épreuve finale --- final exam

Étudier --- to study

Comprehension Questions

1. Où Louis suit-il des cours d'économie ?

A) Chez lui, via un programme en ligne

B) A l'université locale

C) Dans un collège communautaire

D) Chez lui, avec un professeur particulier

2. L'expression "défi redoutable" indique que le défi est...

A) facile à relever.

B) impossible à relever.

C) intimidant.

D) réalisable.

3. Quel était le problème lié au cours ?

A) Les cours avaient lieu tard le soir.

B) Les amis de Louis bavardaient pendant les cours.

C) Les explications du professeur étaient trop compliquées.

D) Le professeur n'aimait pas les étudiants.

4. Qui organisait les groupes de travail ?

A) Les étudiants

B) Les assistants du professeur

C) Louis

D) Le professeur

5. L'examen final incluait...

A) uniquement des questions à choix multiples.

B) un mélange de questions à choix multiples et de questions à développement.

C) un mélange de bachotage et de frais de scolarité élevés.

D) uniquement des questions à développement.

Answers :

1) B

2) C

3) C

4) A

5) D

Conclusion

Thank you for reaching the end of the book French Vocabulary and Grammar. Hopefully, this book was able to demonstrate for you how easy it can be to learn the French language when it is laid out for you in the right way. This book finished with a few short stories so that you could practice everything you have learned by trying to read through a piece of text that contained everything you learned all in one place. From here, you can now go on to find more short stories to read in order to practice your French language skills.

Like I mentioned in the introduction to this book, when it comes to learning a language, practice is key. This means to practice in the form of exposure, as well. Your brain is able to pick up on things even if they are not in your conscious mind, so even having a French audiobook on in the background while you clean the house or do grocery shopping will help you to remember everything you have learned, especially the pronunciations.

The next best thing to do will be to find people to practice with. Whether these people are your friends who are also interested in learning the French language, or you find a pen pal across the world, being able to practice your French with other people is a great way to brush up on your skills and get feedback from other people in real-time. This avoids bad habits and confusion, as there is someone else to bounce your French off of. If you do not have access to this, reading books and watching movies is a great place to start. Beginning with children's books of short stories will help you to start out slow, and as your vocabulary grows, you can progress to harder books in terms of grammar and word choice.

Do not get discouraged if some days become difficult or some days, it is harder to remember the language. Patience will be necessary for you as you are learning, as with anything else. You do not become an expert overnight but the earlier you start practicing, the earlier you will get there. Try to find people to keep you motivated and try to enjoy the learning as it comes. One day you will blurt out an entire French sentence when travelling in France and you will surprise yourself. You will also be glad that you read this book and that you practiced your French language skills so often.

If you would like, share this book with your friends and family and plan a trip to France together! This will not only serve as motivation to study and practice, but it will give you all other people to practice with in the meantime.

Exposing yourself to as many new forms of language as possible is hugely beneficial, as your brain is eager to learn and grow. Language is a beautiful thing in this world, and we should take advantage of the many resources available to us that allow us to enrich our lives with it.

FRENCH COMMON PHRASES

LEARN AND SPEAK FRENCH FAST AND EASY WITH WORDS AND VOCABULARY THAT YOU CAN USE IMMEDIATELY IN YOUR CONVERSATIONS

PAUL BONNET

Introduction

Ah, *français*, the *langue d'amour*! Spoken the world over, this beautiful language sits on the tongues of many all over the globe.

I've helped a lot of people learn foreign languages, primarily French and Spanish. In my time helping people to learn these languages, I've come to hear the same sorts of excuses all the time. The things I heard go along the lines of "I'm just not wired to learn languages!" or "Every time I try, I forget everything I learned."

If you say any of these things, then I have good news for you: you're absolutely and completely lying to yourself. The unfortunate truth is that the academic method that most people use to learn languages isn't exactly well-suited to language learning as it were.

Think back to when you were in high school or college and you were taking language courses. Chances are that you don't exactly remember a lot of the things that you learned. Why is this? Well, think back to what your classes were like.

The academic method of language learning is actually a great method, in terms of academia. It's a fantastic method for teaching you a lot of things to get you up to the point where you can pass a test. However, there's an immense lack of "portability" when it comes to taking the various things that you learned in there to the real world.

After all, the brain isn't really made to keep the information it isn't using, and the number one way to make a language seem unimportant is to try learning it out of a textbook. While you may remember splotches of vocabulary here and there, there's a very, very low chance that you're actually going to remember the breadth of what you learn.

This book offers an alternative solution: help you learn the language naturally and intuitively, using your built-in natural language processing faculties to learn the language.

That's right - you have the natural ability to learn language built into your system. Actually, it's pretty much common sense when you think about how you started speaking a language in the first place.

When you were younger, how did you learn words? By being exposed to them and the contexts in which they're used. A tree isn't naturally a tree - it exists of its own accord, it's only called a tree. However, in Spanish, it's called an *arból*. In French, it's called an *arbre*. You learned the English word the same way that a French or Spanish speaker learned their respective word, by naturally picking it up through context, a need to describe something.

Most polyglots - people who speak multiple languages fluently – absolutely agree that the best way to learn a language is through exposure and deep immersion. Benny the Irish Polyglot, creator of massively popular web-service '*Fluent in Six Months*,' travels the world and stays in a location for six months to a year at a time to learn any given language. He walks away very fluent in it, able to converse with anybody about much of anything.

He and most other language-learning pros will tell you that there is a natural language learning process that you can tap into, and you tap into it by being immersed in the language. This is the same reason that people who move to a new country and don't have any opportunities to speak their mother tongue will often lose their mother tongue, either partly or completely; the brain keeps what it sees as important. If a language is no longer important, it will be forgotten because it won't be used. On the other hand, if a language is deemed as important, the brain will dedicate extra processing power to learning it.

You cannot learn a language intuitively if you don't understand it at the most basic level. Well, you can, but it will slow down your progress tremendously. Building a foundation is immensely important.

In the conclusion, we're going to go over how you can build on top of the foundation that you've made using natural language acquisition techniques so that you can learn the language with relative ease compared to people who are taking classes and forcing themselves to gulp down the language.

Understand this before you get started: French is not an easy language to speak. It differs from many other languages in that the manner in which French is spoken is very morphologically complex. There are a ton of different vowels and nuance and the written form of the language sounds quite different from the spoken form because of this. There are a lot of factors that can make it difficult to speak for somebody who's not used to a language that, well, sounds like how French sounds or is spelled like how French is spelled.

However, at the same time, there are a lot of patterns in French that will make it easier to learn. There are, for example, concepts such as liaison - some of which we'll be explaining here momentarily - that can make it pretty difficult to speak until you catch on to them, but once you know them, the language becomes beautifully expressive and easy to follow.

This also means that there will be a large gap between written French that you learn to read and write and spoken French that you learn to listen to and speak back with. The gap isn't huge, but there is quite a big difference in the received sounds of the language. There are also a huge amount of diphthongs (vowels which are written together as one unit to make one sound, like *head* in English which produces the singular vowel sound of *eh*) that make sounds which seem somewhat counterintuitive - yet another feature which can make this language challenging.

This book intends to make up for this by making itself a clear and easy study guide as well as a field reference for all kinds of different things, not the least of which is how the language itself works.

English and French are rather similar languages. As an English speaker, this can be somewhat of a major perk. There are many things that you aren't going to have to worry about or that will perhaps even make sense to you across different languages. This is because French and English developed alongside each other;

historically, there has been a long rivalry between France and England, and the Normans had a major influence on both the development of English and of French.

To add another element to it, French is derived ultimately from Latin. Because of this, much of French's vocabulary will seem rather familiar to you, since much of English's vocabulary is derived from Latin. That which isn't already familiar *because* of French will likely be familiar because of Latin.

What this leaves for you to learn are essential grammatical categories, the barebones parts of French grammar, and the tendencies and nuances of the language itself. French is one of the easier languages to learn as an English speaker, so fortunately for your travels, you aren't going to have a whole lot of difficulty with it.

Pronunciation is probably one of the most difficult parts of French. It has a very distinct and unique morphology that it's developed over millennia of conquest and interactions with neighboring states. Just like how we discussed that English and French are quite similar because of the impact of the Normans, a variety of socioeconomic and militaristic events have happened that resulted in the French language taking a unique path of development.

This makes it a rather difficult language to follow when you're hearing it spoken for the first time, and it also means that there's a bit of a detachment from what you're *used* to as an English speaker. The letters often will be similar but not quite the same. Right now, we're going to jump into all of that.

One nice benefit of French is that the vowel sounds are relatively consistent. While they aren't as consistent as, say, Spanish or Italian, two languages with very simple vowel syllabaries, they are more consistent than English where context and history decide a vowel's pronunciation more often than not.

There are six *basic* vowel sounds that you need to know:

A—Pronounced like the *ah* in *father*.

E—Pronounced like the *oo* in *book* if at the end of a syllable or like the *eh* in *head* in the middle of a word. At the end of a word, it's silent, but gives sound to the consonant prior which often would be left off. (Unless followed by a vowel in the next word.)

I and *Y*—Pronounced like the *ee* in *reed.*

O—Pronounced like the *o* in *no,* but it doesn't round off at the end; lips stay still.

U—No direct correlative. Just say *ee* like you're saying the letter *i* or *y*, but round your lips like you're saying *o*.

However, French also has a rich collection of accents and diphthongs. Diphthongs are when you combine letters together to produce a new sound.

Here are the accents and their respective sounds:

À—Pronounced like the *ah* in father.

Â—Pronounced like the *ah* in father but open the mouth wider.

É—Pronounced like the "ay" in "day" (though you don't round off the end of the syllable like you do in *day.*)

È—Pronounced like *eh* in *head.*

Ô—Pronounced like *oh* in *no.*

Then, you have the most basic diphthongs:

Oi—Pronounced like the *wah* in *water.*

Ou—Pronounced like the *ooh* in *move.*

Ai—Pronounced like the *eh* in *head.*

Ei—Pronounced like the *eh* in *head.*

Au—Pronounced like the *oh* in *no*, but not rounded.

Eau—Pronounced like the *oh* in *no,* but not rounded.

Eu—Pronounced like the *oo* in *book*, but more open.

Oeu—Pronounced like the *oo* in *book,* but more open.

These are most of the vowel sounds that you're going to need to navigate French. Other than these, you'll rarely ever see the unmentioned ones.

With the vowels out of the way, it's time that we move on to the consonants in French. French consonants are spoken like so:

B—Sounds like the English B in bear.

C—Sounds like an English *s* before an *e* or an *i*. Otherwise, it sounds like an English *k*.

Ç—Called a *cedilla* or *cedille* en français. Makes an English *s* sound.

G—Sounds like a soft English *j* when before an *e* or an *i*. Otherwise, it sounds like an English *g* in *go*.

H—Always silent. Words that start with an *h* will contract with *le* or *la*, e.g. *l'hôtel*. (The hotel)

J—Sounds like an English soft *j*, or like the *s* in *measure*.

L—Sounds like an English *l* in *lamb*.

Ll—Sounds like an English *l* in *lamb*.

Qu—Sounds like an English *c* in *car*.

R — French has an extremely interesting *R* sound. It is somewhat guttural, like the German *R*. It is the only 'Romance language' with a guttural trill instead of a palatal trill like Spanish and Italian. It is similar to the sound we make when we gargle but far softer. It will come naturally to you with time and exposure.

S—Sounds like an English *s* at the beginning of a word, but sounds like an English *z* if between two vowels.

T—Sounds like an English *t*.

V—Sounds like an English *v*.

W—Rare, but sounds like an English *w* when present.

X—Rare, but sounds like an English *x* when present. Follow English *x* pronunciation rules.

Z—Rare, but sounds like an English *z* when present.

With that, you now have a relatively firm understanding of how French consonants and vowels are pronounced. This will come in handy later.

The hardest part about French is hearing and speaking it. Reading and writing the language is an absolute breeze by comparison. One of the biggest lessons you'll have to learn is when to keep syllables and when to drop them. Because of the fact that it has a very vibrant manner of being spoken, French sounds so musical.

The idea of dropping consonants between words and using them to connect one vowel to another is known as '*liaison*.' There are a lot of different rules to liaison, but the gist is that within the context of liaison, you will generally not say the consonant at the end of a word. Exceptions are made for the letters *c, f, l,* and *r*; these consonants are always pronounced.

Moreover, if a consonant is at the end of a sentence, it is generally pronounced. This isn't always the case, but it is certainly generally the case.

This is one of the hardest concepts to master as a new French speaker. It's certainly quite a handful when you're trying to learn the language, at the very least. Every sentence sounds only slightly like what you've practiced, and reading to yourself can be a complete and total drag – you may even read things incorrectly to yourself sometimes until you have a firm grasp on the language.

However, don't worry, this goes away with time. All it takes is time, practice, and actually being around and speaking the language. It's because of this that French is one of the most difficult Romance languages to learn; however, it is also one of the most beautiful and expressive ones to learn at the same time.

There's a rich history underlying the language that has made it what it is today, and every sentence that you speak the language has that unique history underpinning it. It's for this reason that you should continue with your learning of the language and try to become as present within it as you can.

Don’t stress out and think it’s a monumental hurdle, though — it’s definitely not difficult and there is both room and time to grow. It will also be quite familiar to you because French and English are relatively similar as already noted.

Chapter 1 - French Alphabet and Pronunciation

Remember when you were a kid and you had to learn your ABCs? Pretend that you are back in the kindergarten classroom with your crayons and tracing paper, but this time you have an attractive French teacher in front of the class. You want to be curious and eager to please your teacher, so pay full attention to L' Alphabet.

The French Alphabet

One thing that the French language has in common with English is that it has 26 letters in its alphabet. However, many of them are pronounced quite differently.

But before you delve deep into the French alphabet, take note that there are "accentuated vowels" and special characters that are not found in written English. These are:

- The grave accent *è*, which sounds like the "e" in the word "bet". It is also found in the vowels "a"and "u".

- The acute accent *é*, which sounds like "ei". It can only be found above the letter e.

- The circumflex accent *ê*, which is placed over all vowels. It causes the vowel to sound longer, such as the "ay" in "play".

- The French/*ə*/, which is a unique sound that sounds like a short "u" sound.

- The *cedilla*, which turns the "k" sound into the "s" sound. For example, the French word "*garçon*" (which means boy or waiter) is pronounced as/GHAR son/.

- The diaeresis (called "*tréma*" in French), which is placed on the second of two consecutive vowels. It is to show that the vowels are pronounced separately. For example, the French word for Christmas, *Noël*, is pronounced as/no EL/.

To help you understand these unique French sounds better, go online and listen to them using free applications such as Google Translate.

Now, practice saying the following letters based on the description below each. Keep in mind that the words used to help describe the sounds are based on the Standard American English accent.

Aa/ah/

Sounds like the "a" in "father".

Bb/bé/

Sounds like the "e" in "bed".

Cc/sé/

Sounds like "k", but if there is a cedilla, it becomes the sound "s".

Dd/dé/

Sounds like

Ee/ə/

Sounds like the "a" in "again".

Ff/ef/

Sounds like the "f" in "food".

Gg/ g/

Sounds like the "s" in "measure" if it comes after "e" or "i". Other than that, it sounds like the "g" in "girl".

Hh/ashe/

It is often not pronounced. For example, "*heureux*", which is French for "happy", is pronounced as/EUH reuh/.

Ii/ee/

Sounds like the “ee” in “seen”.

Jj/dji/

Sounds like the second “g” in “garage”.

Kk/ka/

Sounds like the “k” in “kite”.

Ll/el/

Sounds like the “l” in “love”.

Mm/em/

Sounds like the “m” in “man”.

Nn/en/

Sounds like the “n” in “neck”.

Oo/o/

Sounds like the “o” in “holiday”.

Pp/pe/

Sounds like the “pe” in “pellet”.

Qq/ku/

Sounds like the “k” in “kick”.

Rr/er/

Sounds like the “r” in “error”.

Ss/ess/

Sounds like the “s” in “sat”.

Tt/te/

Sounds like the “t” in “tent”.

Uu/y/

A uniquely French sound, which is similar to the “oo” in “too”.

Vv/ve/

Sounds like the “v” in “vow”.

Ww/doblé vee/

Sounds like the “w” in “weekend”.

Xx/iks/

Sounds like the “x” in “xylophone”.

Yy/y/

Pronounced as/I grec/ when alone. Other than that, it is like the sound “ea” in “each”.

Zz/zed/

Sounds like the “z” in “zebra”.

French Pronunciation Guidelines

- If two/*k*/ sounds are together, only the first one is not changed, such as *accepter*/AK sep tee/ (“accept”).

- The sound/*ks*/ becomes/*z*/ or/*gz*/, such as *exact*/EG zakt/.

- If the sounds/*k*/ and/*g*/ precede “*e*” or “*i*”, they become/*s*/ and/*ʒ*/, respectively.

- If the letters “*gu*” is succeeded by “*e*” or “*i*”, the/u/ is silent., such as *guerre*/GEH/ (“war”).

- If the “*s*” is between vowels, it becomes/*z*/, such as *chose*/shooz/ (“thing”).

- The/*t*/ becomes/*s*/ if followed by “*ie*”, “*ia*”, and “*io*”, such as *patient*/PEH syun/ (“patient”).

- If the word-final/*il*/ comes after a vowel, it becomes/ee/, such as *œil*/uh Y/ (“eye”).

• If "ill" is not at the start of a word, it turns into/ee/, such as *oreille*/ooh REYH/ ("ear").

• If no vowel is placed before "*ill*", the sound/i/ is pronounced, such as *fille/fee yh/* ("girl"). However, the/l/ is pronounced in the words *distiller/distile/* ("to distill") and mille/mil/ ("thousand").

• If the letter "o" comes after the letter "y", it is pronounced as/wa/, such as *voyage*/VWA yaj/ ("travel").

• If "*i*", "*u*", and "*y*" are placed before a vowel in a word, they become glides, such as *pied/pye/* ("foot"), *oui/wi/* ("yes"), and *huit*/oo weet/ ("eight").

• The final "*e*" is not pronounced, such as *bouche*/boosh/ ("mouth").

• In French there is a phenomenon called "*liaison*", wherein a consonant which is usually silent is pronounced right before the word that it precedes. For example, "*vous avez*" is pronounced as/vou zavee/ ("you have").

• Also, when a word ends with a silent "e", the liaison is present in the vowel that follows it. For example, *reste à côté* is pronounced as/rest ah cotei/ ("stay next").

• "*Enchaînement*" is another French language phenomenon and it involves transferring the consonant sound at the end of a word to the start of the word that it precedes. For instance, *elle est is* pronounced as/e le/ ("she is").

• Most of the time, the final e in French words is not pronounced. For example: *jambe/jamb/* (leg), *bouche/bush/* (mouth), *lampe/lamp/* (lamp).

• If the *e* is followed by a double consonant, it becomes the sound/ei/, but more open and without the glide from e to i. For example: *pelle/pèl/* (shovel), *lettre/lètr/* (letter)

• Memorize the mute consonants in the French language, which are: the final -b that follows an m- (such as *plomb/plon* (the 'om' sounds more like the 'on' in wrong)/ [metal]), final -d (such as *chaud/shoh/* [warm]), final -p (such as *trop/tro/* [very much]), final -s (such as *trés/treh/* [very much]), final -t (such as *part/par/* [part]), final -x (such as *prix/pri/* [price]), and the final -z (such as *assez/ase/* [enough]).

Pronunciation of the Single Vowels

/***a***/ -sounds like the first/a/ in marmalade, but not as open. The more open vowel sound that is similar to this one is â.

Examples: *table* (table), *chat* (cat), *sac* (bag), *baggage* (luggage), *rat* (rat), *matin* (morning), *bras* (arm)

/***e***/ -sounds like the the English indefinite article 'a' but make the sound sharper, such as the second/a/ in *marmalade.* Sounds that are similar to this one are/eu/ which is a more open e and/*oeu*/ which is a more open eu.

Examples: *deux* (two), *oeuvre* (master works), *cheveu* (hair), *soeur* (sister), *beurre* (butter), *heure* (hour)

Keep in mind that the final e in French words is always silent. For example: *Notre Dame, Anne*

Also, the e in the middle of a French word is glided over. For example: *boulevard, Mademoiselle*

/***i***/ -sounds like the/ee/ sound in the English language but shorter.

Examples: *courir* (to run), *pipe* (pipe), *midi* (midday), *minute* (minute), *nid* (nest)

/***o***/ -there are two different sounds with the letter o in French. The first sound is an open/o/ that sounds like the o in the following English words: not, more, and for.

The second sound is a more closed/o/ like the one in the English low and go.

Majority of the/o/ sounds in French pronunciation are open. It is only closed when it is placed at the end of the word.

Examples of the open/o/: *botte* (botte), *homme* (man),

Examples of the closed/o/: *indigo* (indigo), *vélo* (bicycle), *développer* (to develop)

Sounds that are similar to the closed/o/ are/*eau*/,/*au*/, and/*ô*/. For example: *auto* (car), *contrôle* (control), and *eau* (water)

/***u***/ -the French pronunciation for u is not actually present in the English language. While the English pronunciation of/u/ is the sound of it in the word push, in French it is quite different. However, the u in push is present in the French language, but it is for the vowel combination/ou/.

Examples: *minute, voiture* (car), *humain* (human)

/***y***/ -the pronunciation of this is similar to the French double/i/ sound.

Examples: *loyer*/loi ier/ (lease), *noyer*/noi ier/ (to drown), *rayer*/rai ier/ (to scratch), *pays*/pai i/ (country)

Practice pronouncing the following:

si => sou => su

rue => rit => roue

sous => assure => assis

écrou => écrit => écru

repu => tous => asile

tisse => sucre => rousse

git => joue => jus

revit => revue => couve

Accentuated Vowels

One of the most obvious differences between English and French is that the latter uses accented characters. Most vowel sounds, with the exception of/*y*/, can be accentuated.

/**è**/ -this is pronounced like the/e/ in pet. The grave accent is also placed on top of a as well as u to create *à* and *ù*, respectively, although these do not change the pronunciation.

Examples: *Hélène*/hei len/ (Helen), *où*/oo/ (where)

/**é**/ -the special character above the e is called the acute accent and it is only used over e.

Example: *égoïste*/ei go ist/ (selfish), *comédie*/ko mei dee/ (comedy)

/**ê**/ -the circumflex accent, which is the special character over e, can also be placed on top of all the other vowels. What it does is that it lengthens the sound.

Example: *à côté de*/ah co tei deuh/ (beside), *s'il te plaît*/silt te ple/ (please)

/**ë**/ -this special character is called the dieresis mark and it is placed over a vowel to show that the sound is a separate syllable from the other vowel next to it. For instance, if you have two vowel put together such as ai, it is usually pronounced as/e/, but if you place a dieresis on top of the/i/, the sound becomes/ai/.

Example: *naïf/na eef/* (naive), *haïr/a eer/* (to hate).

Vowel Combination Pronunciation

/***ou***/ -this vowel combination sounds like something in between the sounds of the u in bush and the oo in cool.

Example: *cou/coo/* (neck), *genou*/g like the ge in 'garage' and 'e' like 'a' in english:/geuh noo/ (knee)

/***au***/ and/eau/ -this is pronounced the same way as/ô/.

Example: *bateau*/bah toh/ like the 'o' in 'go'/ (ship), *eau*/oh/ like the 'o' in 'go'/ (water)

/***oi***/ -to pronounce this vowel combination, make the/wa/ sound.

Example: *doigt*/doo wa/ (finger), *oie*/oo wa/ (goose)

/***ai***/ -this is pronounced the same way as/*ê*/.

Example: *j'ai*/zhei/'j' sounds like 'ge' in 'garage'/ (I have), *maison*/mei son/('on' sounds like 'on' in 'wrong')/ (house)

/***ui***/ -to produce the sound of this vowel combination, the diphthong/oo wee/.

Example: *fruit*/froo ee/ (fruit), *aujourd'hui*/oo zhoor dui/('j' like 'ge' in 'garage')/(today)

/***eu***/ and/***oeu***/ -pronounced the same way as the short/*u*/ sound.

Example: *bleu*/blu/ (blue),*feu*/fu/ (fire)

/***er***/,/***et***/ and/***ez***/ -these vowl combinations have a sound that is similar to/*é*/.

Example: *boulanger*/boo lan ge/('g' like 'ge' in 'garage')/ (baker), *hier*/ee yer/ (yesterday)

Practice pronouncing the following:

mêle => meule => molle

coeur => corps => caire

sol => sel => seule

Plaire => pleure => implore

l'or => l'air => leur

peur => port => père

gueule => guerre => encore

Nasal Vowel Pronunciation

/***on***/ - it is not possible to find an exact English sound that is similar to this unique French sound. However, the closes vowel would probably be the long/o/ such as the o in long (but without fully pronouncing the/ng/ sound).

Example: *oncle*/ohng kl/ (uncle), *bon*/bohn/ (good)

/***an***/ and/***am***/ -if a vowel combination is followed by the letter n or m, it does not immediately mean that the sound would be nasal, unless the n or m is the final letter of the word. However, if there is only one vowel before the n or m, the vowel is a nasal sound.

Example: *détient*/dei ti ahn/ (holds), *sens*/sahns/ (sense)

/***en***/ and/***em***/ -the closest sound that is similar to these French nasal vowels would be the a in swan.

Example: *souvent*/soo vahn/ (often), *ensemble*/ahn sahm bl/ (together)

/***in***/,/***ain***/,/***ein***/, and/***aim***/ -the closest sound in the English language that is similar to this one would be the an in hang.

Example: *main*/mahn/ (hand), *pain*/pahn/ (bread)

/***un***/ and/***um***/ -to produce the nasal vowel sound, find the sound between/*o*/ and/*e*/.

Example: *un*/unh/ (one or a), *brun*/brunh/ (brown)

<u>Practice pronouncing the following:</u>

bain => banc => bond

sain => cent => son

daim => dans => don

fin => faon => fond

gain => gant => gond

geint => jean => jonc

lin => lent => long

main => ment => mont

pain => paon => pont

rein => rang => rond

thym => tant => ton

vin => vent => vont

Exercise

Here is a list of words that will let you practice most of the sounds in the French alphabet. Use a sound recorder and a free online application such as Google Translate to compare your pronunciation with that of a native speaker.

Consonant Sounds

- *Beau*
- *Doux*
- *Fête*
- *Guerre*
- *Cabas*
- *Loup*
- *Femme*
- *Nous*
- *Agneaux*
- *Passé*
- *Roue*
- *Option*
- *Choux*
- *Tout*
- *Vous*
- *Hasard*
- *Joue*

Semi-Vowel Sounds

- *Travail*
- *Oui*
- *Huit*

Vowel Sounds

- *Là*
- *Pâte*
- *Aller*
- *Faite*
- *Maître*
- *Monsieur*
- *Régie*
- *Jeune*
- *Queue*
- *Haut*
- *Minimum*
- *Roue*
- *Sûr*

Nasal Vowel Sounds

- *Sans*
- *Pain*
- *Parfum*
- *Nom*

Chapter 2 - Structure of a Sentence

In this chapter, we will take your knowledge a step further and examine the structure of a sentence. This includes things like nouns, adverbs, and adjectives. In French, there is a little more that goes into structuring a sentence than in English, as there are a few more rules and the order of words is quite specific. We will look into this in-depth in this chapter, and by the end, you will be quite comfortable with structuring your own sentences.

Articles

The first part of a sentence that we will look at are articles. Articles are words that are attached to nouns. In English, we use the words *the, an* or *a* in front of nouns. These serve to set up the listener or reader for what is coming next, whether it is something specific or general. For example, *the boy* or *a boy.*

In French, every word is assigned a gender. Now, this may sound odd, but it is true. Everything from a chair to a kettle and everything else in between has an assigned gender. This gender is not assigned for no reason. The gender of a word informs which of the forms of *the* or you will use when speaking about that word. The gender of a word does not change. In French, there are many different forms of the words *the* and *a,* and you will choose which of these you use according to the gender of the word about which you are speaking. As you learn French nouns, you will need to learn its gender along with it. The best way to do this is to learn the noun along with the article that accompanies it because this article will tell you the gender of the noun. In this section, we will look at all of the different articles you will come across and some examples of nouns you will see them with. In the section that follows, we will go deeper into our study of nouns because then you will understand the articles that you will see them with.

L'Article Defini

In English, we do not have feminine and masculine nouns, so when we are talking about **something specific,** we use the word to describe it. This is called the definite article or *l'article defini,* [l-ar-tee-k-le][day-fee-nee]. We will first look at the singular form before moving onto the plural form.

Singular Definite Article

Masculine, *le,* [l-uh]

Feminine, *la,* [l-ah]

Vowel or h, *l',* [l]

All three of these mean *the,* and this is where French gets more complicated than English. In English, you only need to know that *the* is used in definite cases. In French, you must know that it is definite as well as the gender of the thing you are describing.

When attaching an article before a verb that starts with a vowel or with the letter *h* (which is a silent sound in French), you will use the letter *L,* followed by an apostrophe. This is so that there isn't the awkward sound of two vowels together, as this would be difficult to pronounce properly.

Some examples of when each article, along with a word which matches its gender are below for you to practice saying and memorizing.

The game, *le jeu,* [l-uh][j-uh]

The casino, *le casino,* [l-uh][k-as-ee-no]

The table, *la table,* [l-ah][tah-b-l]

The cup, *la tasse,* [l-ah][tah-ss]

The bee, *l'abeille,* [l-ah-bay]

The hexagon, *l'hexagone,* [l-ex-a-gone]

Notice how the *l'* before a noun becomes blended into the noun itself when you are saying it aloud. Practice this a few times before moving on.

Plural Definite Article

In English, when we are speaking about a group of nouns in a specific way, we would still use the word. In French, there is a different definitive article *(l'article defini)* than those explained above (le, la, l') that are found with plural nouns.

Plural (either masculine or feminine), *Les,* [l-ay]

We will use the same article for plural nouns regardless of whether they are feminine or masculine. Some examples of this are below;

The books, *les livres,* [l-ay][lee-v-re]

The oranges, *les oranges,* [l-ay][oh-ron-j]

L'Article Indefini

We will now move on to the Indefinite Article, or *l'article indefini.* This is used when we are speaking about something unspecific, where in English we would say the word *a* or *an*. We would use these to describe a noun in general instead of one specific item.

Singular

Masculine, *un,* [uhn]

Feminine, *une,* [oo-n]

A few examples of this are below,

An orange, *un orange* [uhn][oh-ron-j]

A book, *un livre,* [uhn][l-ee-v-r]

An apple, *une pomme,* [oo-n][p-uh-m]

Plural

When it comes to the plural form of unspecific or indefinite articles, there is not an exact equivalent of an article in English, but the closest thing would be when we use the word *multiple* or *many*. This is not an article by definition in English, but for our purposes, it will be.

Some, *des,* [d-ay]

Multiple books, *des livres,* [d-ay][l-ee-v-rs]

Many apples, *des pommes,* [d-ay][p-uh-m]

Notice how one of the above examples is feminine, and one of them is masculine (as we saw above with *un et une*), but when it comes to the plural form, they both are attached to the article *des*.

L'Article Partitif

The Partitive Article is used when we are talking about only a part of something, rather than the whole of it. This is often used when we are speaking about food. This is used when the noun is something we cannot count, which is why it is usually used with food.

Singular

In English, we would use the word *some* in this place. You will find examples of this below.

Masculine, *du,* [doo]

Feminine, *de la,* [d-uh][lah]

Vowel or h, *de l',* [d-uh][l]

Notice again how either starts with a vowel or the letter *h* (which would be silent), *de* is used, followed by the letter *l* and an apostrophe.

Some cheese, *du fromage,* [doo][fr-oh-mah-j]

Some pie, *de la tarte,* [d-uh][lah][tar-t]

Some money, *de l'argent,* [d-uh][l-ar-j-ont]

Plural

Plural Partitive Articles are used when we are talking about a portion of food that contains multiple items. Examples are below in order for you to better grasp this concept. Notice that this article is the same one used when speaking about indefinite items in multiples (as above).

Des, [d-ay]

Some Spinach, *des épinards,* [d-ay-s][eh-pee-n-ar-d]

Some Pasta, *des pâtes,* [d-ay][pah-t-s]

Nouns

We will now talk about nouns. As we know from speaking English, a noun is a *place,* a *person,* or a *thing*. If you know a few words from the French language already, many of these are likely nouns. If you know how to say chair or cereal, for example, these would be nouns. All of the words we attached to articles were nouns. There will be more pronunciation practice in this section, so continue to read the new words you learn aloud. The one major takeaway that you should get from this section is that in the French language, everything is gendered. Everything has a gender associated with it. There is no trick that will tell you if a noun is feminine or masculine, you will have to remember this for the most part. To make this easier for you, as you are learning nouns they will all be paired with their appropriate article.

Before we get there, we will learn the French word for noun;

A Noun, un *nom,* [n-om]

Masculine and Feminine Nouns

As you know by now, there are some nouns that are feminine and some that are masculine, while others are plural. The articles that are placed with nouns are different depending on if the noun is masculine, feminine, or plural. Now that you are familiar with articles and the different forms and uses for them, we will look at some examples of nouns that use each of these articles. To help you remember which nouns are feminine and which are masculine more easily, we will now look at them in terms of the categories of nouns that tend to be feminine and others that tend to be masculine, so that you can group them in your brain and remember them later. Keep in mind, in the French language there will always be exceptions, but those will be learned later.

Feminine Nouns And Their Articles

We will begin by looking at the categories of nouns that contain feminine nouns. As you read through this section, read the nouns and their articles aloud to practice pronunciation.

School subjects are feminine, such as;

Chemistry, *la chimie,* [l-ah][shee-mee]

Gym, *la gymnastique* [l-ah][j-eem-nas-tee-k]

Language, *la langue* [l-ah][l-on-g]

Cars and car names are feminine. For example;

In French, there are two different words that mean car. They are both feminine nouns.

A car, *une auto* [oo-n][oh-toe]

A car, *une voiture* [oo-n][v-wah-too-r]

A Mazda 3, *la Mazda Trois,* [l-ah]Mazda][tr-wah](rolled r)

Most **foods that end with the letter *e*** are feminine nouns. For example;

A banana, *la banane,* [l-ah][bah-na-n]

A tomato, *la tomate,* [l-ah][t-oh-mat]

An apple, *la pomme,* [l-ah][po-m]

Continents are feminine nouns. For example;

Australia, *l'Australie,* [l-os-t-ra-lee]

Europe, *L'Europe* [l-you-rup]

Asia, *L'Asie,* [l-ah-see]

Mostly all **countries whose French names end with the letter *e*.** These are going to be feminine nouns. The countries below may not seem like they end with the letter *e,* but their French names do. For example;

France, *la France,* [l-ah][f-ron-s] (rolled r)

China, *la Chine,* [l-ah][sh-een]

Patagonia, *La Patagonie,* [l-ah][pat-a-go-nee]

Masculine Nouns And Their Articles

We will now look at some examples of noun categories that are masculine.

The **calendar** itself is a masculine noun as well as all of the **days in a week,** the **months** as well as the **seasons.**

Calendar, *le calendrier,* [l-uh][k-al-on-dree-ay]

December, *le décembre,* [l-uh][day-s-om-br-uh]

Summer, *l'ete,* [l-ay-tay]

Tuesday, *le Mardi,* [l-uh][mar-dee]

When speaking about a **specific date**, this is masculine.

June 6th, *le six juin,* [l-uh][s-ee-s][j-w-an]

October 12th, *le douze octobre,* [l-uh][doo-z][o-k-toh-b-ruh]

Colors are masculine nouns, as well.

Red, *le rouge,* [l-uh][roo-j]

Orange, *l'orange,* [l-oh-ron-j]

Pink, *le rose,* [l-uh][r-oh-z](rolled r)

Drinks are most often masculine.

Coffee, *le cafe,* [l-uh][k-af-ay]

Juice, *le jus,* [l-uh][j-oo-s]

Tea, *le the,* [l-uh][t-ay]

Foods that don't end with the letter *e* are masculine nouns.

Corn, *le mais,* [l-uh][mah-yee-s]

Sandwich, *le sandwich,* [l-uh][s-and-wee-ch]

Countries that end in any letter other than *e* are masculine nouns.

Canada, *le Canada,* [l-uh][k-ana-da]

Japan, *le Japon,* [l-uh][j-ap-on]

Directions on a compass are masculine nouns.

North, *le nord,* [l-uh][n-or]

South, *le sud,* [l-uh][soo-d]

East, *l'est,* [l-ess-t]

West, *l'ouest,* [l-oo-ess-t]

Languages are masculine nouns, although, as we saw above in the feminine noun categories, the actual school subject of languages and the word *language (la langue)* [l-ah][l-on-g] itself is feminine.

French, *le francais,* [l-uh][f-ron-say]

Greek, *le grec,* [l-uh][g-rek]

When we speak about **letters of the alphabet** on their own, these are masculine nouns.

A, *le a,* [l-uh][ah]

D, *le d,* [l-uh][d-ay]

P, *le p,* [l-uh][pay]

Plural Nouns

In the French language, some nouns are always plural and therefore are always associated with a plural article (les, des). While most of the time in English, a noun can be either plural or singular depending on what you are talking about, in French there are nouns that can only be used in a plural sense and therefore can only be used with a plural article. These plural nouns will either be accompanied by the article *les* or *des*. Examples of these can be seen below.

Business, *les affaires,* [l-ay][ah-f-air]

Asparagus, *les asperges,* [l-ay][ah-s-pair-j]

Luggage, *les bagages,* [l-ay][bah-g-ah-j]

Advice, *les conseils,* [l-ay][k-on-say]

All of these nouns will only be seen in their plural form. This is similar to the words *pants* or *glasses* in English. It is one item, but we talk about it as if it is more than one.

Pronouns

We will now move on to our study of another part of a sentence, the pronouns. Pronouns in French are called *les pronoms,* [l-ay][p-r-oh-no-m](rolled r). Pronouns are used English and French; in French, however, they have much more of an effect on the rest of the sentence than they do in English. In English, pronouns are things like: *I, we, they, she* and so on.

Personal Pronouns

Personal pronouns or, *les pronoms personnels,* [l-ay][p-r-oh-no-m][pair-s-on-el] are pronouns which are used in place of a grammatical person.

I, *Je,* [j-uh]

You, *Tu,* [too]

He, *il,* [ee-l]

She, *elle* [el]

We, on,* [oh-n](light *n* sound)

We, *Nous,* [new]

You (plural), *Vous,* [v-oo]

They (masculine or feminine), ***ils/elles,* [eel][el]

**on* is an informal pronoun that can replace *nous* to mean *we,* though the proper way to say *we* are by using *nous.*

** Notice that *'they'* has two different forms, one for masculine and one for feminine. Both French words for this (*ils* and *elles)* are pronounced in exactly the same way as their singular forms; *he* and *she* (il and elle), as the letter *s* is silent in these words.

Impersonal Pronouns

Impersonal pronouns or *les pronoms impersonnels* [eh-m-pair-soh-n-el] are pronouns that replace something in a sentence that is not a grammatical person. This could be a noun, an amount of something, a place, or a quantity. Examples are below.

This, *Ce,* [suh]

That, *ça,* [sah]

Multiple, *plusieurs,* [p-loo-see-uhr-s]

Who, *qui,* [k-ee]

What, *que,* [k-u-h]

Which One, *lequel,* [leh-k-el]

Adjectives

Adjectives or *les adjectifs* [l-ay][a-j-ek-teef] describe nouns. We use these in both French and English. Now that you are familiar with various French nouns and their articles, we will look at the adjectives that describe these nouns and more. Adjectives give a sentence more life, more description, and more life-like quality.

These can be things like the color of something, the shape, the size or if it is ugly or pretty. In English, adjectives have only one form, but in French, they will have one of four forms.

Adjectives must be in agreement when it comes to the gender of the noun, and whether it is plural or singular, so we adjust the adjective to agree with this, just like we do with an article. The article of a noun will give you the information on how to make the adjective agree with the gender as well. The default form of every adjective in French is the masculine form, and from there we add letters to adjust the ending to make it feminine or plural or both.

Masculine(nothing added)

Feminine -e

Masculine plural -s

Feminine plural -es

We will now look at some examples of adjectives before adding them to nouns and adjusting their endings accordingly. As you read through these examples, say them aloud and practice the pronunciation.

Small, *petit* [p-uh-tee]

Big, *grand* [g-ron] (rolled r)

Ugly, *laid* [l-ed]

Sharp, *pointu* [pwa-n-too]

Hot, *chaud* [sh-oh]

Cold, *froid* [f-r-wa] (rolled r)

If the adjective ends with the letter -a, -e or -o, then both masculine and feminine form will be the same because we don't want to add another vowel (an *e)* on to the end of a word already ending in a vowel. Examples of this are below.

Damp, *humide*, [hoo-mee-d]

Masculine, *humide*

Feminine, *humide*

Masculine plural, *humides*

Feminine plural, *humides*

Try adding the appropriate endings to the example below using what you learned with the adjective *humide.*

Pretty, *belle* [b-el]

Masculine, *belle*

Feminine, *belle*

Masculine plural, *belles*

Feminine plural, *belles*

If the adjective ends with the letter -s or -x, then the masculine singular and masculine plural forms are the same. These adjectives are somewhat irregular, especially those ending in -x, so pay close attention. An example of this is below, and further is one for you to try.

Delicious, *Delicieux* [day-lee-s-yuh]

M: delicieux

F: delicieuse*

MP: delicieux

FP: delicieuses

*Notice how the -x has been removed and replaced by -se to make the feminine form. This is because 'delicieuxse' would not make much sense and would be a mouthful to try and say. We make it an adverb ending in -s and then add the appropriate feminine ending for both singular and plural feminine forms.

Try changing the endings of this adjective to make it in agreement with the gender. Be especially careful with the feminine forms; look above for assistance if need be!

Happy, *heureux,* [euh-ruh]

M: heureux

F:heureuse

MP: heureux

FP: heureuses

Surprised, *surpris,* [s-oo-r-pree]

M: Surpris

F; Surprise

MP: surpris

FP: surprises

Notice in this example how the masculine singular and plural forms are exactly the same.

We will now do a little practice on the things we have just learned about adjectives by combining it with what we know about articles and nouns. For each pair below, you can see them put together by adjusting the adjective to the gender of the noun.

The fairy and small, *La fée et petit,* **La** fée petit**e**

The apple and juicy, *La pomme et juteux, La pomme juteuse*

February and cold, *Le février et froid, Le février froid*

China and big/large, *La Chine et grand, La Chine grande*

The fairies and small, *Les fées et petit, Les fées petites*

Adverbs

Adverbs are another type of description word, much like adjectives. Adverbs can modify a verb, an adjective, and they can even modify themselves. There are different categories of adjectives, depending on the type of modification that they make. We will look at those different types now.

Chapter 3 - The First Impression Is Very Important

Everyone knows the old saying "you only get one chance to make a first impression."

Therefore, it's no surprise that one of the first things every child learns is to say hello and introduce themselves. Even J.K. Rowling, the famous author of that young wizard's adventures, said "A good first impression can work wonders", and I completely agree.

Just a simple "Hello" can make all the difference in a conversation. That's exactly the reason why we will begin this exciting adventure, learning greetings in French. You will learn how to introduce yourself and greet people at different times of the day, among other useful things.

Ready to start? I really hope you are as excited as I am!

So, let's start with the most common ways to greet someone in French:

Hello.	Bonjour /Salut

Bon-joor – Sah-luh

The word "Bonjour" is probably one of the most popular French words and is now used as a friendly salutation around the world.

Salut, which is more informal, is also used quite often, but applies more to people you know personally, such as friends and family.

Good morning.	Bonjour

Translated literally, "Bonjour" means "good day". It is also used as a greeting upon waking up. You can use it in the morning and afternoon.

Contrary to English, the greetings don't change depending on the time of the day. As such, in the afternoon, you also say "Bonjour".

As the afternoon sets in, you should say "Good evening".

Good evening.	Bonsoir

Bon-swar

You can use this greeting on both formal and informal occasions. It is used both for when you are arriving and leaving a place.

Finally, at bedtime, you will say:

Good night.	Bonne nuit

Boh-nuh nu-ee

Remember! You should use "Bonne nuit" only when you are saying goodbye late at night. It is also used to wish sweet dreams.

Last one. When departing, you say:

Goodbye.	Au revoir / Ciao

Au revoir – Tchah-oh

You should remember that, depending on whether you are greeting a friend or a stranger, you would use a different salutation.

For example, when leaving a restaurant (or in any other formal occasion), you will say "Au revoir" if you want to sound polite. Although, you can use "Ciao" if you are saying goodbye to some old friends or to someone you know well (informal occasion).

Farewell.	Adieu
Farewell. I love you.	**Adieu**. Je t'aime

Ah-dee-euh

"Adieu" is used as a final salutation when you are pretty sure you are not going to see someone ever again. It's a phrase very rich in drama, sadness, or irony.

There is also a more informal version of "Au revoir"

See you later.	A plus tard.
Great! **See you later.**	Parfait! **À plus tard.**

Ah-plu-tar

How is your pronunciation? Hope you are starting to make progress.

See you in a few.	À tout à l'heure
Ok! **See you in a few.**	Okl! **À tout à l'heure.**

A-toot-a-leur

When greeting, you may also want to ask how someone is doing.

How are you?	Comment ça va? / ça va?

Ko-man-sah-vah

Asking "Comment ça va?" is a really good way to start a friendly conversation. It is an informal greeting and can also be used between people you are familiar with to ask about their health or mood. You can also simply say: ça va?

There is no big difference between the two. Here's the literal translation of both expressions:

-Comment ça va? "How are you doing?"

-ça va? Are you alright/Are you okay?

How can I help you?	Comment je peux t'aider?

Koh-man-guh-puh-teh-deh

At this point, you have probably figured out the connection between two words: "how" and "comment", and you know how important the word "how" is in any language.

Let's see another sentence that uses the word "Comment":

What is your name?	Comment tu t'appelles?

Ko-man-tah-pel-tu

To say what your name is in French you use:

My name is	Je m'appelle
My name is John.	**Je m'appelle** John.

Juh-ma-pell

I am	Je suis
I am new around here.	**Je suis** nouveau ici.

Juh-suee

Thanks/Thank you.	Merci

Mer-see

"Merci" is used to say both "thanks" or "thank you". However, if you wish to show more gratitude, you could say "Thanks a lot" which translates to "Merci beaucoup".

Mer-see-bo-koo

I am sorry.	Je suis désolé.

Juh-suee-dé-zo-lé

Nice to see you again.	Ravi de te revoir.

Ra-vee-duh-tuh-ruh-vwar

Was it too hard? Don't worry. Greetings are basic phrases you will need to memorize, but I promise that following sentences will be shorter and easier to remember.

What is new?	Quoi de neuf?

Kwa-duh-neuf

Another sentence with similar meaning is "Qu'est-ce que tu racontes?" What do you say?

Ke-suh-kuh-tu-ra-ko-ntuh

How are you doing?	Comment vas-tu? Comment ça va?

Ko-man-va-tu

As you might know, "Ok" is an English expression. Nevertheless, it's universally used worldwide, even among French speakers. You should be aware, however, that there is a French equivalent:

Ok.	D'accord

Da-kor

How is it going? Is it easy? Or maybe you need to practice a little bit more. Practice is the key to mastery. Anyway, before we move to another topic, let's take a look at a short conversation that uses some of the words we have just learned.

You'll now listen to a short dialog between John and a Vendor.

You'll listen to the sentences, first in English and then in French.

Vendor (Vendeur):	*Good morning!* Bonjour
John:	*Good morning to you, too.* *Bonjour à vous.*

Vendor: *How can I help you?*

Comment puis-je vous aider?

John: *I am here to pick up a cake.*

Je suis ici pour récupérer un gâteau.

Vendor: *Sure. What is your name?*

Bien-sûr. Quel est votre nom?

John: *My name is John Hill.*

Je m'appelle John Hill.

Vendor: *Oh, I am sorry. Your bday cake is not ready yet.*

Oh, je suis désolé. Votre gâteau d'anniversaire n'est pas encore prêt.

John: *Ok. When can I come pick it up?*

D'accord. Quand est-ce que je peux venir le récuperer?

Vendor: *It will be ready in one hour.*

Ce sera prêt dans une heure.

John: *Great. I will run some errands and come back.*

Super. Je vais faire quelques courses et je reviens.

Vendor: *Thanks for understanding. See you in a few.*

Merci de votre compréhension. A tout à l'heure.

John: *Sure. See you later!*

Bien-sûr. A plus tard!

I hope John is not getting low blood sugar, because he will have to wait for a while. In the meantime, shall we go and learn some new words and phrases that relate to family and relatives? This could be really handy if you are going to celebrate your birthday!

Chapter 4 - Enchanté
(Nice To Meet You)

Conjugation of the Irregular Verb "Venir"

Venir: To come

Je viens = I come

Tu viens = You come

Il/ Elle / On vient = He comes/ She comes/ We come

Nous venons = We come

Vous venez = You come

Ils/ Elles viennent = They come

Examples of the verb:

-Je viens de Lyon - (I come from Lyon.)

-Nous venons au restaurant avec notre famille. - (We are coming to the restaurant with our family.)

-Vous venez à la banque? - (You are coming to the bank?)

To Make Negative Sentences

The rule for negation is: **ne + verb + pas**

And in case of vowels, it is: **n' +verb + pas**

Example:

1. Je regarde le film. = (Meaning -> I watch the film)

   ne+verbe+ pas

   Je ne regarde pas le film. = (Meaning -> I do not watch the film)

2. Tu danses

   (You dance.)

Tu ne danses pas.

(You do not dance.)

3. Il habite à Paris.

   (He lives in Paris.)

   Il n'habite pas à Paris.

   (He does not live in Paris.)

4. Nous travaillons ensemble.

   (We work together.)

   Nous ne travaillons pas ensemble.

   (We do not work together.)

5. Elle est mariée.

   (She is married.)

   Elle n’est pas mariée.

   (She is not married.)

6. Vous chantez bien.

   (We sing well.)

   Vous ne chantez pas bien.

   (We do not sing well.)

7. Ils sont riches.

   (They are rich.)

   Ils ne sont pas riche.

   (They are not rich.)

8. Je suis canadien.

   (I am Canadian.)

Je ne suis pas canadien.

(I am not Canadian.)

9. Tu es belle.

(You are beautiful.)

Tu n'es pas belle.

(You are not beautiful.)

10. Il est beau.

(He is handsome.)

Il n'est pas beau.

(He is not handsome.)

To Respond to a Question by Saying Yes/ Non

(OUI/ NON/ SI)

Tu es marié ? = (Meaning -> Are you married?)

Oui, Je suis marié. = (Meaning -> Yes, I am married.)

Non, Je ne suis pas marié. = (Meaning -> No, I am not married.)

Vous êtes français ? = (Meaning -> You're French?)

Oui, Je suis français. = (Meaning -> Yes, I am French.)

Non, Je ne suis pas français. = (Meaning -> No, I am not French.)

Tu habites à Lyon? = (Meaning ->Do you live in Lyon?)

Oui, J'habite à Lyon.

Non, Je n'habite pas à Lyon.

Vous parlez espagnol? = (Meaning ->You speak Spanish?)

Oui, Je parle espagnol.

Non, Je ne parle pas espagnol.

Vous invitez vos parents? = (Meaning ->Are you inviting your parents?)

Oui, J'invite mes parents.

Non, Je n'invite pas mes parents.

Ils travaillent chez AIR FRANCE? = (Meaning ->They work at AIR FRANCE?)

Oui, Ils travaillent chez AIR FRANCE.

Non, Ils ne travaillent pas chez AIR FRANCE.

When the question is negative, we use <<***si***>> instead of <<***oui***>>

Tu n'es pas marié ? = (Meaning -> Are you not married?)

Non, Je ne suis pas marié. = (Meaning -> No, I am not married.)

Si, Je suis marié. = (Meaning ->Yes, I am married.)

Tu n'habites pas à Lyon? = (Meaning ->Don't you live in Lyon?)

Non, Je n'habite pas à Lyon.

Si, J'habite à Lyon.

Vous ne parlez pas espagnol? = (Meaning ->You don't speak Spanish?)

Non, Je ne parle pas espagnol.

Oui, Je parle espagnol

Tu n'aimes pas les galces ? = (Meaning ->You don't like ice cream?)

Non, Je n'aime pas les glaces.

Si, J'aime les glaces.

The Numbers 30-100 (Les Nombres 30-100)

30 Trente

31 Trente – et – un

32 Trente – deux

33 Trente – trios

34 Trente – quatre

35 Trente – cinq

36 Trente – six

37 Trente – sept

38 Trente – huit

39 Trente – neuf

40 Quarante

41 Quarante – et – un

42 Quarante – deux

43 Quarante – trios

44 Quarante – quatre

45 Quarante – cinq

46 Quarante – six

47 Quarante – sept

48 Quarante – huit

49 Quarante – neuf

50 Cinquante

51 Cinquante – et – un

52 Cinquante – deux

53 Cinquante – trois

54 Cinquante – quatre

55 Cinquante – cinq

56 Cinquante – six

57 Cinquante – sept

58 Cinquante – huit

59 Cinquante – neuf

60 Soixante

61 Soixante – et – un

62 Soixante – deux

63 Soixante – trios

64 Soixante – quatre

65 Soixante – cinq

66 Soixante – six

67 Soixante – sept

68 Soixante – huit

69 Soixante – neuf

70 Soixante – dix

71 Soixante – onze

72 Soixante – douze

73 Soixante – treize

74 Soixante – quatorze

75 Soixante – quinze

76 Soixante – seize

77 Soixante – dix – sept

78 Soixante - dix – huit

79 Soixante – dix – neuf

80 Quatre – vingts

81 Quatre – vingt – un

82 Quatre – vingt – deux

83 Quatre – vingt – trios

84 Quatre – vingt – quatre

85 Quatre – vingt – cinq

86 Quatre – vingt – six

87 Quatre – vingt – sept

88 Quatre – vingt – huit

89 Quatre – vingt – neuf

90 Quatre – vingt – dix

91 Quatre – vingt – onze

92 Quatre – vingt – douze

93 Quatre – vingt – treize

94 Quatre – vingt – quatorze

95 Quatre – vingt – quinze

96 Quatre – vingt – seize

97 Quatre – vingt – dix – sept

98 Quatre – vingt – dix – huit

99 Quatre – vingt – dix – neuf

100 Cent

Number	*Pronunciation*
Trente	Th – roh – t
Quarante	Keh – roh – t
Cinquante	She – koh – t
Soixante	Suaah – soh – t
Soixante – dix	Suaah – soh – t di – c
Quatre – vingts	Keh – th – r – veh
Quatre – vingt – dix	Keh – th – r – veh di – c
Cent	S – oh

Conjugation of the Irregular Verb “Avoir”

Avoir: To have

J'ai = I have

Tu as = You have

Il/Elle/On a = He has/ She has/ We have

Nous avons = We have

Vous avez = You have

Ils/Elles ont = They have

The verb avoir is used in two cases:

1.When you want to express your possession.

For example:

-J'ai un stylo. (I have a pen.)

-Paul a trois crayons. (Paul has 3 pencils.)

-Tu as deux portables? (You have 3 phones?)

2.In case you want to ask or tell about the age.

For example:

-J'ai vingt-trois ans. (I am 23 years old.)

-Il a trente-deux ans. (He is 23 years old.)

-Elle a cinquante ans. (She is 50 years old.)

To Ask Someone His/Her Age: (What is your age?)

Formal	***Informal***
Vous avez quel âge?	Tu as quel âge?

Professions (Les Professions/Les Métiers)

MASCULIN	*FÉMININ*	***Meaning***
Il est	Elle est	He is/ She is
Chauffeur	Chauffeur	Driver
Avocat	Avocate	Advocate
Journaliste	Journaliste	Journalist
Artiste	Artiste	Artist
Peintre	Peintre	Painter
Pilote	Pilote	Pilot
Dentiste	Dentist	Dentist
Secrétaire	Secrétaire	Secretary
Musicien	Musicienne	Musician

Mécanicien	Mécanicienne	Mechanic
Serveur	Serveuse	Waiter
Éditeur	Éditerice	Editor
Directeur	Directerice	Director
Chanteur	Chanteuse	Singer
Danseur	Danseuse	Dancer
Facteur	Factrice	Post man
Vendeur	Vendeuse	Sales man
Médecin	Médecin	Doctor
Professeur	Professeur	Professor
Infirmier	Infermière	Nurse
Boulanger	Boulangère	Baker
Cusinier	Cusinière	Chef
Ingénieur	Ingénieure	Engineer
Homme au foyer	femme au foyer	Househusband/ House wife
Homme d'affaires	femme d'affaires	Business man
Docteur	Docteur	Doctor

How to Introduce Someone/Something:

Qu'est ce-que c'est? (Utilisé pour les objets)
What is it? (Used for the objects)

The Answer ***(La réponse)***

Singular	*Meaning*	*Plural*	*Meaning*
C'est un stylo.	This is a pen	Ce sont des stylos	These are pens
C'est un crayon.	This is a pencil	Ce sont des crayons	These are pencils
C'est une gomme.	This is an eraser	Ce sont des gommes	These are erasers
C'est une règle.	This is a scale	Ce sont des règles	These are scales
C'est un livre.	This is a book	Ce sont des livres	These are books
C'est un cahier.	This is a notebook	Ce sont des cahiers	These are notebooks
C'est un taille crayon.	This is a sharpener	Ce sont des taille crayons	These are sharpeners
C'est un portable.	This is a phone	Ce sont des portables	These are phones
C'est un ordinateur.	This is a computer	Ce sont des ordinateurs	These are computers
C'est un ventillateur.	This is a fan	Ce sont des ventilateurs	These are fans
C'est une télévision.	This is a television	Ce sont des télévisions	These are televisions

C'est un climatiseur.	This is a air conditioner	Ce sont des climatiseurs	These are air conditioners
C’est une poubelle	This is a dustbin	Ce sont des poubelles	These are dustbins
C’est un sac	This is a bag	Ce sont des sacs	These are bags

Un, Une, Des are the articles. Un is used with masculine nouns. Une is used with feminine nouns, and des is used with plural nouns.

Qui est-ce ? C'est qui ? {Utilisé pour les personnes}
Who is it? {Used for people}

The Answer *(La réponse)*

Sentence	***Meaning***	***Formal/Informal***
Il s'appelle Paul	His name is Paul	Formal/Informal
Elle s'appelle Paul	Her name is Paul	Formal/Informal
Je vous présente Paul	I present to you Paul	Formal
Je te présente Paul	I present to you Paul	Informal
C'est Paul	This is Paul	Formal/Informal
Voici Paul	This is Paul	Formal/Informal

To Describe the Professions:

Sentence	***Meaning***
Il est directeur.	He is a director.

Elle est directrice.	She is a director.
c'est un directeur	It's a director.
c'est le directeur de HCL.	It's the director of HCL.
c'est le réalisateur de film<< Avengers>>.	It's the director of the film"Avengers"

To write a profession with C'est, the two types of articles can be used. Definite articles (Le, La, Les, L') or Indefinite articles (Un, Une, Des).The indefinite articles are used when the information is not precise. For example: C'est un journaliste. The definite articles are used when the information is precise. For example: C'est le journaliste de l'émission <<RFI>>.

The articles:

Le -> masculine

La -> feminine

Les -> plural

L' -> vowel

Un -> masculine

Une -> feminine

Des -> plural

Possessive Adjectives (Les Adjectifs Possessifs)

What are the Possessive Adjectives?
It is used to demonstrate the possession of something. For instance, My pen, His car, Our house, Their friend etc. In the French language, the noun bears genders (masculine, feminine or plural), henceforth the possessive adjectives are divided into 3 categories explained as following:

Subject	***Masculine possessive adjectives***	***Pronunciation***	***Feminine possessive adjectives***	***Pronunciation***	***Plural possessive adjectives***	***Pronunciation***	***Meaning***
Je	Mon	M – oh	Ma	M - aa	Mes	M – eh	My___
Tu	Ton	T – oh	Ta	T – aa	Tes	T – eh	Your____
Il/Elle/On	Son	S – oh	Sa	S – aa	Ses	S – eh	His ____
Vous	Votre	Voh – th - r	Votre	Voh – th – r	Vos	Voh	Your____
Nous	Notre	No – th – r	Notre	No – th – r	Nos	Noh	Our ____
Ils/Elles	Leur	L – r	Leur	L – r	Leurs	L – r	Their___

If the noun is masculine then a masculine possessive adjective is used. If the noun is feminine then a feminine possessive adjective is used. If the noun is plural then a plural possessive adjective is used.

Examples:	***Meaning:***	***Examples:***	***Meaning:***
Mon stylo	My pen	Notre maison	Our house
Ma voiture	My car	Leur ami	Their friend
Ses parents	His parents	Nos sacs	Our bags

Exception Rule: If the noun starts with a vowel then it will always be masculine possessive adjective, irrespective of the gender. For example, Amie is feminine, hence it should use a feminine possessive adjective. But it will be incorrect as Amie starts with A i.e. a vowel. Hence it can be: Mon amie Sylvie, Ton amie Sylvie, Son amie Sylvie, Notre amie Sylvie, Votre amie Sylvie, Leur amie Sylvie.

Let us see another example: Université is feminine i.e Une université - but it starts with a vowel. So it will always appear with Mon, Ton, Son etc.

Vocabulary Words

Word	***Meaning***	***Pronunciation***
Chercher	To search	*Sh – r – sh – ay*
Avoir peur	To fear	*Aa – vuah – r*
Carte	Card	*Ka – r – t*
Enfin	At last	*Oh – fah*
Divertissement	Entertainment	*Di – veh – r – ti – z – moh*
Vêtements	Clothes	*Veh – t – moh*
Inoubliable	Unforgettable	*In – ooh – b – li – aa – b – l*
Autre	Another	*Oh – th – r*

Lunettes de soleil	Sunglasses	*Looh – neh – t*
Montre	Watch	*Moh – th – r*
Roman	Novel	*Roh – moh*
Clés	Keys	*K – lay*
Jeux	Games	*Jeh*
Choix	Choice	*Sh – uah*
Coin	Corner	*K – uah*
Amour	Love	*Aa – mooh – r*
Acheter	To buy	*Aa – sh – tay*
Argent	Money	*Aar – goh*
Billet	Ticket	*Bi – ay*
Bijou	Jewellery	*Bi – jooh*
Chanceuse	Lucky	*Sh – oh – s – z*
Chez	At somebody's place	*Sh – ay*
Devoir	Homework	*D – vuah – r*
Culturel	Cultural	*Kul – tuh – rel*
Côte à côte	Side by side	*Koh - t – aa – koh - t*
Contraire	Contrary	*Kon – th – reh – r*
Complèter	To complete	*Kom – pleh – the*
Enfant	Kid	*Oh – foh*
Faux	False	*Ph – oh*
Femme	Woman	*Ph – a – m*

Homme	Man	*O – m*
Endroit	Place	*Oh – druah*
Ensemble	Together	*Oh – soh – m – b - l*
Exemple	Example	*Eh – zom – pl*
Fêter	To party	*Feh – the*
École	School	*Eh – ko – l*
Histoire	Story or history	*Is – tuah – r*
Maintenant	Now	*Meh – n – the – noh*
D'accord	Alright	*Daa – korh*
Immeuble	Building	*I – m – bleh*
Jardin	Garden	*Jaar – dah*
Inviter	To invite	*Ahn – vi – tay*
Note	Note	*Noh – t*
Lire	To read	*Li – r*
Ouvrir	To open	*Oh – v - rir*
Recevoir	To receive	*Reh – c – vuah – r*
Favori(e)	Favourite	*Ph – aa – voh – ri*
Auteurs	Authors	*Oh – th – r*
Coeur	Heart	*K – r*

Chapter 5 - Finding the Way/Directions

When traveling, finding your way is very important, and asking people you pass by on the street or people working in stores or hotels is very useful. Being able to ask people is not only important when you are in an English-speaking place but also when in a new place where they primarily speak another language that is not your own. With the knowledge gained in this chapter, you will be able to ask people for directions in French-speaking places in order to ensure you can get to where you are going with as little trouble as possible.

Addresses

We will now look at the way we say addresses in French. When we are talking about street addresses, there are a few differences between French and English. First, we will break it into pieces and look at each section contained in an address.

Streets

Rue [roo], street

Route [roo-t], road

Chemin [sh-uh-m-an], trail, path

Allee [ah-lay], driveway

Ruelle [roo-el], alley

Terrain de stationnement [tuh-r-an](rolled r)[duh][st-ah-si-on-mon-t], parking lot

Numbers

We will now look at the numbers from 1 to 10 in French. While there are differences in the way we say larger numbers, for your purposes, as long as you can say the numbers themselves, you will be fine. I will show you an example of what I mean below.

325 Example St.

Instead of having to say “three hundred and twenty five example street,” as long as you can say “three two five example street,” you will be able to adequately get your point across to the person you are asking, such as a taxi driver. As you now know, numbers from 1 to 20 and multiples of 10 from 20 to 100, you will be able to say many many address numbers. If you aren’t sure, however, you can simply state the numbers that you see that you do remember, and the person you are talking to will likely be able to understand what you are trying to say. As a refresher, the numbers from 1 to 10 are below for your reference.

1, 2, 3, 4, 5, 6, 7, 8, 9, 10

Un, deux, trois, quatre, cinq, six, sept, huit, neuf, dix

One, two, three, four, five, six, seven, eight, nine, ten

As an example, we will use the following address and look at it in more detail:

9 Rue Ste. Catherine

In French, when there is the word Saint, or St. in an address, like the street name *St. Catherine Street or St. Andrew street,* it is written as “Ste.” instead of “St.” like in English. This is because, in French, the word is *Sainte*. So when talking about any word or street with the word Saint in it, it will be written in this way:

Ste. Catherine, Sainte Catherine

Ste. Andrew, Sainte Andrew

Address Examples

When we write addresses, we write them in this order: number + street type (road, crescent, etc.) + street name. It is a bit of a different order than in English as the word street is moved to the front of the street name instead of after it.

9 St. Catherine Street is what we would say in English. In French, this would be written as *9 Rue Ste. Catherine* and said as *neuf, rue sainte catherine, à Paris, en France.*

13 Chemin Georges, un trois chemin georges, treize chemin georges. 13 Georges Street

100 chemin arbres, québec, québec, Canada. Cent chemin arbres, à québec, québec au Canada. 100 Arbres Trail, Quebec, Quebec, Canada.

À Washington vs. Au Washington

When we are talking about being or having been someplace, there are different ways to say this, depending on what type of place you're talking about. For example, in the United States, there are two different places called Washington. One is a state, and the other is a city. When speaking in English, we can tell which is being refered to because if they are talking about the state, they will say Washington State. In French, we don't do this, but there is another way that we can actually tell which of these somebody is talking about based on the word that precedes it. If we are talking about a city or town, we would say **À Washington**, which would indicate to the person we are speaking to that we are talking about the city. If we are talking about the state, we would say **Au Washington.**

One more thing to note is that if the province, state, or country we are talking about begins with a vowel, then using *au* would be quite a mouthful. In this case, we would say **en.** For example, "Je suis allé **en France**," which means, "I went to France." If you were talking about going to Paris, which is a city, you would say "Je suis allé **à Paris**."

Asking for Directions

This section will focus on the phrases you will need when you are traveling. These are related to transportation and directions so that you can get around with ease.

If you need to ask someone where something is, you can ask them in the following way:

Excusez-moi, est-ce que vous savez où est ____? This means Excuse me, do you know where is ______? You will then insert something like *La Tour Eiffel* (The Eiffel Tower.)

You could also say *Est ce que vous pouvez m'aider a trouver ______?* This means, "Could you help me find _____?"

Alternatively, you could also say *Est ce que vous savez ou est ce que c'est ________?* This means, "Do you know where ______ is?"

After asking this, you will likely hear one of the following responses:

Gauche, right

Droite, left

C'est..., It is / It's...

C'est à droite, It's to the right

C'est à gauche, It's to the left

C'est à côté de [s-eh][ah][k-oh-tay][duh], It's beside (something)

C'est près de [s-eh][pr-eh][duh], It's close to (something)

C'est près d'ici [s-eh][pr-eh][d-ee-see]], It's close to here

C'est loin d'ici [s-eh][l-w-ah-n][d-ee-see], It's far from here

C'est loin de [s-eh][l-w-ah-n][duh], It's far from (something)

Vocabulary List

Excusez-moi, où [oo] est [ay] ____?

Est ce que vous pouvez [poo-vay] m'aider [ay-day] a trouver [t-roo-vay] ______?

Est ce que vous savez [sah-vay] ou est ce que c'est ________?

La Tour Eiffel [lah][too-r][ee-fell]

Gauche [g-oh-sh], right

Droite [dr-wah-tuh] (rolled r), left

C'est [s-eh], It is / It's

C'est à gauche. It's to the left.

C'est à droite. It's to the right.

C'est à côté de [s-eh][ah][k-oh-tay][duh]. It's beside (something).

C'est près de [s-eh][pr-eh][duh]. It's close to (something).

C'est près d'ici [s-eh][pr-eh][d-ee-see]]. It's close to here.

C'est loin de [s-eh][l-w-ah-n][duh]. It's far from (something).

C'est loin d'ici [s-eh][l-w-ah-n][d-ee-see]. It's far from here.

Rue [roo], street

Route [roo-t], road

Chemin [sh-uh-m-an], trail / path

Allee [ah-lay], driveway

Ruelle [roo-el], alley

Terrain de stationnement [tuh-r-an](rolled r)[duh][st-ah-si-on-mon-t], parking lot

1 [uhhn],

2 [duuh],

3 [t-r-wah] (rolled r),

4 [cat-ruh](rolled r),

5 [sank],

6 [see-s],

7 [set],

8 [wee-t],

9 [nuuf],

10 [dee-s]

9 Rue Ste. Catherine, 9 St. Catherine Street

Sainte

neuf, rue sainte catherine, a Paris en France

13 chemin georges, un trois chemin georges. 13 Georges Street

100 chemin arbres, québec, québec, Canada. Cent chemin arbres, à québec, québec au Canada. 100 Arbres Trail, Quebec, Quebec, Canada.

A Washington, to Washington (city)

Au Washington, to Washington State

Chapter 6 - Travel, Transportation and How to Book/Buy A Ticket

Buying a Ticket

This section will tell you how to buy a ticket and other phrases that will come in handy when you need to travel and find your way around transportation in general. We will look at a variety of scenarios, and you will be well on your way to traveling around with ease.

The first thing we will look at is the metro, the train, or a bus. These types of transportation will require you to buy a ticket before you get on, so you will need to know how to buy a ticket or how to ask for help if you aren't sure how. We will first look at some words that you will come across in the stations and on signs leading to these stations.

Un Billet [bee-yay], a ticket

Les Billets, tickets

You will likely see a sign that says, *Guichet de la Billetterie,* which means "Ticketing Counter." This is where you will go with your ticket questions or buy a ticket. When you get to the counter, you will say *Bonjour, je veux acheter un billet,* which means, "Hello, I would like to buy a ticket." *Un billet* (a ticket) *s'il vous plaît* (please), which means, "One ticket, please" will also work. If you want to be more specific, you can specify where exactly you are going so that you can get a ticket to the right place. To do this, you will insert the name of the place you are going or the station you want to get to right after the word "ticket," such as *Un billet <u>à Paris</u> s'il vous plaît.*

When it comes to buying tickets, if you are doing so at a counter or even online, the following terms will help you to ensure you clearly understand what you are buying so that you end up in the right place!

Un billet aller-retour, a return ticket

Un billet aller-simple, a one-way ticket

Un siège, a seat

Je dois acheter un billet de retour pour la Grèce. I need to buy a return ticket to Greece.

S'il vous plaît réservez-moi le vol de 21 heures. Please book me the 9 PM flight.

Payer par carte bancaire, pay by debit

Combien coûte le billet? In English, this means, *How much does the ticket cost?*

Donnez-vous un rabais pour une personne âgée? Qu'en est-il d'un étudiant? Do you give a discount for a senior? What about a student?

Avez-vous de rabais pour une personne plus âgée? Do you have a discount for a senior person?

Je dois arriver à quelle heure? What time should I arrive?

When you are ready to go to the station for your train, bus, or flight, you can say to your taxi driver one of the following:

Je veux aller à l'aéroport. I want to go to the airport

Est-ce que vous pouvais me conduire à la station de train/ à la gare? Can you drive me to the train station?

Station de train/gare, train station

Station d'autobus, bus station

Aéroport, airport

Then, once you get to the station, you can ask for directions by saying:

Est-ce que vous pouvais m'aider à trouver ma porte? What this means is, "*Can you help me find my gate?*"

J'ai un vol pour attraper, I have a flight to catch.

Checking In

When checking into a flight, you would call this *enregistrer.*

If you want to ask someone where you can go to check into your flight, you can ask for *la reception.* If you want to tell someone that you are looking for the check-in desk, you can say, *je veux me presenter a la reception.* Once you get there, you will want to tell them that you have a reservation. To say this, you will say *J'ai une reservation.*

Upon check-in, you will be able to ask any questions, and you will be able to check your bags there. When they ask you which bags are for check-in, you will say:

J'ai une valise et trois sacs à main. I have one suitcase and three carry-on bags.

When you get to where you are going, you would say that you or someone else has:

Arriver, to arrive

More Travel Words and Phrases

Voyager, to travel

Un Passeport, a passport

Une Valise, a suitcase

Les bagages, baggage

Un plan, a map

Sortie, exit

Entrée, entrance

Un Guide Touristique, a tour guide

Vocabulary List

Un Billet [bee-yay], a ticket

Les Billets, Tickets

Guichet [gee-sh-ay] de la Billetterie, ticketing counter

Acheter[ah-sh-uh-tay] un billet, to buy a ticket

Un billet, s'il vous plaît [uhn][bee-yay][seel][v-oo][p-l-eh]

If you want to get more specific, you can specify where exactly you are going so that you can be sure you will get a ticket to the right place.

Un billet à Paris s'il vous plaît [uhn][bee-yay][ah][pah-ree][seel][v-oo][p-l-eh].

Un billet aller-retour [ah-lay-ruh-too-r], a return ticket

Un billet aller-simple [ah-lay-s-ah-m-p-luh], a one-way ticket

Un siège [see-y-eh-j], a seat

Je veux aller à la porte. I want to go to the gate

Je veux aller à l'aéroport. I want to go to the airport

Je veux réserver un billet. I would like to reserve a ticket.

Je dois acheter un billet de retour pour la Grèce. I need to buy a return ticket to Greece.

S'il vous plaît réservez-moi le vol de 21 heures. Please book me the 9 PM flight.

A quelle heure est ce que je dois [d-wah] arriver? What time should I arrive?

J'ai un valise et trois sacs à main. I have one suitcase and three carry-on bags.

Valise [vah-lee-suh]

Combien coûte le billet? How much should I pay for the ticket?

Combien [k-om-bee-yen]

Coûte [k-oo-tuh]

Donnez-vous un rabais pour une personne âgée? Qu'en est-il d'un étudiant? Do you give a discount for a senior? What about a student?

Rabais [rah-bay]

Etudiant [ay-tto-dee-y-on-t]

Avez-vous de rabais pour une personne plus âgée? Do you have a discount for a senior person?

Plus âgée, [p-loo][ah-j-ay]

Acheter un billet, to buy a ticket

J'ai un vol pour attraper

Vol [v-oh-l]

Payer par carte bancaire, pay by debit

Bancaire [b-on-k-ee-air]

Enregistrer [on-ray-gee-s-t-ray]

Voyager [v-oy-ah-j-ay], to travel

Un Passeport, a passport

Une Valise [v-ah-lee-z], a suitcase

Les bagages, baggage

Un plan, a map

Sortie, exit

Entrée [on-t-ray], entrance

Un Guide Touristique [g-ee-d][too-ree-s-t-ee-k], a tour guide

Common phrases used by traveller

Traveling to France is a wonderful journey where you will have the chance to experience local culture, as well as all the beautiful artwork and exquisite cuisine! As you are getting ready for your trip, it is essential that you try to learn some new languages skills. If you are interested by the common phrases used by travellers, please keep reading. It will help you to navigate throughout France and any french-speaking territory with ease. Remember, the best way to experience your journey is to immerse yourself completely by talking with the local population. We hope this section will give you many opportunities to practice your French.

Standard conversational sentences in French	
Bonjour! Bonsoir!	Hello! Good evening!
Bienvenue.	Welcome.
Madame, mademoiselle, monsieur.	Madam, miss, sir.
Excuse- moi.	Excuse me.
Je ne parle pas francais.	I don't speak French
Parlez-vous anglais?	Do you speak English?
Merci beaucoup.	Thank you very much.
De rien.	You're welcome.
A plus tard.	See you later.

GETTING INFORMATION	
Pourriez-vous m'aider?	Could you help me?
Je ne comprends pas.	I don't understand.
Parlez lentement, s'il vous plaît.	Speak slowly, please.
Répétez, s'il vous plaît.	Repeat, please.
Où sont les toilettes ?	Where are the toilets?
Où puis-je trouver un bon restaurant?	Where can I found a good restaurant?
Où se trouve (la ville, la plage, la rue St Michel...)?	Where is (the city, the beach, St Michel street...)?
Je cherche (le métro, la gare, l'aéroport...) ?	I'm looking for (the metro, the train station, the airport...)?
Je cherche (l'hôtel x, la police, le distributeur...).	I'm looking for (the hotel x, the police, the atm...).
Pourriez-vous nous prendre en photo?	Could you take us in photo?

ASKING FOR DIRECTIONS	
C’est tout droit	It’s straight away.
C'est sur la gauche.	It’s to the left.
C'est sur la droite.	It’s to the right.
C'est loin ? C'est proche ?	Is it far? Is it close?
Où sommes-nous ?	Where are we?

TRANSPORTATION	
Puis-je regarder les horaires?	Can I look at the schedule?
Puis-je réserver un billet ?	Can I reserve a ticket?
Puis-je acheter un billet aller simple/aller-retour ?	Can I purchase a one-way ticket/a round-trip ticket?
A quelle heure doit-il arriver ?	At what time should it arrive?

HOTEL	
Avez-vous une chambre disponible?	Do you have a room available?
Avez-vous la climatisation?	Do you have air conditioning?
Avez-vous une chambre disponible?	Do you have a double room?
Puis-je annuler ma réservation ?	Can I cancel my booking?
Quand est le check-out ?	When is the check-out?

SHOPPING	
Où est le centre commercial?	Where is the mall?
Où sont les magasins ?	Where are the shops?
Acceptez-vous les cartes de crédit ?	Do you accept credit card?
A quelle heure ouvrez vous ?	At what time do you open?
A quelle heure fermez vous ?	At what time do you close?

Je cherche (un livre, une robe, une carte...).	I am looking for a (book, dress, card...).
Combien cela coûte-t-il ?	How much does it cost?
C'est une bonne affaire.	It's a great deal.
C'est trop cher.	It's too expensive.
C'est génial/mauvais	It's great/bad

RESTAURANT	
Je voudrais (un café, de l'eau, une bière, un verre de vin, un jus, un thé...).	I would like (a coffee, water, a beer, a glass of wine, a juice, a tea....).
Le menu, s'il vous plaît.	The menu, please.
La note, s'il vous plaît.	The bill, please.
Puis-je réserver une table pour ce soir ?	Can I book a table for tonight?
C'est délicieux, merci.	It's delicious, thank you.

Chapter 7 - Traveling and Going About

We are now getting to some pretty useful things, especially if you are planning a trip to France or any French speaking country. Foreigners are usually easily helped by locals to find their way, especially if they speak a little French. So don't hesitate to leave your GPS in your pocket and use the opportunity of looking for your way to talk to people and ask them for guidance. If you stick to English when asking your way to others, it might very well be considered as a rude attitude. Don't forget that you are asking a "favor", so the least you can do is to try to ask in French.

But that won't be much of a problem, since you are now reading this chapter about "indications" (directions). So let's start with the basics, and what you should definitely start your sentence with: "excusez moi".

Excusez-moi : excuse me

Pardon : pardon me

Je cherche: I'm looking for

Où est/sont: Where is/are

Dans quelle rue se trouve : In which street is the ... located ?

Est-ce que ... est loin d'ici ? Is the ... far from here ?

Où puis-je trouver : Where can i find

Comment est-ce que je vais à/au... : How do I get to the...

Pouvez-vous m'aider : Can you help me

Pouvez-vous me montrer: Can you show me

Pouvez-vous me dire : Can you tell me

Est-ce que ... est loin/près d'ici ? Is the... far/close from here ?

Pouvez-vous m'emmener : Can you take me to

Centre ville : city center

Le prochain/ la prochaine : the next

À gauche : on the left

À droite : to the right

Tout droit: go straight

Traverser : to cross

Demi tour: U turn

Derrière: behind

À coté: next to

Devant: in front of

En face: opposite

Bout de la rue: end of the road

Le feu rouge: the traffic light

Le rond point : the round about

Une carte: a map

Nord/sud/est/ouest: North, south, east, west

What do you need exactly? Here is a list of things you might suddenly have the need for. Good luck !

Les toilettes : toilets

La gare : the train station

Le supermarché : the supermarket

La piscine : swimming pool

La banque : bank

Le distributeur de billets : ATM

La boulangerie : bakery (that's a very useful one)

Le magasin : the shop

La pharmacie : the pharmacy

L'hôpital : the hospital

Le restaurant: the restaurant

At the train station

How do I book a train ticket in French? How do I find out which track I should go to? How do I complain if my train has been canceled? Don't worry, in this section we will go through a certain number of easy sentences to help you survive in the train station.

Prendre le train: to take the train

Un ticket: guess?

Aller simple: one way

Aller retour: round trip

Première/seconde classe: first/second class

Tarif spécial : special fare

Réduction : discount

Combien coûte : how much is...

À quelle heure part/arrive: at what time leaves/arrive?

Le quai : the platform

Être en retard : to be late

Le train est en retard : the train is late

Rater le train : to miss the train

Composter: to validate a ticket

Annuler: to cancel

Échanger : to exchange

Remboursable : non refundable

Les renseignements : information (desk)

La grève : the strike (happens more than you think)

Les horaires: timetable

Le TGV: High speed train

Le wagon restaurant: bar compartment

Hotels

How do I book a hotel room in French? What do I say to the friendly receptionist who doesn't speak a word of English? How do I get my breakfast in my room? How do I cancel my expensive booking? Here again, we will take a look at some basic sentences that will help you to answer these questions. Do note, though that in touristic areas, hotel staff are supposed to speak some English, so don't you get robbed through expensive extras just because you absolutely want to get things done in French. Do try to get friendly contacts with employees; it might very well be helpful.

L'hôtel: the hotel

La reception: reception

Une chambre disponible : an available room

Réserver une chambre : book a room

Lit simple/double : single/double bed

Quel est le prix d'une chambre double ? how much is a double room ?

Un lit de bébé : a cot

Un lit d'appoint : a spare bed

Admis : allowed

Une clé : a key

Une clé magnétique : magnetic card

Petit-déjeuner compris : breakfast included

Demi-pension: half board

Pension complète : full board

Servi : served

Le service en chambre / d'étage : room service

Réserver en ligne : to book online

Sous le nom : under the name

Une chambre avec vue : room with a view

A partir de quelle heure ? : from what time ?

Prendre possession de la chambre : check in

Libérer la chambre : check out

Code Wifi : Wifi code

Ne marche pas : doesn't work

La douche : the shower

Trop chaud/ froid : too hot/cold

L'ascenseur: the elevator

Premier étage: second floor (US)

Annuler une réservation : cancel a booking

Remboursé : refunded

Garer la voiture : park the car

Se lever tôt: to wake up early

Faire la grasse matinée: to sleep in

Faire la sieste: to take a nap

Ne pas déranger : do not disturb

Merci de faire ma chambre : please clean up my room

Le savon : soap

La serviette : towel

La robe de chambre : robe

La télécommande : remote control

Service de blanchisserie : cleaning service

Centre de bien être : wellness center

Supplement : extra charge

Service voiturier : valet service

L'auberge de jeunesse : youth hostel

Appartement de location : private renting appartment

Camping : guess ?

Surviving French airports

Not an easy task, friends... Now that we have already gotten to know the word "grève", let's carry on with more fun! This section will help you in finding your way through check in, security, duty free and boarding hassle. Information at both Paris' airports is written in English, but you might come across some folks not speaking English, or simply not in the mood. Keep your cool attitude, smile, and surprise them by your awesome French vocabulary. C'est parti!

L'aéroport: the airport

Prendre l'avion: taking the plane

Rater l'avion: to miss the plane

Le retard: the delay

Le comptoir d'enregistrement: the check-in desk

Un aller simple/retour : one-way ticket/ a round trip

Combien coûte: how much

Par personne: per person

La porte d'embarquement: the boarding gate

La compagnie aérienne : the airline company

Les départs : the departures

Les arrivées : the arrivals

Les horaires : time schedule

Les baggages/ valises : luggage/ suitcases

Assistance personnelle : personal assistance

À votre disposition : at your disposal

Annulé : cancelled

Échanger : exchange

La douane : customs

Nationalité : nationality

Tamponner : to stamp

Postuler pour un visa : apply for a visa

Formulaire de déclaration : declaration form

Les renseignements : information

Le parking dépose-minute : drop-off point

Le parking souterrain : underground parking

La sortie : exit

L’entrée : entrance

La grève : the strike

Objets trouvés : lost property

Perdre ses baggages : to lose your luggage

Le contrôle des passeports : passports control

atterrir : to land

décoller : to take off

La ceinture de sécurité : the seat belt

L’altitude : the altitude

Les turbulences : turbulence

L’équipage : the crew

La sortie de secours : the emergency exit

La cabine : the cabin

Le plateau : the tray

Le siège : the seat

Le couloir : the aisle

Le hublot : the window

L’hôtesse de l’air : the air hostess

Le steward : the steward

La soute : the hold

La correspondance: the connection

Chapter 8 - Ordering In a Restaurant

One of the most important things to learn, especially when travelling is how to order in a restaurant. So, this section is dedicated to discussing how to order in French. This can come really handy when you visit smaller towns and places which may not normally cater to an international audience. Therefore, they may not have menus in English or servers who can help you in English.

So, let's start off with the three meals of the day

- petit déjeuner (breakfast) /puh-tee day-zhoo-nay/
- déjeuner (lunch) /day-zhoo-nay/
- diner (dinner) /dee-nay/

These are the basics of meals. Most French restaurants will have any number of these items on their menus, so it is always best to check out what they have in store for you.

Now, let's look at some expressions which can be used to order and ask about menu items.

- Je voudrais ______. (I would like ______), for example:

- Je voudrais du vin. (I would like some wine)

- Je voudrais une pizza, s'il vous plaît. (I would like a pizza, please)

- Je voudrais des fruits. (I would like some fruit)

- Servez-vous ______. (Do you serve ______?) for example:

- Servez-vous de la bière? (Do you serve beer?)

- Servez-vous des fruits de mer frais? (Do you serve fresh seafood?)

- Servez-vous des plats végétariens? (Do you serve vegetarian dishes?)

- Quelle sorte ______. (What kind of ______?)

- Quelle sorte de boissons servez-vous? (What sort of drinks do you serve?)

- Quelle sorte de viande servez-vous? (What sort of meat do you serve?)

- Quelle sorte de desserts avez-vous? (What sort of desserts do you have?)

• Quelle sorte de possoins servez-vous? (What kind of fish do you serve?)

• Quel est le plat du jour? (What is the dish of the day?)

Please keep in mind that the expression for “please” is “s’il vous plaît”, which roughly equates to “if you please.” Also, to say “thank you,” the standard “merci” will never go wrong. You can also use the expression “merci beaucoup” (thank you very much) or the more formal “je vous remercie” which means “thank you” but is roughly equivalent to “I thank you.”

Here are some other helpful expressions which you can use to talk about food and restaurants.

• J’ai faim. (I am hungry)

• Je veux manger. (I want to eat)

- Je veux manger de la pizza. (I want to eat pizza)

- Je veux manger une soupe. (I want to eat a soup)

- Je veux manger une salade. (I want to eat a salad)

Please note that regardless of the type of food, you would say “eat” whenever you are talking about meals. In this case, you might be thinking that “eating” a soup sounds weird. So, it is worth taking these nuances into account.

Now, let’s take a look at foods that you can have either at a restaurant or at home.

English	French
breakfast	le petit déjeuner
bacon	bacon
cereal	céréale
coffee	café
eggs	des œufs
fruit	fruit
milk	lait
oatmeal	gruau
orange juice	jus d'orange
pancakes	crêpes
tea	thé
toast	pain grillé
waffles	gaufres

After looking at these breakfast foods, let's take a look at the foods which are typically eaten for lunch or dinner.

English	French
lunch	le déjeuner
dinner	dîner
appetizer	apéritif
baked	cuit

beef	boeuf
beer	bière
bread	pain
chicken	poulet
dessert	dessert
fish	poisson
fried	frit
grilled	grillé
main course	plat principal
pasta	pâtes
pork	porc
rice	riz
salad	salade
soda	soda
soup	soupe
vegan	végétalien
vegetables	des légumes
vegetarian	végétarien
water	eau
wine	vin

Now, let's talk about some other foods which can be found in menus or prepared at home.

English	**French**
baked potato	pomme de terre au four
barbecue	barbecue
cheese	fromage
chocolate	chocolat
fat-free	sans gras
french fries	frites
fresh	frais
fried chicken	poulet frit
frozen	congelé
fruit juice	jus de fruit
gluten	gluten
grilled salmon	saumon grillé
light	allégée
non-alcoholic	non alcoolique
pepper	poivre
pork chop	côtelette de porc
raw	cru
roast beef	rôti de bœuf
salt	sel
sandwich	sandwich
skinless chicken	poulet sans peau
sparkling mineral water	eau minérale gazeuse

steamed vegetables	légumes à la vapeur
strawberry	fraise
sugar	sucre
vanilla	vanille

Let's move on and have a look at fruits and vegetables.

English	**French**
fruits	fruits
apple	pomme
avocado	avocat
banana	banane
blueberry	myrtille
cherry	cerise
coconut	noix de coco
cranberry	canneberge
grapes	les raisins
lemon	citron
mango	mangue
orange	orange
papaya	papaye
peach	pêche
pear	poire

pineapple	ananas
plum	prune
strawberry	fraise
watermelon	pastèque

Please note that the pronunciation of “fruit” in English is /froot/ whereas the French pronunciation would be /froo-ee/. As such, it is common to find words which have identical spelling, or very similar, yet have very distinct pronunciation.

Let’s look at vegetables now.

English	**French**
Vegetables	Des légumes
Asparagus	Asperges
Broccoli	brocoli
Brussels sprouts	choux de Bruxelles
Cabbage	Chou
Carrot	Carotte
Celery	Céleri
Corn	Blé
Cucumber	Concombre
Eggplant	Aubergine
Lettuce	Salade
Onion	Oignon

Peas	Pois
Potato	Patate
Pumpkin	Citrouille
radish	radis
Red pepper	poivron rouge
Spinach	épinard
Tomato	Tomate

With this healthy list, you'll be able to navigate your way through restaurants, grocery stores, and practically any conversation related to food. Now, let's take a closer look at more expressions which you can use when talking about food and ordering in restaurants. So, let's talk about desserts.

English	**French**
brownie	lutin
cake	gâteau
cheesecake	cheesecake
chocolate	chocolat
cookies	biscuits
crepes	crêpes
doughnuts	donuts
fruit cocktail	cocktail de fruits
ice cream	crème glacée

pie	tarte
pudding	pudding
tiramisu	tiramisu

With this vocabulary, you can now order from the most delicious part of the menu. In addition, you will be able to order in bakeries and cake shops.

Let's move on now to more expressions about ordering in restaurants.

When it comes time to pay, you can say:

- Puis-je avoir la note s'il vous plait? (Can I have the bill, please?)
- Puis-je payer en espèces? (Can I pay in cash?)
- Puis-je payer avec ma carte de crédit? (Can I pay with my credit card?)
- Acceptez-vous des dollars? (Do you accept dollars?)

Also, here are some other phrases which will certainly come in handy.

- Puis-je prendre cela pour aller? (Can I take this to go?)
- Serveur! (waiter!)
- S'il vous plaît donner le meilleur au chef. (Please give my best to the chef)
- Tout va bien. (Everything is fine).

At this point, let's run through a practice dialogue.

Serveur: Bonjour, êtes-vous prêt à commander? (are you ready to order?)

Client: Excusez-moi, quelles sont vos spécialités? (Excuse me, what are your specials?)

Serveur: Nous avons du saumon grillé avec des légumes et du canard rôti à la sauce à l'orange. (We have grilled salmon with vegetables and roast duck in an orange sauce)

Client: Je voudrais le canard rôti, s'il vous plaît.

Serveur: Et pour boire? (And to drink?)

Client: Puis-je voir votre carte des vins?

Serveur: Voilà

Client: Merci, Je voudrais une bouteille de votre meilleur vin rouge. (Thank you, I would like a bottle of your best red wine)

Serveur: Bien sûr. Rien d'autre? (Of course. Anything else?)

Client: Non, ce sera tout, merci. (No, that will be all, thank you)

A few moments later...

Serveur: Voulez-vous commander un dessert?

Client: Oui, puis-je voir votre menu de desserts, s'il vous plaît? (Yes, may I see your dessert menu, please?)

Serveur: Voilà

Client: Merci, je voudrais le tarte aux pommes. (I would like apple pie)

Serveur: Excellent choix.

And now... to get the bill....

Client: Serveur! (waiter!)

Serveur: Oui monsieur / madame? (Yes, sir / ma'am)

Client: Puis-je avoir la note s'il vous plait? (Can I have the bill, please?)

Serveur: Voilà

Client: Puis-je payer avec ma carte de crédit? (Can I pay with my credit card?)

Serveur: Bien sûr. (Of course)

Client: Voilà... merci.

At this point, you are ready to navigate the world of restaurants in French-speaking countries. So, do take the time to go over any words or expressions which you happen to find particularly useful and important. Please remember that the more you practice, the better you will become.

Home

In this section, we are going to be talking about words and phrases which you can use to talk about your home. So, let's look into how you can discuss this topic, both when dealing with people you meet when traveling, or with other learners of French, you interact with.

The first word to consider in this section is "la maison" (the house). Now, it should be noted that French does not make any distinction between "house" and "home." The term which is used in either case is the same "maison." As such, don't be surprised to see that French speakers use this term when talking about their home and their family.

Another very important expression to learn is "chez moi" (at my place). This expression is used to make reference to your home either in terms of having others visit it, or simply referencing it, or anything related to it.

Here are some useful expressions:

- Ma maison est très grande. (My house is very big)
- Ma maison est mon endroit préféré. (My home is my favorite place)
- J'ai un chien chez moi. (I have a dog at my place)
- Rendez-vous chez moi. (Let's meet at my house)

Let's take a look at some vocabulary related to house and home.

English	**French**
at my place, at my home, at my house	chez moi
build	construire
buy a house	acheter une maison
decorate	décorer
House / home	maison
mortgage	hypothèque
paint	peindre
real estate agent	agent immobilier
remodel	remodeler
renovate	rénover
search for a house	rechercher une maison
sell a house	vendre une maison

Also, please note that "maison" is feminine. So, the proper possessive adjective is "ma," article is "la," and the indefinite would be "une." For example:

- La maison est très chère. (The house is very expensive)
- La maison est dans un bon quartier. (The house is in a good neighborhood)
- Cette maison a trois chambres. (This house has three bedrooms)
- Je veux une maison avec une grande cuisine. (I want a house with a big kitchen)
- Je cherche une maison dans un quartier familial. (I'm looking for a house in a family neighborhood)

As you can see, the use of “la” and “une” highlight the feminine nature of “maison.” Getting used to the masculine and feminine of nouns is just a matter of practice and experience with the language.

Let’s take a look now at the part of the house.

English	**French**
attic	le grenier
backyard	l’arrière-cour
basement	le sous-sol
bathroom	la salle de bains
bedroom	la chambre à coucher
dining room	la salle à manger
driveway	l’allée
garage	le garage
garden	le jardin
hallway	le couloir
Home decorator	le décorateur
housekeeper	une domestique
Inside	À l'intérieur
Interior designer	le décorateur d'intérieur
kitchen	la cuisine
living room / den	le salon
office / study	le bureau / l’étude
playroom	la salle de jeux
room	la pièce
stairs	l’escaliers

With this vocabulary, you can talk about your home or homes that you are interested in looking at. Here are some questions you can ask when taking a look at a home.

• Combien de chambre y a-t-il? (How many bedrooms does it have?)

• Combien de salles de bains a-t-il? (How many bathrooms does it have?)

• Combien coûte le loyer? (How much is the rent?)

• At-il un garage? (Does it have a garage?)

• Quand est-il disponible? (When is it available?)

• La cuisine est-elle neuve? (Is the kitchen new?)

These are some very useful questions you can ask when you are looking at a potential rental property. If you are looking to purchase a property, you can use phrases such as:

• Est-ce une maison ou un appartement? (it is a house or an apartment?)

• Quel est le prix demandé? (What is the asking price?)

• Quel est le prix du marché? (What is the market price?)

• Quel est le taux d'intérêt? (What is the interest rate?)

• Quel est le paiement mensuel? (What is the monthly payment?)

• Qui est l'agent immobilier? (Who is the real estate agent?)

• Nous voudrions faire une offre. (We would like to make an offer)

• Nous acceptons leur contre-offre. (We accept their counteroffer)

With these questions and phrases, you are now ready to make a good deal on the property of your choice.

Now, to further expand your vocabulary, let's take a look at other words used to describe the house, furniture, appliances, and other features of a home or apartment.

English	**French**
an alarm clock	un réveil
an individual furniture item	un meuble
a bathroom sink	un lavabo
a bed	le lit
bed linen	le linge de lit
a bookshelf	un étagère à livres
a cabinet	un cabinet
a carpet	un tapis
a ceiling	le plafond
a chair	la chaise
a clock	l'horloge
a closet	le placard
a computer	un ordinateur
a couch	un canapé
a curtain	le rideau
designer furniture	le mobilier design
a desk	un bureau
a door	la porte
a dresser	une commode
a floor	le sol
a furniture	des meubles
a kitchen sink	un évier de cuisine

a lamp	la lampe
a laptop computer	un ordinateur portable
a microwave	un four micro onde
a mirror	le miroir
an oven	le four
a painting	la peinture
a picture	l'image
a pillow	un oreiller
a poster	une affiche
a printer	une imprimante
a radio	la radio
a refrigerator	le réfrigérateur
a rug	le couverture
a shower	la douche
a stereo system	le système stéréo
a stove	le poêle
a table	la table
a telephone	le téléphone
a television	la télévision
a toilet	une toilette
a wall	le mur
a window	la fenêtre

Let's have a look at some examples of how you can use these expressions in regular conversation.

- Il a une sofa plus grande dans la maison. (He has a very large sofa in the house)
- Ella a un beau horloge sur le mur. (She has nice clock up on the wall)
- Le poêle dans la cuisine est neuf. (The stove in the kitchen is new)
- Nous avons une belle table avec six chaises autour. (We have a beautiful table with six chairs around it)
- Les meubles de la maison sont antiques. (The furniture in the home is antique)
- La maison a besoin d'une nouvelle peinture. (The house needs some new paint)
- Le tapis a été récemment installé. (The carpet has been recently installed)
- La salle de bain est moderne. (The bathroom is modern)
- Il a un grand placard dans la chambre principale. (He has a big closet in the master bedroom)
- Le miroir est très joli. (The mirror looks very nice)

As you can see, these phrases can be used in virtually any situation that you find yourself talking about houses and apartments. Of course, you can play around with this vocabulary to suit your particular needs and address what you are looking to communicate.

Lastly, here are some addition words which you can use to talk about homes.

English	**French**
a balcony	un balcon
a bench	un banc

a fence	une clôture
a flower bed	un lit de fleurs
a flower garden	un jardin de fleurs
a fountain	une fontaine
a guest house	une maison d'hôtes
a guest room	une chambre d'amis
a patio	un patio
a swimming pool	une piscine
a vegetable garden	un potager
an awning	un auvent
an outdoor barbecue	un barbecue en plein air
outside	à l'extérieur

So, do take the time to go over this vocabulary. That way, you can make the most of your interactions with other French speakers. Best of all, we have taken the guess work out of this topic. With these lessons, learning French doesn't have to be overly complex or difficult.

Chapter 9 - Eating, drinking, and visiting

Now that you have safely landed in France or any other French-speaking country, and hopefully on time, you now deserve to move on to the real thing: enjoy yourself without too much trouble. French culture has so much to offer, it would be a shame not to enjoy it, and that in French. So get ready to learn everything an English speaking tourist needs to know in order to have a great time!

In a restaurant:

Nothing better than going to a French restaurant in France. It even feels better if you are able to order your meal, understand what that strange looking plate is made of, make your compliments to the chef, get some more wine, and even ask for the bill. Who knows, you might be able to get to know some people, and exchange about culture, food, and language! Bon apétit !

Réserver une table : to book a table

Pour ce soir : for tonight

Pour 2 personnes : for two

Au nom de : in the name of

Une table en terrasse : a table on the terrace

A l'intérieur : inside

Le menu/la carte : the menu

La carte des desserts/ des boissons : the dessert/ drinks menu

Les toilettes : toilets

Que recommandez-vous ?: What do you recommend ?

Le plat du jour : dish of the day

Commander : to order

Être prêt: to be ready

Végétarien/végétalien: vegetarian/vegan

Nous allons prendre: We are going to have

Le vin rouge/blanc de la maison : the house red/white wine

Un verre : a glass

Une bouteille : a bottle

La même chose : the same thing

De l'eau du robinet / en carafe : tap water

L'eau gazeuse: sparking water

L'eau plate : plain water

Délicieux : delicious

Formidable : amazing

Miam miam : yummy

Aigre-doux: sweet and sour

Epicé : spicy

Mes compliments au chef : my compliments to the chef

Sel/poivre : salt/pepper

Une serviette : a napkin

Un couteau : a knife

Une fourchette : a fork

Une cuillère : a spoon

Une paille : a straw

Une tasse : a cup

Une petite/grande assiette : a small/large plate

Un plateau : a tray

Du pain : some bread

Le plat : dish

La viande : meat

Le poulet : chicken

Le bœuf : beef

Le veau : veal

Le canard : duck

Le porc : pork

L'agneau : lamb

La saucisse : saussage

Le poisson : fish

Fruits de mer : seafood

Du riz : some rice

Des pâtes : some pasta

Des frites : french fries

Des légumes : vegetable

La pomme de terre : potato

La tomate : tomato

La salade : salad

Le menu/plat enfant : kids menu/dish

Entrée : starter

Plat de résistance : main dish

Dessert : dessert

La glace : ice cream

Le gateau : cake

Digestif : digestive (strong) alcohol after a meal

L'addition: the bill

Payer en liquide: pay cash

Payer avec la carte : pay with a credit card

Quelle cuisson pour votre viande? : How would you like your meat to be cooked?

Bleu: very rare

Saignant: rare

À point: medium

Bien cuit: well done

Le service est inclus : service is included

Serveur/serveuse : waiter/waitress

Un pourboire : a tip

Offert: free of charge

Froid : cold

Brûlé : burned

Je ne veux pas payer : I don't want to pay

Je veux parler patron : I want to speak to the boss

Acting like a pro in a bar or café

Bars and cafés are probably the best places to practice your language skills. This is where the atmosphere is laid back, good music is playing (sometimes), and holding a drink in your hand may very well be a secret weapon for some people (it certainly is for me) to push back their linguistic barriers. So go on, share some relaxed conversation, practice your small talk, pay a round, and don't forget the main goal: have fun! Santé! (cheers!)

Practical hint: service in French bars and restaurants are always included unless specified so. Do leave a tip if you find the service to be of higher quality or if you want to impress that sexy waitress.

Prendre/boire un verre : have a drink

Boire un coup : have a drink, less formal

L'apéro: aperitif, a truly magical word in French

Quu'est-ce que vous prenez ?: What will you have ?

Un verre de... : a glass of...

Une bière pression : a draft beer

Un panaché : a shandy (mix of beer and lemonade)

Une bouteille de... : a bottle of...

Trinquer : to drink to

Santé/ à la tienne/ à la vôtre/tchin-tchin : cheers !

Une/ma tournée : a/my round

Un/e autre : another

La même chose : the same

Etre gai/e, pompette: to be tipsy

Être saoul/e, ivre: to be drunk

Être bourré : to be wasted

Avoir la gueule de bois : to have a hangover

Un pourboire : a tip

La bière : beer

Le vin : wine

Un demi : 25cl beer

Un demi de vin rouge/blanc : 50cl of red/white wine

Une girafe : a huge beer container with a tap at the bottom. Useful for a group.

Le café noir/au lait : a coffee black/ with milk

Le chocolat chaud : a hot chocolate

Le lait : milk

Un jus d'orange/de pomme : orange/apple juice

Un soda : a soda

Un coca light : diet coke

Une lemonade : lemonade

Le garçon : the bar waiter

La serveuse : the bar waitress

Activities

Now that you have arrived well, rested your bones in a nice bed, had some tasty food in your belly, you are now ready to get down to business. France being the most visited country in the world, you will have enough to do. But how are you going to express your needs? Just read the following--you will find the most useful words for your touristic activities.

Touriste : tourist

Bruyant : noisy*

Faire le touriste : beeing all touristy

Guide touristique : guidebook/ tour guide

Visiter : to tour

Découvir: to discover

Louer : to rent

Acheter : to buy

Caution : deposit

Assurance : insurance

Recommandé : recommend

L'église : church

Le château : castle

La grotte : cave

Les ruines : ruins

La forêt : forest

Le chemin de randonné : hicking trail

La piste cyclable : bike way

La rivière : river

La plage : beach

La montagne : mountain

La ville : city

Le musée : museum

La campagne : country side

Le parc d'attraction : theme park

Le parc nautique : water park

La piscine couverte/découverte : indoor/outdoor swimming pool

La discotèque/la boite : disco/club

Aller à un concert : to go to a concert

Itinéraire : itinerary

Planifier : to plan

Flâner: to stroll

Ne rien faire/ glander: to do nothing/ familiar

Prendre une photo/un selfie : take a picture/a selfie

Se baigner : to go for a swim

Se promener: to walk around

Faire une marche/une promenade: to hike

Courir: to run

Faire du jogging: to jog

Faire du vélo: to bike

Jouer: to play

Money!

Money is of course a central subject when it comes to traveling. You will need to have some knowledge about it to get through lots of situations. How do you find a bank, an exchange office, or tell someone that this wonderful painting is way too expensive? Let's look at some important sentences you will need.

L'argent: money

Combient ça coûte? : How much does it cost?

Cher/ ce n'est pas donné : expensive

Pas cher/ bon marché : cheap

Carte bancaire : credit card

Payer : pay

Payer en espèce/liquide : to pay cash

Payer par chèque: pay by check

Un billet de... : a ...note

Une pièce de... : a... coin

La monnaie : change

Chèque de voyage : traveler's cheque

Le distributeur (automatique de billet) : ATM

Code : PIN code

La banque : bank

Le bureau de change : foreign exchange office

Changer de l'argent : to change money

Le taux de change : the exchange rate

Retirer : to withdraw

Déposer : to make a deposit

Virer/ faire un virement: to transfer money

Dépenser : to spend

Economiser : to save money

Être à découvert: to be overdrawn

Emprunter : to borrow

Prêter : to lend

Clothes shopping!

Would you know your way around a clothes shop in France? Well let me tell you that even though I speak perfect French, I still encounter lots of challenges when going to such god-forsaken places. Guys, you can skip this section if you want to (and practice ordering a “bière pression, while she’s getting the credit card). Girls, rejoice!

Essayer: to try/ to try on

Pantalon : pants

La cabine d’essayage : the changing room

La taille : size

Trop grand(e)/petit(e) : too big/ too small

Autre couleur : other color

Une réduction : a discount

A quelle heure fermez-vous le magasin ce soir : At what time do you close the shop tonight?

Les heures d’ouverture/ de fermeture : opening/closing times

En solde : on sale

Échanger : exchange

Se faire rembourser : to be reimbursed

Un avoir : a credit note

Le bon d’achat : a voucher

Le ticket de caisse : receipt

Le miroir : mirror

Rendre : to return

Aller : to fit

Cette jupe vous va bien : This skirt fits you well.

Les chaussures : shoes

Les baskets : sneakers

Les chaussettes : socks

Le pantalon : pants

La jupe : skirt

La robe : dress

Le T-shirt : practice your accent !

Le débardeur : longshoreman

Le pull : sweater

La veste : jacket

Le manteau : coat

L'imperméable : raincoat

Le chapeau : hat

La casquette : baseball cap

La culotte : panties

Soutien-gorge : bras

Sous-vêtements : underwear

Maillot de bain : bathing suit

Les lunettes : glasses

Chapter 10 - Health and Fitness

Exercising on a regular basis can significantly improve your health and reduce your risk of having chronic diseases, such as type 2 diabetes, cancers, and heart diseases. It can also improve your mental state, boost your mood levels, and improve your sleep pattern.

Likewise, eating healthy and living a healthy lifestyle can improve the quality of your life. You can manage your weight better, lower your blood pressure and blood cholesterol, and have a better overall health.

French - English

Pourquoi il est important d'être en bonne santé

- Why it is important to be healthy

Être en bonne santé est un investissement à long terme

- Being healthy is a long-term investment

Il réduit le risque de certaines maladies

- It reduces the risk of certain diseases

Avoir une bonne santé améliore l'humeur et renforce la confiance en soi

- Having a good health improves the mood and boosts self confidence

Cela augmente la longévité

- It increases longevity

Réduit le risque de décès prématuré chez les individus

- It reduce likelihood of premature death among individuals

Il augmente le niveau d'énergie et renforce le système immunitaire

- It increases energy level and strengthen the immunity system

Il y a beaucoup de façons simples et différentes d'être en bonne santé

- There are many different and simple ways to be healthy

Écoutez votre corps

- Listen to your body

Dormez suffisamment

- Get enough sleep

Visitez le médecin pour un contrôle de temps en temps

- Visit the doctor for check-up once in a while

Évitez les environnements et les activités pouvant engendrer du stress

- Avoid environments and activities that may lead to stress

Penser sainement

- Think healthy thoughts

Manger équilibré

- Eat a balanced diet

Prendre des vitamins

- Take vitamins

Obtenez assez de calcium et de vitamine D

- Get enough Calcium and Vitamin D

Ne comptez pas sur les supplements

- Do not depend on supplements

Boire beaucoup d'eau

- Drink plenty of water

Ne pas fumer

- Do not smoke

Ne sautez pas de repas

- Don't skip meals

Évitez les aliments avec trop de sucre et de caffeine

- Avoid foods with too much sugar and caffeine

Surveillez votre fréquence cardiaque

- Monitor your heart rate

Toujours se laver les mains

- Always wash your hands

Pratique une bonne hygiene

- Practice good hygiene

Pratique une bonne hygiene

- Take a bath everyday

Faire une pause de temps en temps

- Take a break from time to time

Faites de l'exercice régulièrement et faites de l'activité physique

- Exercise regularly and be physically active

Buvez de l'alcool avec moderation

- Drink alcohol in moderation

Couper les aliments gras et sales

- Cut down oily and salty foods

Surveillez votre poids

- Monitor your weight

Construire une relation forte avec la famille et les pairs

- Build a strong relationship with family and peers

Trouvez des recettes plus saines et préparez votre propre nourriture

- Find healthier recipes and make your own food

Je voudrais renseigner un cours de fitness

- I would like to inquire for a fitness class

Y a-t-il encore des créneaux disponibles?

- Are there still slots available?

Avez-vous un entraîneur de fitness?

- Do you have a fitness trainer?

Combien coûte l'adhésion au club?

- How much does gym membership cost?

Pouvez-vous me parler des forfaits que vous proposez?

- Could you tell me about the packages that you offer?

Cela semble un peu cher.

- It sounds kind of expensive.

Quel genre d'installations avez-vous?

- What kind of facilities do you have?

Votre équipement est-il neuf?

– Is your equipment new?

Nous aimerions avoir une visite du gymnase.

- We would like to have a tour of the gym.

Pouvez-vous me montrer comment utiliser le matériel?

- Can you show me how to use the equipment?

J'aimerais perdre du poids.

- I would like to lose weight.

J'aimerais renforcer mes muscles

- I would like to strengthen my muscles

J'aimerais améliorer mon endurance

- I would like to improve my stamina

Je veux grosser

- I want to get fat

Pensez-vous que vous avez besoin de grossir?

- Do you think you need to get fat?

Êtes-vous également ouvert le weekend?

- Are you also open on weekends?

Tous vos instructeurs de fitness sont-ils certifiés?

- Are all your fitness instructors certified?

Génial! Je suis impatient de commencer.

- Great! I can't wait to get started.

Où puis-je acheter des vêtements de fitness?

- Where can I buy fitness clothes?

Où avez-vous acheté vos écouteurs?

- Where did you buy your earphones?

Jogging en place pendant une minute

- Jog in place for one minute

Respirez, expirez

- Breathe in, breathe out

Je te verrai en cours d’aérobic.

- I’ll see you in Aerobics class.

À quelle fréquence dois-je faire du yoga?

- How often should I do Yoga?

Ai-je besoin d'un certificat médical pour ces cours?

- Do I need medical certificate for these courses?

Que devrais-je manger pendant l'entraînement?

- What should I eat during training?

Dois-je prendre des suppléments?

- Should I take supplements?

Prendre des suppléments, c'est vous qui décidez

- Taking supplements is up to you

Que proposez-vous?

- What do you suggest?

Je suggère de prendre des suppléments de protéines pour les clients qui développent leurs muscles

- I suggest taking protein supplements for clients who are building their muscles

Combien de calories devrais-je manger par jour?

- How many calories should I eat per day?

Je veux être en forme.

- I want to get in shape.

Salut! Comment allez vous?

- Hi! How are you doing?

Mes muscles me font déjà mal!

- My muscles are already hurting!

J'ai soif

- I'm thirsty

Vous devriez rester hydrate

- You should stay hydrated

Restez concenter

- Just stay focused

Tu peux le faire!

- You can do it!

Le programme vous sera très utile

- The program will benefit you a lot

Vous devriez maintenir votre régime

- You should maintain your diet

Est-ce votre première fois d'aller à un gymnase?

- Is this your first time to go to a gym?

Depuis combien de temps travaillez-vous?

- How long have you been working out?

À quelle fréquence vas-tu au gymnase?

- How often do you go to the gym?

Quels types d'exercices connaissez-vous?

- What types of exercise do you know?

Soulevez-vous des poids?

- Have you been lifting weights?

Tu as de grands muscles

- You have great muscles

J'ai commencé à soulever des poids il y a deux mois

- I started lifting weight two months ago

Où travaillez-vous?

- Where do you work out?

Combien d'heures alloues-tu pour ton travail?

- How many hours do you allot for your work out?

Je passe habituellement deux à trois heures par jour

- I usually spend two to three hours a day

Je fais du jogging tous les jours

- I jog every day

Je n'utilise le tapis roulant que lorsqu'il pleut

- I only use the treadmill when it rains

Vous devriez porter des chaussures confortables

- You should wear comfortable shoes

Comment aimez-vous nos installations, monsieur?

- How do you like our facilities, sir?

J'aime que la salle de sport soit grande et bien ventilée

- I like it that the gym is large and well-ventilated

Avez-vous un programme spécial pour les clients ayant des antécédents médicaux?

- Do you have a special program for clients with past medical records?

Avez-vous un dossier médical dans le passé?

- Do you have a medical record in the past?

Existe-t-il un type spécifique de programme de conditionnement physique pour une cinquantaine d'années?

- Is there a specific type of fitness program for a fifty year old?

Nous avons des formateurs spéciaux en particulier pour les aînés et les personnes ayant des problèmes de santé

- We have special trainers particularly for elders and people with health conditions

Dois-je suivre un régime strict?

- Do I need to follow a strict diet?

Une fois que vous serez inscrit ici, vous recevrez un programme d'entraînement complet et un programme alimentaire.

- You will be given with a complete workout and dietary program once you have been enrolled here

Combien de formateurs avez-vous?

- How many trainers do you have?

Nous vous fournirons votre entraîneur personnel

- We will provide you with your personal trainer

En plus des formateurs, nous avons également des aides pour vous aider à soulever des poids

- Aside from trainers we also have helpers to assist you in weight lifting

L'haltérophilie est-elle effrayante?

- Is weight lifting frightening?

Ne vous inquiétez pas, nos formateurs veilleront à votre sécurité.

- Don’t worry, our trainers will ensure your safety

Ils enseigneront toute la manipulation appropriée de l’équipement

- They will teach all the proper handling of equipment

Vous devez avoir une bonne alimentation pour avoir le plein d'énergie tout en travaillant

- You must eat a proper diet to have full enery while working out

À quelle fréquence tombez-vous malade chaque année?

- How often do you get sick in a year?

Mangez-vous toujours des aliments malsains?

- Do you always eat unhealthy foods?

Qu'est-ce qu'une nourriture saine pour vous?

- What is healthy food for you?

À quelle fréquence consultez-vous votre médecin pour un examen médical?

- How often do you visit your doctor for medical examination?

Combien de fois travaillez-vous?

- How often do you work out?

Pensez-vous que vous êtes en bonne santé?

- Do you think you are healthy?

Combien de repos ai-je besoin entre les sessions?

- How much rest do I need between sessions?

Puis-je faire de l'exercice même quand je suis stressé?

- Can I exercise anyway, even when I'm stressed?

Quel est le meilleur moyen de perdre de la graisse?

- What is the best way to lose fat?

Comment aplatir mon ventre?

- How do I flatten stomach?

Quels types d'exercices devrais-je effectuer?

- What types of exercises should I perform?

Puis-je toujours manger mes aliments préférésmême lorsque je suis en entraînement?

- Can I still eat my favorite foods even when I am on a workout?

Combien d'exercice dois-je avoir pour rester en forme?

- How much exercise do I need to stay fit?

Combien de calories est-ce que je brûle quand je cours pendant un mile?

- How many calories do I burn when I jog for one mile?

Quels sont les meilleurs exercices à faire chaque jour?

- What are the best exercises to do every day?

Quels sont les exercices simples pour ceux qui travaillent à la maison?

- What are some simple exercises for those who work at home?

Commencez par un échauffement de dix minutes

- Start with a ten- minute warm up

Comment commencer l'exercice cardio

- How to start cardio exercise

Quels sont les avantages de l'exercice cardio?

- What are the benefits of cardio exercise?

Les exercices cardio-vasculaires maintiennent les poumons et le cœ-ur en bonne santé

- Cardio exercise keeps the lungs and heart srong

Cela donne plûs d'énergie à la personne

- It gives the person more energy

Il vous aide à brûler des calories

- It helps you burn calories

Il vous aide à prévenir le cancer et le diabète

- It helps you to prevent cancer and diabetes

Il réduit le stress et l'anxiété

- It reduces stress and anxiety

Choisissez une activité simple qui vous convient

- Choose a simple activity that works for you

Marcher, danser, nager

- Walking, dancing, swimming

Course, aérobic, escalade

- Running, aerobics, climbing

Reposez-vous entre vos entraînements

- Take a rest between workouts

Ne vous poussez pas trop fort

- Do not push yourself too hard

Concentrez-vous sur votre objectif

- Focus on your goal

Augmentez votre temps d'exercice quotidian

- Increase your daily exercise time

Vous pouvez changer le type de votre activité

- You can change the type of your activity

Relevez le défi

- Challenge yourself

Après les exercices, faire des étirements

- After work out, do some stretchings

Motivez-vous

- Motivate yourself

Faites un horaire de votre travail

- Make a schedule of your work out

Faire du yoga

- Do some yoga

Où est mon tapis de yoga?

- Where is my yoga mat?

J'utilise des kettlebells

– I am using kettlebells

C'était une routine d'entraînement intense

– That was an intense workout routine

Chapter 11 - Phrases I

Relations - Relationships

-Famille = Family

Ma famille est étroite.

My family is tight.

-Oncle = Uncle

Mon oncle est gentil.

My uncle is nice.

-Tante = Aunt

Ma tante est une vieille dame.

My aunt is an old lady.

-Cousin = Cousin

Le nom de mon cousin est Peter.

My cousin's name is Peter.

-Mère = Mother

Ma mère est morte

My mother is dead.

-Père = Father

Mon père habite ici.

My father lives here.

-Maman = Mum

Ma maman aime la mer.

My mum loves the sea.

-Père = Dad

Mon père aime les chiens.

My dad loves dogs.

-Grand-père = Grandfather

Mon grand-père aime les chats.

My grandfather loves cats.

-Grand-mère = Grandmother

Ma grand-mère aime cuisiner.

My grandmother loves cooking.

-Grands-parents = Grandparents

Mes grands-parents arriveront demain.

My grandparents will arrive tomorrow.

-Belle-sœur = Sister-in-law

Ma belle-sœur est américaine.

My sister-in-law is American.

-Beau- frère = Brother-in-law

Mon beau-frère a les cheveux roux.

My brother-in-law has red hair.

-Belle-fille = Daughter-in-law

Ma belle-fille cuisine très bien.

My daughter-in-law cooks very well.

-Beau-fils = Son-in-law

Son beau-fils est très intelligent.

His son-in-law is a very smart person.

-Beau-père = Father-in-law

Hier, je suis allé rendre visite à mon beau-père. Il m'a fait des pâtes.

Yesterday I went to visit my father-in-law. He cooked me pasta.

-Belle-mère = Mother-in-law

Ma belle-mère aime faire du shopping.

My mother-in-law loves shopping.

-Fils = Son

Le fils de Mario étudie en Angleterre et il parle très bien anglais.

Mario's son studies in England and he speaks English very well.

-Fille = Daughter

Ma fille est une écrivaine très connue.

My daughter is a very well-known writer.

-Seul enfant = Only child

Mario est le seul enfant car ses parents étaient trop vieux pour avoir d'autres enfants.

Mario is an only child because his parents were too old to have other children.

-Nièce = Niece

Ma nièce adore nager.

My niece loves swimming.

-Neveu = Nephew

Le nom de mon neveu est Carlo.

My nephew's name is Carlo.

-Petite-fille ou petit-fils = Granddaughter or Grandson

J'aime mon petit-fils et ma petite-fille; Je joue souvent avec eux.

I love my grandson and my granddaughter; I often play with them.

-Soeur = Sister

Ma sœur est intelligente.

My sister is smart.

-Frère = Brother

Mon frère est jaloux.

My brother is jealous.

-Proches = Relatives

Mes proches arriveront demain.

My relatives will arrive tomorrow.

-Amitié = Friendship

L'amitié est une chose magnifique.

Friendship is a magnificent thing.

-Ami = Friend

Marco est mon ami.

Marco is my friend.

-Amie = Friend

Laura est mon amie

Laura is my friend.

-Ennemi = Enemy

Dans Breaking Bad, Tuco est l'ennemi de Walter.

In Breaking Bad, Tuco is Walter's enemy.

-Rival = Rival

Mattia est le rival romantique de Marco.

Mattia is Marco’s romantic rival.

-Meilleur ami = Best friend

Luca est mon meilleur ami.

Luca is my best friend.

-Copine = Girlfriend

La copine de Matteo est Roberta

Matteo's girlfriend is Roberta.

-Copain = Boyfriend

Le copain de Roberta est Matteo.

Roberta's boyfriend is Matteo.

-Mari = Husband

Hier, Mirko est devenu le mari de Michela.

Yesterday Mirko became Michela's husband.

-Femme = Wife

Hier, Michela est devenue la femme de Mirko.

Yesterday Michela became Mirko's wife.

-Liaison = Bond

L'amitié est un lien très fort.

Friendship is a very strong bond.

-Garçon = Boy

Il a 14 ans, ce n'est qu'un garçon.

He is 14 years old, he’s just a boy.

-Fille = Girl

Elle a 12 ans; elle est une fille.

She is 12 years old; she is a girl.

-Mariage = Marriage

Notre mariage est heureux.

Our marriage is a happy one.

-Couple = Couple

Nous sommes un vrai couple.

We are a real couple.

-Divorce = Divorce

Le divorce est traumatisant pour les enfants.

Divorce is traumatic for children.

-Caliner = To hug

Je câline toujours ma fille.

I always hug my daughter.

-Aimer = To love

J'aime les fraises!

I love strawberries!

-Admirer = To admire

Mara admire votre travail.

Mara admires your work.

-Embrasser = To kiss

La maman embrasse le bébé.

The mom kisses the baby.

-Se marier = To marry

John a marié Maria.

John married Maria.

Temps - Time

-Lundi = Monday

Aujourd'hui, c'est lundi.

Today is Monday.

-Mardi = Tuesday

Demain sera être mardi.

Tomorrow will be Tuesday.

-Mercredi = Wednesday

Je pars en Hollande mercredi.

I am going to Holland on Wednesday.

-Jeudi = Thursday

Ma maman est décédée jeudi.

My mom died on Thursday.

-Vendredi = Friday

Vendredi, il fera beau.

On Friday it will be sunny.

-Samedi = Saturday

Samedi j'irai à l'école.

On Saturday I will go to school.

-Dimanche = Sunday

Le dimanche est mon jour de repos.

Sunday is my day of rest.

-Seconde = Second

Cette voiture peut passer de 0 à 100 km / h en moins de 7 secondes.

This car can go from 0 to 100 km/h in less than 7 seconds.

-Minute = Minute

Il nous restait sept minutes avant le début de l'examen.

We had seven minutes to go before the start of the exam.

-Heure = Hour

Il faut deux heures et demie pour y arriver.

It takes two and a half hours to arrive there.

-Avance = Advance

Le train est arrivé dix minutes à l'avance.

The train arrived ten minutes in advance.

-Chronomètre = Chronometer

J'utilise le chronomètre pour pratiquer mon discours.

I use the chronometer to practice my speech.

-Temps = Time

Le temps de départ reste à déterminer.

The departure time is still to be determined.

-Minuit = Midnight

Pourquoi tu ne dors pas?! C'est minuit.

Why aren't you sleeping?! It's midnight.

-Douze heures = Twelve o'clock

Il est douze heures et j'aimerais manger une pizza en ce moment.

It's twelve o'clock and I would like to eat a pizza right now.

-20 heures et quart = Quarter past eight p.m.

Hier, j'ai dîné à huit heures et quart.

Yesterday I had dinner at a quarter past eight p.m.

-Trois heures et demie de l'après-midi. = Half past three p.m.

Je suis allé chez Marco à trois heures et demie de l'après-midi.

I went to Marco's at half past three p.m.

-Cinq heures = Five o'clock

Hier, je me suis réveillé à cinq heures.

Yesterday I woke up at five o'clock.

-L'heure d'été = Daylight saving time

La plupart des pays ont l'heure d'été en été, mais avec des dates de début différentes.

Most countries have daylight saving time during summer, although with different beginning dates.

-Heure solaire = Solar time

Je n'ai jamais compris comment fonctionne l'heure solaire.

I have never understood how solar time works.

-Compte à rebours = Countdown

La foule a retenu son souffle au début du compte à rebours pour le lancement.

The crowd held their breath as the countdown to launch began.

-Heure locale = Local time

L'avion devrait atterrir à 4 h, heure locale.

The plane should land at 4 a.m. local time.

-Fuseau horaire = Time zone

Mon amie vit dans un fuseau horaire différent, je ne peux donc l'appeler que le matin.

My friend lives in a different time zone, so I can only call her in the morning.

-Janvier = January

Janvier est toujours le mois le plus froid.

January is always the coldest month.

-Février = February

Février est mon mois d'anniversaire!

February is my birthday month!

-Mars = March

En mars, le printemps commence et les fleurs fleurissent.

In March, spring begins and flowers bloom.

-Avril = April

En avril, le temps est toujours instable.

In April, the weather is always unstable.

-Mai = May

Mai est un mois important pour la religion catholique.

May is an important month for the Catholic religion.

-Juin = June

En juin, les écoles sont terminées.

In June schools are over.

-Juillet = July

En juillet, toutes les mamies emmènent les enfants au bord de la mer.

In July all grandmas take children to the seaside.

-Août = August

En août, les entreprises sont fermées.

In August companies are closed.

-Septembre = September

En septembre, les écoles sont de retour: il est temps d'étudier.

In September schools are back: it's time to study.

-Octobre = October

En octobre, l'automne arrive enfin.

In October autumn finally arrives.

-Novembre = November

En novembre, le ciel est toujours gris

In November the sky is always grey.

-Décembre = December

En décembre, c'est l'heure de Noël et du nouvel an.

In December it's time for Christmas and New Year's Eve.

-Printemps = Spring

Le printemps est plein de parfums et de couleurs.

Spring is full of scents and colours.

-Été = Summer

L'été, c'est quand les fruits les plus lisses mûrissent.

Summer is when the smoothest fruits ripen.

-Automne = Autumn

En automne, toutes les collines sont colorées de mille nuances et ressemblent à des images

In autumn all hills are coloured by thousand shades and they look like pictures.

-Hiver = Winter

En hiver, je joue avec la neige.

In winter I play with snow.

-Bonne année! = Happy New Year!

Après le toast, bonne année!

After the toast, Happy New Year!

-Joyeux Noël! = Merry Christmas!

Je vous remercie tous d'être venus et joyeux Noël!

I thank you all for coming and Merry Christmas!

-Joyeuses Pâques ! = Happy Easter!

C'est l'occasion de vous souhaiter de joyeuses Pâques!

This is an occasion to wish you a Happy Easter!

-Joyeuses Fêtes ! = Happy Holidays!

Joyeuses fêtes à vous tous!

Happy Holidays to you all!

-Réveillon du Nouvel An = New Year's Eve

Où allons-nous célébrer la veille du Nouvel An?

Where will we celebrate New Year's Eve?

-Carnaval = Carnival

Le carnaval est la fête où tout le monde peut être quelqu'un d'autre.

Carnival is the feast where all can be someone else.

-Noël = Christmas

Le jour de Noël est le 25 Décembre

Christmas Day is on December 25th.

-Jour de libération = Liberation day

L'un des symboles de Pâques est le lapin de Pâques.

Liberation Day is on April 25th.

-Lapin de Pâques = Easter bunny

L'un des symboles de Pâques est le lapin de Pâques.

One of Easter symbols is the Easter bunny.

-Dimanche des Rameaux = Palm Sunday

Pendant le dimanche des Rameaux, les oliviers sont bénis.

During Palm Sunday olive trees are blessed.

-Épiphanie = Epiphany

Epiphanie a lieu le 6 Janvier.

Epiphany occurs on January 6th.

-Vacances mi- août = Mid-August Holiday

Les vacances de la mi-août, nous mangeons tous ensemble.

On Mid-August Holiday we all eat together.

-Fête des pères = Father's Day

La fête des pères est appréciée de ma fille.

Father's Day is well-liked by my daughter.

-Journée de la femme = Women's Day

La journée de la femme est un jour heureux.

Woman's Day is a happy day.

-Fête des mères = Mother's Day

La fête des mères est une douce fête.

Mother's Day is a sweet feast.

-Halloween = Halloween

Allez-vous sortir pour un tour ou un régal pour Halloween?

Will you go out for trick or treat on Halloween?

-Festivité = Festivity

Chaque Festivité est l'occasion de célébrer.

Every festivity is a chance to celebrate.

-Pâques = Easter

Pâques amène la fin du printemps.

Easter brings the late spring along.

-Saint Valentin = Valentine's Day

La Saint Valentin est la fête des amoureux.

Valentine's Day is the lovers feast.

-Donner = To give

Que donnerez-vous à vos parents pour Noël?

What will you give to your parents for Christmas?

-Célébrer = To celebrate

Ma famille et moi célébrons le réveillon du Nouvel An tous ensemble.

My family and I celebrate New Year’s Eve all together.

Chapter 12 - Phrases II

Colors

Gold

Doré *Doh-rey*

Red

Rouge

Roozh

Orange

Orange

Oh-rãnzh

Yellow

Jaune

Zhohn

Green

Vert

Vehr

Blue

Bleu

Bluh

Light blue

Bleu ciel

Bluh syehl

Violet

Violet

Vee-oh-leh

Pink

Rose

Rohz

Brown

Marron

Maa-ron

Purple

Mauve

Mohv

White

Blanc

Blãn

Black

Noir

Nwahr

Gray

Gris

Gree

Silver

Argenté

Aar-zhan-tey

What color is that sign?

De quelle couleur est ce panneau ?

Duh kehl koo-luhr eh suh paa-noh ?

Is the cartoon in color?

Le dessin animé est en couleur ?

Luh deh-sĩn aa-nee-mey eh_tãn koo-luhr ?

Is this television show in color?

Cette émission télé est en couleur ?

Seht eh-mee-syõn tey-ley eh_ tãn koo-luhr ?

This is a red pen.

Ceci est un stylo rouge.

Suh-see eh_tũn stee-loh roozh.

This piece of paper is blue.

Ce morceau de papier est bleu.

Suh mohr-soh duh paa-pee-ey eh bluh.

What color is that car?

De quelle couleur est cette voiture ?

Duh kehl koo-luhr eh seht vwah-tur ?

What color are your clothes?

De quelle couleur sont tes vêtements ?

Duh kehl koo-luhr son tey veht-mãn ?

Is this the right color?

Est-ce la bonne couleur ?

Ehs laa bohn koo-luhr ?

What color is the stop light?

De quelle couleur est le feu d'arrêt ?

Duh kehl koo-luhr eh luh fuh daa-rey ?

Does that color mean danger?

Est-ce que cette couleur signifie un danger ?

Ehs-kuh seht koo-luhr see-nyee-fee ũn dãn-zhey ?

That bird is red.

Cet oiseau est rouge.

Seh_twah-zoh eh roozh.

What color is that animal?

De quelle couleur est cet animal ?

Duh kehl koo-luhr eh seh_taa-nee-maal ?

The sky is blue.

Le ciel est bleu.

Luh syehl eh bluh.

The clouds are white.

Les nuages sont blancs.

Leh nu-aazh sõn blãn.

That paint is blue.

Cette peinture est bleue.

Seht pĩn-tur eh bluh.

Press the red button.

Appuyez sur le bouton rouge.

Aa-pwee-yey sur luh boo-tõn roozh.

Don't press the red button.

N'appuyez pas sur le bouton rouge.

Naa-pwee-yey pah sur luh boo-tõn roozh.

Black and White

Noir et Blanc

Nwahr ey blãn

Look at all the colors.

Regardez toutes les couleurs.

Ruh-gaar-dey toot ley koo-luhr.

Is that a color television?

Est-ce une télévision couleur ?

Ehs un tey-ley-vee-zee-yõn koo-luhr ?

What color do you see?

Quelle couleur voyez-vous ?

Kehl koo-luhr vwah-yey voo ?

Can I have the color blue?

Puis-je avoir la couleur bleue ?

Pweezh aa-vwar laa koo-luhr bluh ?

What colors do you have for these frames?

Quelles couleurs avez-vous pour ces cadres ?

Kehl koo-luhr aa-vey voo poor sey kahdr ?

Don't go until the color is green.

N'allez pas tant que ce n'est pas vert.

Naa-ley pah tãn kuh suh ney pah vehr.

Colored pencils

Crayons de couleur

Kreh-yõn duh koo-luhr.

Coloring pens

Stylos à colorier

Stee-loh aa koh-loh-ree-ey

The sharpie is black.

Le feutre est noir.

Luh fuh-tr eh nwahr.

I passed with flying colors.

Je suis passé avec brio.

Zhuh swee pah-sey aa-vehk bree-oh.

Do you have this in another color?

Avez-vous ceci dans une autre couleur ?

Aa-vey voo suh-see dãn_zun ohtr koo-luhr ?

Do you have this in a darker color?

Avez-vous ceci dans une couleur plus foncée ?

Aa-vey voo suh-see dãn_zun koo-luhr plu fõn-sey ?

Do you have this in a lighter color?

Avez-vous ceci dans une couleur plus claire ?

Aa-vey voo suh-see dãn_zun koo-luhr plu klehr ?

Can you paint my house blue?

Pouvez-vous peindre ma maison en bleu ?

Poo-vey voo pĩndr maa meh-zõn ãn bluh ?

Can you paint my car the same color?

Pouvez-vous peindre ma voiture de la même couleur ?

Poo-vey voo pĩndr maa vwah-tur duh laa mehm koo-luhr ?

The flag has three different colors.

Ce drapeau a trois couleurs différentes.

Suh draa-poh ah trwah koo-luhr dee-fey-rãnt.

Is the color on the flag red?

Est-ce que la couleur sur le drapeau est rouge ?

Ehs kuh laa koo-luhr sur luh draa-poh eh roozh ?

Numbers

Zero

Zéro

Zey-roh

One

Un

Ũn

Two

Deux

Duh

Three

Trois

Trwah

Four

Quatre

Kaatr

Five

Cinq

Sĩnk

Six

Six

Sees

Seven

Sept

Seht

Eight

Huit

Weet

Nine

Neuf

Nuhf

Ten

Dix

Dees

Eleven

Onze

Õnz

Twelve

Douze

Dooz

Thirteen

Treize

Trehz

Fourteen

Quatorze

Kaa-tohrz

Fifteen

Quinze

Kĩnz

Sixteen

Seize

Sehz

Seventeen

Dix-sept

Dee-seht

Eighteen

Dix-huit

Dee_zweet

Nineteen

Dix-neuf

Dee_znuhf

Twenty

Vingt

Vĩn

Twenty-one

Vingt-et-un

Vĩn_tey-ũn

Twenty-two

Vingt-deux

Vĩnt-duh

Twenty-three

Vingt-trois

Vĩnt-trwah

Twenty-four

Vingt-quatre

Vĩnt-kaatr

Twenty-five

Vingt-cinq

Vĩnt-sĩnk

Twenty-six

Vingt-six

Vĩnt-sees

Twenty-seven

Vingt-sept

Vĩnt-seht

Twenty-eight

Vingt-huit

Vĩnt-weet

Twenty-nine

Vingt-neuf

Vĩnt-nuhf

Thirty

Trente

Trãnt

Forty

Quarante

Kaa-rãnt

Fifty

Cinquante

Sĩn-kãnt

Sixty

Soixante

Swah-sãnt

Seventy

Soixante-dix

Swah-sãnt-dees

Eighty

Quatre-vingts

Kaa-truh-vĩn

Ninety

Quatre-vingt-dix

Kaa-truh-vĩn-dees

One hundred

Cent

Sãn

Two hundred

Deux cents

Duh-sãn

Five hundred

Cinq cents

Sĩn-sãn

One thousand

Mille

Meel

One hundred thousand

Cent mille

Sãn-meel

One million

Un million

Ũn-mee-lee-yõn

One billion

Un milliard

Ũn-mee-lee-yahr

What does that add up to?

C'est quoi le total ?

Sey kwah luh toh-tahl ?

What number is on this paper?

C'est quoi le chiffre sur ce papier ?

Sey kwah luh sheefr sur suh paa-pyey ?

What number is on this sign?

C'est quoi le chiffre sur ce panneau ?

Sey kwah luh sheefr sur suh paa-noh ?

Are these two numbers equal?

Est-ce que ces deux chiffres sont égaux ?

Ehs kuh sey duh sheefr sõn_tey-goh ?

My social security number is one, two, three, four, five.

Mon numéro de sécurité sociale est un, deux, trois, quatre, cinq.

Mõn nu-mey-roh duh sey-ku-ree-tey soh-syaal eh_tun, duh, trwah, kaatr, sĩnk.

I'm going to bet five hundred euros.

Je vais parier cinq cents euros.

Zhuh veh paa-ree-eh sĩn sãn_zuh-roh.

Can you count to one hundred for me?

Pouvez-vous me compter jusqu'à cent ?

Poo-vey voo muh kõn-tey zhus-kaa sãn ?

I took fourteen steps.

J'ai fait quatorze pas.

Zhey feh kaa-tohrz pah.

I ran two kilometers.

J'ai couru deux kilomètres.

Zhey koo-ru duh kee-loh-mehtr.

The speed limit is 30 km/h.

La limite de vitesse est 30 km/h.

Laa lee-meet duh vee-tehs eh trãnt kee-loh-mehtr luhr.

What are the measurements?

Quelles sont les mesures ?

Kehl sõn ley muh-zur ?

Can you dial this number?

Pouvez-vous composer ce numéro ?

Poo-vey voo kõm-poh-zey suh nu-mey-roh ?

One dozen.

Une douzaine.

Un doo-zehn.

A half-dozen.

Une demi-douzaine.

Un duh-mee doo-zehn.

How many digits are in the number?

Combien y a-t-il de chiffres dans ce numéro ?

Kõm-byĩn yah-teel duh sheefr dãn suh nu-mey-roh ?

My phone number is nine, eight, five, six, two, one, eight, seven, eight, eight.

Mon numéro de téléphone est le neuf, huit, cinq, six, deux, un, huit, sept, huit, huit.

Mon nu-mey-roh duh tey-ley-fon eh luh nuhf, weet, sĩnk, sees, duh, ũn, weet, seht, weet, weet.

The hotel's phone number is one, eight hundred, three, two, three, five, seven, five, five.

Le numéro de téléphone de l'hôtel est le un, huit cents, trois, deux, trois, cinq, sept, cinq, cinq.

Luh nu-mey-roh duh tey-ley-fon duh loh-tehl eh luh ũn, wee-sãn, trwah, duh, trwah, sĩnk, seht, sĩnk, sĩnk.

The taxi number is six, eight, one, four, four, four, five, eight, one, nine.

Le numéro du taxi est le six, huit, un, quatre, quatre, quatre, cinq, huit, un, neuf.

Luh nu-mey-roh du taak-see eh luh sees, weet, ũn, kaatr, kaatr, kaatr, sĩnk, weet, ũn, nuhf.

Call my hotel at two, one, four, seven, one, two, nine, five, seven, six.

Appellez mon hôtel au deux, un, quatre, sept, un, deux, neuf, cinq, sept, six.

Aa-puh-ley mõn_noh-tehl oh duh, ũn, kaatr, seht, ũn, duh, nuhf, sĩnk, seht, sees.

Call the embassy at nine, eight, nine, eight, four, three, two, one, seven, one.

Appellez l'ambassade au neuf, huit, neuf, huit, quatre, trois, deux, un, sept, un.

Aa-puh-ley lãm-baa-saad oh nuhf, weet, nuhf, weet, kaatr, trwa, duh, ũn, seht, ũn.

Medical

I would like to set up an appointment with my doctor.

J'aimerais prendre rendez-vous avec mon médecin.

Zheh-muh-reh prãndr rãn-dey-voo aa-vehk mõn meyd-sĩn.

I am a new patient and need to fill out forms.

Je suis un nouveau patient, et je dois remplir des formulaires.

Zhuh swee_zũn noo-voh paa-syãn ey zhuh dwah rãn-pleer dey fohr-mu-lehr.

I am allergic to certain medications.

Je suis allergique à certains médicaments.

Zhuh swee_zaa-lehr-zheek aa sehr-tĩn mey-dee-kaa-mãn.

That is where it hurts.

C'est là que ça fait mal.

Sey lah kuh saa feh maal.

I have had the flu for three weeks.

J'ai la grippe depuis trois semaines.

Zhey laa greep duh-pwee trwah smehn.

It hurts when I walk on that foot.

Ça fait mal quand je marche sur ce pied.

Saa feh maal kãn zhuh maarsh sur suh pyey.

When is my next appointment?

C'est pour quand mon prochain rendez-vous ?

Sey poor kãn mõn proh-shĩn rãn-dey-voo ?

Does my insurance cover this?

Est-ce couvert par mon assurance ?

Ehs koo-vehr paar mõn_naa-su-rãns ?

Do you want to take a look at my throat?

Voulez-vous examiner ma gorge ?

Voo-ley voo ehg-zaa-mee-ney maa gohrzh ?

Do I need to fast before going there?

Dois-je être à jeun avant d'y aller ?

Dwahzh ehtr aa zhũn aa-vãn dee aa-ley ?

Is there a generic version of this medicine?

Y a-t-il un générique pour ce médicament ?

Ee_yah teel un zhey-ney-reek poor suh mey-dee-kaa-mãn ?

I need to get back on dialysis.

Je dois me remettre en dialyse.

Zhuh dwah muh ruh-mehtr ãn dee-aa-leez.

My blood type is A.

Mon groupe sanguin est A.

Mõn groop sãn-gĩn eh ah.

I will be more than happy to donate blood.

Ça me ferait plaisir de faire un don de sang.

Saa muh fuh-reh pley-zeer duh fehr ũn dõn duh sãn.

I have been feeling dizzy.

J'ai des vertiges.

Zhey dey vehr-teezh.

The condition is getting worse.

La condition s'empire.

Laa kõn-dee-syõn sãn-peer.

The medicine has made the condition a little better, but it is still there.

Le médicament a amélioré un peu la condition, mais elle est toujours présente.

Luh mey-dee-kaa-mãn ah aa-mey-lee-oh-rey ũn puh laa kõn-dee-syõn, meh ehl eh too-zhoor prey-zãnt.

Is my initial health examination tomorrow?

C'est demain mon premier examen de santé ?

Sey duh-mĩn mon pruh-myey_regz-aa-mĩn duh sãn-tey ?

I would like to switch doctors.

J'aimerais changer de médecin.

Zheh-muh-reh shãn-zhey duh meyd-sĩn.

Can you check my blood pressure?

Pouvez-vous vérifier ma tension artérielle ?

Poo-vey voo vey-ree-fyey maa tãn-syõn aar-tey-ryehl ?

I have a fever that won't go away.

J'ai une fièvre persistante.

Zhey un fyeh-vruh pehr-see-stãnt.

I think my arm is broken.

Je pense que mon bras est cassé.

Zhuh pãns kuh mõn brah eh kah-sey.

I think I have a concussion.

Je pense que j'ai une commotion cérébrale.

Zhuh pãns kuh zhey un koh-moh-syõn sey-rey-braal.

My eyes refuse to focus.

Mes yeux ne veulent pas se focaliser.

Mey_zyuh nuh vuhl pah suh foh-kaa-lee-zey.

I have double vision.

Je vois double.

Zhuh vwah doobl.

Is surgery the only way to fix this?

La chirurgie est-elle le seul recours ?

Laa shee-rur-zhee ey_tehl luh suhl ruh-koor ?

Who are you referring me to?

À qui me référez-vous ?

Aa kee muh rey-fey-rey voo ?

Where is the waiting room?

Où se trouve la salle d'attente ?

Oo suh troov laa saal daa-tãnt ?

Can I bring someone with me into the office?

Puis-je amener quelqu'un avec moi dans le bureau ?

Pweezh ah-muh-ney kehl-kũn aa-vehk mwaa dãn luh bu-roh ?

I need help filling out these forms.

J'ai besoin d'aide pour remplir ces formulaires.

Zhey buh-zwĩn dehd poor rãm-pleer sey fohr-mu-lehr.

Do you take Cobra as an insurance provider?

Prenez-vous Cobra comme assurance ?

Pruh-ney voo koh-brah kohm aa-su-rãns ?

What is my copayment?

Quelle est ma quote-part ?

Kehl eh maa koht-pahr ?

What forms of payment do you accept?

Quels modes de paiement acceptez-vous ?

Kehl mohd duh pey-mãn aak-sehp-tey voo ?

Do you have a payment plan, or is it all due now?

Vous avez un plan de paiement, ou il faut tout régler maintenant ?

Voo_zaa-vey ũn plãn duh pey-mãn, oo eel foh too rey-gley mĩn-tuh-nãn ?

My old doctor prescribed something different.

Mon ancien médecin me préscrivait autre chose.

Mõn_nãn-syĩn mehd-sĩn muh prey-skree-veh oh-truh shohz.

Will you take a look at my leg?

Pouvez-vous regarder ma jambe ?

Poo-vey voo ruh-gaar-dey maa zhãmb ?

I need to be referred to a gynecologist.

J'ai besoin qu'on me réfère à un gynécologue.

Zhey buh-zwĩn kõn muh rey-fehr aa ũn zhee-ney-koh-log.

I am unhappy with the medicine you prescribed me.

Je ne suis pas satisfait du médicament que vous m'avez prescrit.

Zhuh nuh swee pah saa-tees-feh du mey-dee-kaa-mãn kuh voo maa-vey prey-skree.

Do you see patients on the weekend?

Consultez-vous le week-end ?

Kõn-sul-tey voo luh wee-kehnd ?

I need a good therapist.

J'ai besoin d'un bon thérapeute.

Zhey buh-zwĩn dũn bõn tey-raa-puht.

How long will it take me to rehab this injury?

Combien de temps il me faudra pour me remettre de cette blessure ?

Kõm-byĩn duh tãn eel muh foh-drah poor muh ruh-mehtr duh seht bleh-sur ?

I have not gone to the bathroom in over a week.

Je ne suis pas allé aux toilettes depuis plus d'une semaine.

Zhuh nuh swee pah_zaa-ley oh twah-leht duh-pwee plus dun suh-mehn.

I am constipated and feel bloated.

Je suis constipé, et je me sens ballonné.

Zhuh swee kõn-stee-pey ey zhuh muh sãn baa-loh-ney.

It hurts when I go to the bathroom.

Ça fait mal quand je vais aux toilettes.

Saa feh maal kãn zhuh veh oh twah-leht.

I have not slept well at all since getting here.

Je n'ai pas du tout bien dormi depuis mon arrivée.

Zhuh ney pah du too byĩn dohr-mee duh-pwee mõn_naa-ree-vey.

Do you have any pain killers?

Avez-vous des antidouleurs ?

Aa-vey voo dey_zãn-tee-doo-luhr ?

I am allergic to that medicine.

Je suis allergique à ce médicament.

Zhuh swee_zah-lehr-zheek aa suh mey-dee-kaa-mãn.

How long will I be under observation?

Combien de temps je dois rester sous observation ?

Kõm-byĩn duh tãn zhuh dwah rehs-tey soo_zohb-sehr-vaa-syõn ?

I have a toothache.

J'ai un mal de dents.

Zhey ũn maal duh dãn.

Do I need to see a dentist?

Est-ce que je dois voir un dentiste ?

Ehs-kuh zhuh dwah vwahr ũn dãn-teest ?

Does my insurance cover dental?

Est-ce que mon assurance prend en charge les soins dentaires ?

Ehs-kuh mõn_naa-su-rãns prãn ãn shaarzh ley swĩn dãn-tehr ?

My diarrhea won't go away.

J'ai des diarrhées persistantes.

Zhey dey dee-aa-rey pehr-see-stãnt.

Can I have a copy of the receipt for my insurance?

Puis-je avoir une copie du reçu pour mon assurance ?

Pweezh aa-vwahr un koh-pee du ruh-su poor mõn_naa-su-rãns ?

I need a pregnancy test.

J'ai besoin d'un test de grossesse.

Zhey buh-zwĩn dũn tehst duh groh-sehs.

I think I may be pregnant.

Je pense que je suis enceinte.

Zhuh pãns kuh zhuh swee_zãn-sĩnt.

Can we please see a pediatrician?

Pouvons-nous voir un pédiatre s'il vous plaît ?

Poo-võn noo vwahr ũn pey-dee-ahtr seel voo pleh ?

I have had troubles breathing.

J'ai eu du mal à respirer.

Zhey u du maal aa rehs-pee-rey.

My sinuses are acting up.

Mes sinus me dérangent.

Mey see-nus muh dey-rãnzh.

Will I still be able to breastfeed?

Pourrais-je encore allaiter ?

Poo-rehzh ãn-kahr aa-ley-tey ?

How long do I have to stay in bed?

Combien de temps je dois rester au lit ?

Kõm-byĩn duh tãn zhuh dwah rehs-tey oh lee ?

How long do I have to stay under hospital care?

Combien de temps je dois rester hospitalisé ?

Kõm-byĩn duh tãn zhuh dwah rehs-tey ohs-pee-taa-lee-zey ?

Is it contagious?

Est-ce contagieux ?

Ehs kõn-taa-zhyuh ?

How far along am I?

Je suis à combien de mois ?

Zhuh swee_zaa kõm-byĩn duh mwah ?

What did the x-ray say?

Que montre la radio ?

Kuh mõntr laa raa-dyoh ?

Can I walk without a cane?

Est-ce que je peux marcher sans canne ?

Ehs-kuh zhuh puh maar-shey sãn kaan ?

Is the wheelchair necessary?

Le fauteuil roulant est-il nécessaire ?

Luh foh-tuh-y roo-lãn eh_teel ney-sey-sehr ?

Am I in the right area of the hospital?

Suis-je dans la bonne section de l'hôpital ?

Sweezh dãn laa bohn sehk-syõn duh loh-pee-taal ?

Where is the front desk receptionist?

Où est la réceptionniste ?

Oo eh laa rey-sehp-syoh-neest ?

I would like to go to a different waiting area.

Je veux aller dans une autre salle d'attente.

Zhuh vuh aa-ley dãn_zun_nohtr saal daa-tãnt.

Can I have a change of sheets, please?

Pouvez-vous changer les draps, s'il vous plaît ?

Poo-vey voo shãn-zhey ley drah seel voo pleh ?

Excuse me, what is your name?

Excusez-moi, quel est votre nom ?

Ehk-sku-zey mwah, kehl eh vohtr nõn ?

Who is the doctor in charge here?

C'est qui le médecin responsable ici ?

Sey kee luh med-sĩn rehs-põn-saabl ee-see ?

I need some assistance, please.

J'ai besoin d'aide, s'il vous plaît.

Zhey buh-zwĩn dehd seel voo pleh.

Will my recovery affect my ability to do work?

Ma convalescence va-t-elle affecter ma capacité à travailler ?

Maa kõn-vaa-leh-sãns vah-tehl aa-fehk-tey maa kaa-paa-see-tey aa traa-vah-yey ?

How long is the estimated recovery time?

Quelle est la durée de convalescence prévu ?

Kehl eh laa du-rey duh kõn-vaa-leh-sãns prey-vu ?

Is that all you can do for me? There has to be another option.

C'est tout ce que vous pouvez faire pour moi ? Il doit y avoir une autre option.

Sey too suh kuh voo poo-vey fehr poor mwah ? Eel dwah ee_yaa-vwahr un ohtr ohp-syõn.

I need help with motion sickness.

J'ai besoin d'aide pour le mal des transports.

Zhey buh-zwĩn dehd poor luh maal dey trãns-pohr.

I'm afraid of needles.

J'ai peur des aiguilles.

Zhey puhr dey_zey-gwee-y.

My gown is too small; I need another one.

Ma blouse est trop petite ; il m'en faut une autre.

Maa blooz eh troh puh-teet ; eel mãn foh un ohtr.

Can I have extra pillows?

Est-ce que je pourrais avoir des oreillers supplémentaires ?

Ehs-kuh zhuh poo-reh aa-vwahr dey_zoh-rey-yey su-pley-mãn-tehr ?

I need assistance getting to the bathroom.

J'ai besoin d'aide pour aller aux toilettes.

Zhey buh-zwĩn dehd poor_raa-ley oh twah-leht.

Chapter 13 - Phrases III

Bank
Banque

I want to make a withdrawal

Je veux faire un retrait

Could you give me some smaller notes?

Pourriez-vous me donner quelques billets plus petits?

I'd like to pay this in ..., please

Je voudrais payer cela en ... , s'il vous plaît

How many days will it take for the check to clear?

Combien de jours faut-il pour encaisser un chèque?

Can the passport serve as an ID?

Le passeport peut-il servir de pièce d'identité?

Here's my ID card

Voici ma carte d'identité

I'd like to transfer some money to this account

Je tiens à transférer l'argent sur ce compte

Could you transfer ... from my current account to my deposit account?

Pouvez-vous transférer... à partir de mon compte courant sur mon compte de dépôt?

I'd like to open an account

Je voudrais ouvrir un compte

I'd like to open a personal account

Je voudrais ouvrir un compte personnel

Can I open a business account?

Puis-je ouvrir un compte d'affaires ?

Could you tell me my balance, please?

Pourriez-vous me donner mon solde, s'il vous plaît?

Could I have a statement, please?

Pourrais-je avoir un relevé de compte, s'il vous plaît?

I'd like to change some money

Je voudrais changer de l'argent

I'd like to order some foreign currency

Je voudrais commander des devises étrangères

What's the exchange rate for euros?

Quel est le taux de change des euros?

I'd like to exchange euros to dollars

Je voudrais changer des euros en dollars

Where's the nearest cash machine?

Où est le distributeur de billets le plus proche?

What's the interest rate on this account?

Quel est le taux d'intérêt sur ce compte?

What's the current interest rate for personal loans?

Quel est le taux d'intérêt des prêts personnels?

I've lost my bank card

J'ai perdu ma carte bancaire

I want to report a lost card

Je veux signaler la perte de ma carte

I think my card has been stolen

Je pense que ma carte a été volée

We've got a joint account

Nous avons un compte joint

I'd like to tell you about a change of address

Je voudrais vous signaler un changement d'adresse

I've forgotten my Internet banking password

Je l'ai oublié mon mot de passe de services bancaires par Internet

I've forgotten the PIN number for my card

J'ai oublié le numéro de code de ma carte

I'll have a new one sent out to you

Je vais vous en envoyer un nouveau

Could I make an appointment to see the manager?

Puis-je avoir un rendez-vous avec le directeur?

I'd like to speak to someone about a mortgage

Je voudrais parler à quelqu'un à propos d'un prêt hypothécaire

Bar

Bring me a beer

Apportez-moi une bière

Two beers, please

Deux bières , s'il vous plaît

Three shots of tequila, please

Trois verres de tequila , s'il vous plaît

I would like a glass of wine

Je voudrais un verre de vin

I'll have the same, please

Je voudrais la même chose s'il vous plaît

Nothing for me, thank you

Rien pour moi , je vous remercie

I'll pay for everyone

Je vais payer pour tout le monde

Another round, please

Un autre tour, s'il vous plaît

Are you still serving drinks?

Êtes-vous toujours servant des boissons? Servez-vous encore des boissons?

Do you have any snacks?

Avez-vous un snack?

Do you have any sandwiches?

Avez-vous des sandwiches?

Do you serve food?

Servez-vous de la nourriture?

What time does the kitchen close?

A quelle heure ferme la cuisine?

Are you still serving food?

Servez-vous encore de la nourriture?

What sort of sandwiches do you have?

Quelle sorte de sandwichs avez-vous?

Do you have any hot food?

Avez-vous des aliments chauds?

Could we see a menu, please?

Pourrions-nous voir un menu , s'il vous plaît?

Can I smoke inside?

Puis-je fumer à l'intérieur?

Do you mind if I smoke?

Ça vous dérange si je fume?

Would you like a cigarette?

Voulez-vous une cigarette?

Have you got a light?

Avez-vous du feu?

Boutique

Shopping

Could I try this on?

Pourrais-je essayer ceci?

Could I try these shoes on?

Pourrais-je essayer ces chaussures?

I need the size ...

J'ai besoin de la taille...

Do you have these shoes in size ... ?

Avez-vous des chaussures de taille ...?

Do you have the trousers in size ...?

Avez-vous le pantalon à la taille ...?

Do you have a fitting room?

Avez-vous une cabine d'essayage?

Where's the fitting room?

Où est la cabine d'essayage?

Have you got this in a smaller size?

Avez-vous cela dans une taille plus petite?

Have you got this in a larger size?

Avez-vous cela dans une plus grande taille?

Does this fit me??

Est-ce que ça me va bien?

The shirt is too big, I don’t like it

La chemise est trop grande, je ne l'aime pas

The pants are too small, I can’t fit in them

Les pantalons sont trop petits. Je n'y rentre pas

I need some high heels, can you help me?

Il me faut des talons hauts. Pouvez-vous m'aider?

Do you have this sweater in another color?

Avez-vous ce pull dans une autre couleur?

What material is this made of?

C'est en quelle matière?

Can I wash this skirt at home?

Puis-je laver cette jupe à la maison?

Does this suit require dry-cleaning?

Est-ce que ce costume exige un nettoyage à sec?

Can I use the fitting room?

Puis-je utiliser la cabine d'essayage?

Bus travel

Voyage en bus

Where can I buy tickets?

Où puis-je acheter des billets?

I need one child return ticket

J'ai besoin d'un billet aller-retour enfant

Where's the ticket office?

Où puis-je prendre les billets?

What time's the next bus to ...?

A quelle heure est le prochain bus à ...?

Can I buy a ticket on the bus? **à**

Puis-je acheter un billet dans le bus?

I'd like a ticket to ..., coming back on Sunday

Je voudrais un billet pour ..., avec retour pour dimanche

Where do I change for ...?

Ou dois-je changer pour...?

Can I have a timetable, please?

Puis_je avoir un horaire, s'il vous plait?

How often do the buses run to ...?

Combien y a-t-il de bus pour...?

The bus is running late

Le bus est en retard

The bus has been cancelled

Le bus a été annulé

Does this bus stop at ...?

Est-ce que ce bus s'arrête à ...?

Could you tell me when we get to ...?

Pourriez-vous me dire quand nous arrivons à ...?

Is this seat taken?

Est-ce que cette place est occupée?

Do you mind if I sit here?

Ca vous dérange si je m'assoie içi?

I've lost my ticket. What should I do?

J'ai perdu mon billet. Que dois-je faire?

What time do we arrive in ...?

A quelle heure arrivons-nous à ...?

What's this stop?

Quel est cet arrêt?

What's the next stop?

Quel est le prochain arrêt?

This is my stop. Can you let me get off?

Ceci est mon arrêt. Pouvez-vous me laisser descendre?

I'm getting off here. Could you please move a bit?

Je descends içi. Pourriez-vous me laisser passer s'il vous plaît?

How many stops is it to ...?

Combien d'arrêts reste t-il pour ..?

How much is the ticket to ...?

Combien coûte le billet pour...?

Where is the bus station, please?

Où est la station de bus, s'il vous plaît?

When does the bus leave for...?

Quand part le bus pour ...?

How many stops before...?

Combien d'arrêts avant...?

Business meetings
Les réunions d'affaires

I would like to schedule a meeting with you

Je voudrais programmer une réunion avec vous

Are you available next week?

Êtes-vous disponible la semaine prochaine?

Can I reschedule our meeting?

Puis-je reporter notre rencontre?

I'll call you in the morning to confirm the time

Je vous appellerai dans la matinée pour confirmer l'heure

When should we arrive?

Quand devons-nous arriver?

Where’s the event going to happen?

Où a lieu l'évènement qui va se passer?

Are there going to be some presentations?

Va-t-il y avoir des présentations?

Who is presenting tonight?

Qui est présent ce soir?

What’s this girl’s name?

Quel est le nom de cette jeune fille?

Can you please introduce us?

Pouvez-vous nous présenter s'il vous plaît?

Who is the guy in the corner?

Qui est le gars dans le coin?

Do you know the man in the gray suit?

Connaissez-vous l'homme en costume gris?

What’s your last name?

Quel est votre nom de famille?

Can I get your business card?

Puis-je obtenir votre carte de visite?

Could you write down your number, please?

Pourriez-vous écrire votre numéro, s'il vous plaît?

Can we talk about the job now?

Pouvons-nous parler du travail maintenant?

I would like to see your boss

Je voudrais voir votre patron

Can I speak to your mentor?

Puis-je parler à votre mentor?

This is my associate, Mr. ...

Voicimon associé, M. .....

I hope your secretary gave you my message

J'espère que votre secrétaire vous a donné le message

Should we get out of the office and go for a lunch?

Pouvons-nous quitter le bureau et aller déjeuner?

What do you think about my proposal?

Que pensez-vous de ma proposition?

I would like to know your opinion

Je voudrais connaître votre opinion

I wanted to ask you for an advice

Je voulais vous demander un conseil

I want to talk about investing in my company

Je veux vous parler d'investir dans mon entreprise

Cafe

Café

Can I get a coffee?

Puis-je prendre un café?

I'll have a coffee, please

Je vais prendre un café, s'il vous plaît

An orange juice for me, please

Un jus d'orange pour moi, s'il vous plaît

Bring me a tea

Apportez-moi un thé

Do you have frappes?

Avez-vous du café frappé?

Double espresso with cream, please

Double espresso à la crème, s'il vous plaît

Can I have a macchiato?

Puis-je avoir un macchiato?

Just a glass of water for me

Juste un verre d'eau pour moi

I'll have a hot chocolate

Je vais prendre un chocolat chaud

Do you have any fresh juice?

Avez-vous des jus de fruits frais?

Have you got lemonade?

Avez-vous de la limonade?

I’ve already ordered

J'ai déjà commmandé

How much do I owe you?

Combien je vous dois?

Keep the change!

Gardez la monnaie!

Do you have internet access here?

Avez-vous accès à Internet ici?

Do you have wireless internet here?

Avez-vous l'Internet sans fil ici?

What’s the wi-fi password?

Quel est le mot de passe Wi-Fi?

Can you move my drink, I’ll sit outside

Pouvez-vous apporter mon verre à l'extérieur?

Where is the restroom?

Où sont les toilettes?

Do you serve alcoholic drinks?

Servez-vous des boissons alcoolisées?

What kind of tea do you have?

Quel type de thé avez-vous?

Car accidents

Les accidents de voiture

Can you call the police?

Pouvez-vous appeler la police?

I have a flat tire, can you call help?

J'ai un pneu à plat. Pouvez-vous appeler de l'aide?

I'm out of gas, is there any gas station near?

Je suis en panne d'essence. Y a-t-il une station d'essence à proximité?

My breaks aren't working, what should I do?

Mes freins ne marchent plus. Que dois-je faire?

There was a major collision, what happened?

Il y a eu un gros accident, que va-t-il se passer?

I’m hurt, can you call the ambulance?

Je suis blessé, pouvez-vous appeler l'ambulance?

Is doctor on his way?

Y a-t-il un médecin dans le coin?

Did you see the car coming?

Avez-vous vu venir la voiture?

Where is the nearest hospital?

Où est l'hôpital le plus proche?

Is the ambulance coming?

Est ce que l'ambulance arrive?

Do you have a first aid kit?

Avez-vous une trousse de premiers soins?

Am I getting a ticket?

Est-ce que je dois attendre un billet?

Did you have a car accident?

Avez-vous eu un accident de voiture?

Is this the truck that hit you?

Est-ce le camion qui vous a heurté?

Here's my ID

Voici mon identité

Do you need my license?

Avez-vous besoin de mon permis?

I've witnessed the accident

Je suis témoin de l'accident

Where's the nearest car repair shop?

Ou est le garage le plus proche?

Do you have spare parts for...?

Avez-vous des pièces de rechange pour ...?

Can you help me pull my car?

Pouvez-vous m'aider à tirer la voiture?

Can I leave the car here?

Puis-je laisser la voiture ici?

What’s wrong with my car?

Quel est le problème avec ma voiture?

How much is it going to cost?

Combien cela va coûter?

I got hit by another car, can an insurance cover the cost?

J'ai été heurté par une autre voiture, est ce que l'assurance couvrira le coût?

It wasn’t my fault at all

Ce n'était pas du tout de ma faute

I was on the main road and he came from the side street

J'étais sur la route principale et il est venu de la rue à côté

Car rental
Location de voiture

I would like to rent a car

Je voudrais louer une voiture

Do you have any cars available?

Avez-vous des voitures disponibles?

I have a reservation under the name ...

J'ai une réservation sous le nom de ...

I have a reservation for a small car

J'ai une réservation pour une petite voiture

I'll need it for a week

Je vais en avoir besoin pour une semaine

Can I get a car for the next month?

Puis-je avoir une voiture pour le mois prochain?

Do I need to leave you any documents?

Dois-je vous laisser tous les documents?

How much does the renting cost?

Quel est le coût de la location?

What's the price per kilometer?

Quel est le prix par kilomètre?

Is it manual or automatic?

Est-elle manuelle ou automatique?

Does it take petrol or diesel?

Est-elle essence ou diesel?

Can you show me the controls?

Pouvez-vous me montrer les contrôles?

Does this car have central locking?

Est-ce que cette voiture possède un verrouillage central?

Does it have child locks?

A-t-elle un verrouillage enfant?

Here's my driving license

Voici mon permis de conduire

When do I need to return it?

Quand dois-je la rendre?

Do I have to return it with the full tank?

Dois-je la rendre avec un réservoir plein?

Can you show me how to open the boot?

Pouvez-vous me montrer comment ouvrir le coffre?

Where do I turn on the lights?

Où puis-je allumer les lumières?

Where are the windscreen wipers?

Où sont les essuie-glaces?

Can I get insurance?

Puis-je obtenir une assurance?

Does the car have insurance?

Est-ce que la voiture a une assurance?

Does the car have all the necessary accessories?

Est-ce que la voiture possède tous les accessoires nécessaires?

How much do you charge if I'm an hour late?

Combien facturez-vous si j'ai une heure de retard?

What are your business hours?

Quelles sont vos heures de bureau?

Do you work on Sunday?

Travaillez-vous le dimanche?

Car travel
Voyage en voiture

I'm driving. Can you call me back?

Je conduis. Pouvez-vous me rappeler?

Can you slow down a bit?

Pouvez-vous ralentir un peu?

Can you stop here for a moment?

Pouvez-vous arrêter ici pour un moment?

Can we take a break here?

Pouvons-nous prendre une pause ici?

Are we going to arrive by the evening?

Allons-nous arriver dans la soirée?

When should we arrive?

Quand devons-nous arriver?

Do you know directions to ... ?

Connaissez-vous la direction vers...?

Can you show me the way to ... ?

Pouvez-vous me montrer le chemin vers...?

How do I get to the ... ?

Comment puis-je aller à...?

Is there an alternative road?

Y a-t-il une autre route?

Is there a detour or should I enter the city?

Y a-t-il un détour ou devrais-je entrer dans la ville?

How can I avoid the traffic jam?

Comment puis-je éviter l'embouteillage?

Are we going towards the highway?

Allons-nous vers l'autoroute?

Is this the right road?

Est-ce la bonne route?

Where are you going to park?

Où allez-vous vous garer?

Is this a public parking?

Est-ce un parking public?

There's an empty parking lot

Il y a un parking vide

How do I pay for the parking?

Comment dois-je payer pour le stationnement?

Can I go left here?

Puis-je aller à gauche ici?

Chapter 14 - Phrases IV

Transportation

How much for a first class/second class/economy ticket to...?

Combien coûte un ticket première classe/ seconde classe/ classe économique pour ....?

(*kon-BIENG kuh-teuh eing tee-kay preuh-mee-ay-reuh kla-ss-euh/ ze-kon-deuh kla-ss-euh/ kla-ss-euh ay-ko-no-mee-keuh poor ... ?*)

A one-way/return ticket to... please.

Un aller simple/ aller-retour pour .... s'il vous plait.

(*eing ah-lay ZIN-pleuh/ ah-lay reuh-too-reuh poor ... zeel-vuh-play.*)

Here's my passport.

Voici mon passport. (*Voi-zee m-on pa-see-por*)

What time does the bus/train/plane/ferry from... arrive?

A quelle heure arrive le bus/train/avion/ferry de .... ?

(*ah-KAY-leuh-reuh ah-ree-veuh leuh bu-zeuh/traing/a-vee-on/fay-ree deuh ... ?*)

What time does the bus/train/plane/ferry to... depart?

A quelle heure part le bus/train/avion/ferry pour .... ?

(*ah-KAY-leuh-reuh pa-reuh leuh bu-zeuh/traing/a-vee-on/fay-ree poor...?*)

52) Which platform/gate/terminal?

Sur quel quai/ à quelle porte/à quel terminal ?

(zhuhr KEL kay/ah KEL por-teuh/ ah KEL ter-mee-na-l ?)

Is the bus/train/plane direct?

Est-ce un bus/train/avion direct ?

(AY-ss-euh eing buh-ss/traing/a-vee-on dee-ray-k-t ?)

Do I have to change buses/trains?

Dois-je changer de bus/train ? *(DUH-a-zeuh zan-zay deuh bu-ss/traing ?)*

Do I need a seat reservation?

Dois-je réserver un siège ? *(DUH-a-zeuh ray-zer-vay see-ay-geuh?)*

Is this seat taken?

Ce siège est-il libre ? *(ZEUH see-ay-j ay-tee-l lee-br-euh ?)*

When is the next train/bus/minibus/ferry to...?

A quelle heure est le prochain train/bus/minibus/ferry pour .... ?

(ah KEL euh-reuh ay l-euh pro-sh-eing traing/bu-ss/mee-nee-bu-ss/fay-ree poo-r ... ?)

Could you call me a taxi?

Pourriez-vous m'appeler un taxi ?

(poo-r-i-i-ay VOO ma-peuh-lay un taa-xee ?)

I'd like to go to...

J'aimerais aller à.... *(ZAY-meuh-ray ah-lee ah...)*

Could you let me know when to get off?

Pourriez-vous me dire quand partir ?

(poo-ri-ee voo meuh dee-r kan pa-r-tee-r ?)

Where could I rent a bike/car?

Où puis-je louer un vélo/une voiture ?

(*OO pu-i-ze loo-ee un vee-lo/un-euh vu-a-tu-r ?*)

I'd like to rent a bike/car.

J'aimerais louer un vélo/ une voiture.

(*ZAY-meuh-ray loo-ay un vee-lo/un-euh vu-a-tu-r*)

Eating & Drinking

Could you recommend a good restaurant?

Pourriez-vous me conseiller un bon restaurant ?

(*POO-ri-ee voo meuh kon-say-yee un b-on ray-sto-ran ?*)

What would you recommend?

Que me recommanderiez-vous ?

(*KEUH meuh reuh-ko-man-deuh-ri-ee voo ?*)

What are some local specialties?

Quelles sont les spécialités locales ?

(*KAY-l s-on lay spay-zi-al-i-tay lo-ka-l ?*)

What is the special of the day?

Quel est le plat du jour ? (*KEL ay leuh pla du z-oo-r ?*)

Could I see the menu, please?

Pourrais-je voir le menu s'il vous plait ?

(*PUH-ray-zhuh vu-aa-r l-euh m-euh nuh ?*)

A beer/coffee/tea, please.

Une bière/un café/ un thé, s'il vous plait.

(*uun bi-ay-reuh/ uhn ka-fay/ uhn t-ee z-il-voo-p-lay*)

I'm allergic to...

Je suis allergique à... (*ZHUH ss-u-i a-ler-gi-keuh aa...*)

That was delicious!

C'était délicieux. (*say-tay deli-SYUH*)

This isn't what I ordered.

C'est pas ce que j'ai commandé. (*SAY p-aa ze keuh zh-ay ko-man-day*)

Can I buy you a drink?

Je peux vous offrir à boire ? (*ZHUH p-euh vhuh off-ree-r aa b-u-a-reuh ?*)

Let's have another!

Prenons-en encore ! (*PR-euh-n-on z-en en-ko-r !*)

Directions

How do I get to...?

Comment va-t-on à... ? (*COW-men va-t-on aa... ?*)

It's on the left/on the right/straight ahead/at the corner.

C'est à gauche/à droite/ tout droit/au coin.

(*SAY aa guh-o-sh-euh/ aa dr-u-a-t-euh/ tuh dr-u-a/ o ku-in.*)

How far is...?

Est-ce que .... est loin ? (*EZ-keuh ..... ay lu-in ?*)

Where is the closest bank/post office/exchange office?

Où est la banque/la poste/le bureau de change le plus proche ?

(*UH ay la ban-k/ la p-os-teuh/ l-euh buh-ro deuh sh-an-z-euh l-euh pl-uh p-ro-sh-euh ?*)

Where can I find tourist information?

Où puis-je trouver des informations touristiques ?

(*OO pu-i-zeuh true-vay day in-for-ma-tion too-ris-tee-k ?*)

Do you have a map?

Avez-vous une carte ? (*AA-vay voo uh-n ka-r-t ?*)

Can you show me that on the map?

Pourriez-vous me le montrer sur la carte ?

(*POO-ri-ee voo m-euh l-euh m-on-tray ss-uh-r la ka-rr-t ?*)

Where is the (American) embassy/consulate?

Où est l'Ambassade des États-Unis ?

(*OO ay l-am-bah-ss-a-d day ay-ta-zu-nee ?*)

Sightseeing

What is the entrance fee?

Combien coute l'entrée ? (*KON-bien coo-t l-en-tray ?*)

What is that building?

Quel est ce bâtiment ? (*KEL ay ss-euh ba-tee-men ?*)

What's on at the cinema/theatre/opera tonight?

Qu'y a-t-il au cinéma/théatre/opéra ce soir ?

(*kI-i-a-tee-l o see-nay-ma/tay-a-tr/o-pay-ra ss-euh ss-o-i-ar ?*)

That's a beautiful church/cathedral/building.

C'est une église/une cathédrale/un bâtiment magnifique.

(*SAY uun ay-glee-z/uun ca-tay-dr-a-l / uhn ba-tee-men ma-gnee-fee-k*)

What is there to see around here?

Qu'y a-t-il à voir aux alentours ? (*KEE i a tee-l a vu-ar o za-len-tur?*)

Accommodation

I have a reservation.

J'ai une réservation. (*ZH-ay uun ray-zer-va-ssion*)

Do you have any single/double rooms available?

Avez-vous des chambres simples/doubles libres ?

(*AA-vee vuh day sh-an-br ss-in-pl/ d-ou-bl lee-br ?*)

Could I see the room?

Pourrais-je voir la chambre ? (*POO-ray-zhuh vu-ar la sh-am-br ?*)

I'd like to stay for... nights.

J'aimerais rester .... nuits. (*ZH-ay-meuh-ray ray-stay .... nu-ee.*)

Is breakfast included?

Le petit-déjeuner est-il inclus ?

(*l-euh p-euh-tee day-z-euh-nay ay-tee-l in-clue ?*)

The TV/air conditioner/lamp in my room doesn't work.

La television/climatisation/lampe de ma chambre ne fonctionne pas. (*la tay-LAY-vee-zi-on/clee-ma-TEE-za-ss-ion/ L-HAM-p d-euh ma sh-ham-br n-euh f-on-ct-i-on p-ah.*)

Could I get a different room?

Pourrais-je avoir une autre chambre ?

(*POO-ray-zhuh aa-vu-a-r uun o-tr sh-ham-br ?*)

Is there a restaurant here?

Y a-t-il un restaurant ici ? *(EE a-tee-l uhn ray-ss-to-ran ee-ss-ee ?)*

Health & Emergencies

Help!

Au secours! (*oh suh-KOOR!*)

I need a doctor/dentist/police officer.

J'ai besoin d'un médecin/dentiste/police.

(*zhay buh-ZWAHN dun may-TSAN/den-TIS-teh/POH-lees*)

Is there pharmacy nearby?

Y a-t-il une pharmacie dans les environs ?

(EE a-tee-l uun far-ma-see d-an lay en-vee-r-on ?)

Can I use your phone?

Pourrais-je utiliser votre telephone ?

(*POO-ray-zhuh u-tee-lee-z-ay v-o-tr tay-lay-f-on ?*)

Call the police/ambulance!

Appelez la police/une ambulance !

(*AA-p-euh-lay la po-lee-ss/uun am-bu-lan-ss !*)

Conclusion

Thank you for reaching the end of *French Common Phrases*. I hope that after reading this book, you feel more ready than you ever to go forth and use your French knowledge in new places and with new people. The phrases and words contained within this book will equip you for almost any encounter and situation where you would need these French language skills. I hope this makes you feel more confident going into your travels and well-prepared for anything unexpected. With the skills you have developed from reading this book, you might just become the French speaker in the family or group. Your knowledge will ensure that you get what you want and need, or that you understand what is happening if you ever need to see a doctor when you are in a French-speaking country. Through your knowledge of the language, you can confidently book a hotel with the right type of amenities and services for yourself or your group.

Continue to practice your pronunciation of the terms and phrases in this book, and challenge yourself to develop your own sentences from the tools that this book has given you. Mixing and matching the words and verbs that you have learned in this book will allow you to create virtually any sentence you need when it comes to conversation. Even if you are able to read the signs or websites that you come across in French while planning a trip or while away in a French-speaking country, this knowledge will have proved to benefit you greatly!

If you are looking for what steps to take next, it would be to continue to expose yourself to as many new French words as possible! Listen to French podcasts, watch French films, or engage in as many conversations in French as you can. This will help to keep this French knowledge fresh in your brain and will solidify it in your memory. Doing so will help you to keep this for as long as possible, hopefully for the rest of your life. There is never too much practice that you can have when it comes to learning a language. If you read this book out loud the first time, continue to read it in this fashion, and if you did not, make sure you read it aloud at least once. This will be extremely beneficial for your comprehension of the language and the longevity of the language pronunciation in your memory.

Now, use what you have learned and become a French conversationalist. With an entirely new language under your belt, pick up as much information and knowledge as you can along the way. This book will be available to you the entire time, just in case you need to flip back for a little tune-up.

FRENCH SHORT STORIES

LEARN FRENCH WITH THE MOST COMMON STORIES AND DISCOVER HOW TO IMPROVE YOUR READING AND LISTENING SKILLS LANGUAGE WITH SHORT STORIES

PAUL BONNET

Introduction

To most folks, learning a new language is a truly difficult task. But it doesn't have to be. Of course, it can be nearly impossible if you don't know how to approach it effectively. Well, that is true of anything in life.

Think about that for a moment.

Suppose that your car breaks down and you don't have the slightest idea of what's wrong with it. How could you ever possibly expect to fix it?

The same goes for learning a language. When you are learning a new language, you need to have the right approach in mind in order to help you maximize your personal talents.

It is worth noting that the guidelines that we are outlining here are hardly limited to exceptionally talented people. Actually, they are the type of actions that anyone can take advantage of. When a regular person makes use of them effectively, they can develop their linguistic capabilities to incredible extremes.

Plus, you will find that these top five tips and strategies are actually intuitive. Once you see them in action, they will immediately click in your mind. So, do take the time to go over them in detail. That way, you will be able to make the most of your time and efforts when learning any new language.

The first guideline is consistency.

That's right. Consistency is easily the most important skill you can develop when learning a new language. For most people, learning a new language is like joining a new gym. For the first couple of weeks, motivation in high. But after some time, that motivation begins to wane until it is practically gone. After a while, this new endeavor becomes just another task which did not lead anywhere.

Just like a new gym, learning a new language generally suffers the same fate... unless you engage in consistent and sustainable practices.

The easiest way to build consistent habits is to start off slow and build your way up. Initially, devoting just 15 minutes a day of concerted practice will help you build your skills effectively. Then, you can incrementally build up your stamina until you reach a point where you can realistically devote as much time as possible to learning your chosen language.

The best part of this particular guideline is that you can apply to any language you wish to learn or any other skill for that matter.

So, try your best to carve out a small chunk of your day. From there, you can build on it until you find the optimal amount of time, and time of day, to study French.

The second guideline deals with the time of day that you dedicate to study.

This is a tricky one, as everyone is different. For some folks, the best time to focus and study is first thing in the morning. Others, who are night owls, prefer to stay up a bit later and brush up on their studies. This is why you might have to experiment a bit a first until you find your own groove. When you do find that groove, try to make it as consistent as possible. This is especially true because humans are creatures of habit. If you juggle your study schedule, you might find that you might not be getting as much out of your studies as you would like. Again, consistency is key.

The third guideline which we are going to discuss pertains to concentration.

This guideline is often overlooked, especially with the pace of modern life. In fact, it is quite common for most people to try and build in activities on top of each other.

Now, you might be able to pull that off with some activities. For example, you might be able to listen to an audiobook while you are driving or making dinner. But when you are learning a new language, the ideal setting is to completely focus on the content you are covering. This will help you maximize your time and efforts.

If you choose to incorporate your language learning tasks into other activities, then you might find that you need to constantly go over certain contents or that some of these don't stick quite as well. That leads to duplicate tasks and ineffective study time.

So, the best way to go about this is to devote focused time, even if it is just a few minutes at a time, in which you can really concentrate on what you are learning. This will help you pick up the new language far more easily.

That leads us to the fourth guideline, which deals with memory.

In this book, we won't be asking you to memorize anything. Of course, if you naturally enjoy memorizing words and expressions, then by all means. However, most individuals prefer to practice a new language and new content into practice right away. As such, do take the time to put your newly acquired language into practice at once. This will help you fixate contents into your mind.

The best way in which you can practice is to seek out other folks who speak French. While you may not know many French speakers yourself, there are plenty of groups on social media that are dedicated to language learning. Seek out groups of French learners. You will surely find great opportunities to put your new talents to good use.

The last guideline is a simple one: relax!

For most people, learning a language can be stressful, even if it is nothing more than a personal development goal. The fact of the matter is that anything new can cause stress and anxiety. But unless you have your boss breathing down your neck, learning French ought to be a fun activity for you. Do take it for what it is: a personal development endeavor.

The fact is that speaking multiple languages does not only look good on your resumé, but it is also the type of skill which can make you a more interesting person and give you a great sense of satisfaction. So, please take it for what it is: a wonderful growth opportunity.

Chapter 1 - Most Significant Differences between the English and French Languages

In this chapter, we are going to be taking a closer look at the most significant differences that lie with the English and French and how you can use them to improve your understanding of the way the French language works in practice.

French and English are very similar in many ways, yet they are completely different in others.

First of all, French is a Romance language. While you might feel that French sounds sexy and attractive, the fact is that the term "Romance" is derived from the "Romans" since it is a Latin-based language. As such, the term Romance is shared with other languages that are derived from Latin, such as Italian, Spanish, Portuguese and Romanian.

In fact, French is a type of blend of the language spoken in ancient Gaul (modern-day France) and the Latin spoken by the Romans. This mix of Gallic and Latin led to what is known today as French. As a matter of fact, French was so predominant during its heyday that it was spoken, therefore, Europe. Today, French is one of the working languages of the European Union and is preferred for legal and banking matters.

English, on the other hand, is a Germanic language. The first instances of what would become English were spoken by nomadic tribes that migrated from Upper Bavaria to the British Isles. After their settlement on the British Isles, the language spoken by these tribes underwent considerable influence from other peoples, such as the Vikings, who consistently raided the British Isles. This led to the influence of Old Norse into the English language. The most striking example of this influence is "Thursday," which in Old

English is a derivation from "Thor's Day" named after the well-known Norse God.

Fast forward a few centuries later, the Romans took hold of the British Isles and renamed it Britannia. The Romans tried their best to impose Latin on the settlers of the British Isles but were unsuccessful. The best they could manage was to sneak in some words from Latino into the lexicon on these settlers.

Then, the Norman Conquest of 1066 brought a French King to England. And with this conquest, the English court had French as its working language until early in the 20th century. While French control of England ended in the 15th century, the linguistic imprint of this period led English to acquire a dual nature. This means that a great deal of the more "sophisticated" language seen in English can be traced back to French while the more "common" language in English is directly derived from German.

This is what makes French surprisingly easy to learn For English speakers. In fact, it is said that the easiest language for English speakers to learn is French. While there are some striking differences in verb conjugation and other nuances, the fact is that English has a lot more in common with French than with any other language except for German.

Nevertheless, here are the most striking differences between English and French.

•French has a much more complex verb conjugation system than English. It is based on the ending of the infinitive form of the verb. Then, verb endings are substituted based on the subject that it agrees with. English does not require significant changes in verb conjugation except for the past tense form of irregular verbs.

•French has a masculine-feminine form for nouns. English is a gender-neutral language. As such, this difference is one of the most challenging aspects of the language as there is no clear-cut way of knowing which nouns are masculine and which are feminine save for their spelling.

•Adjectives precede nouns in French while adjectives follow nouns in English.

•Adjectives can be both plural and singular in French. Adjectives in English are never plural.

•The numerical system is highly complex in French. It uses a 60-base system as opposed to the 10-base system in most other languages.

•The pronunciation of French consonants uses the base of the throat a lot more than English ones. Vowels are much more rounded than in English.

•French makes use of far more nasal sounds that English does. This can make it challenging to get the right sound at times.

•French uses a series of accents on vowels for the purpose of illustrating pronunciation, whereas English does not use any save for certain imported words.

•French syntax (word order) is a lot more flexible than English syntax. This means that there are cases in which parts of speech can be moved around to suit the speaker's taste. In English, word order is very restrictive. So, the speaker must know where to place each part of speech.

•While English and French use the same character set, multiple vowels, and consonant combinations tend to produce a single sound.

While this list may seem quite large, the fact of the matter is that it encompasses a concise illustration of the main differences between both languages. Now, it should be pointed out that English and French resemble each other very closely. What this means is that you already have a leg up on many other folks who are looking to learn French as well.

Chapter 2 - Une tarte aux pommes (Apple Pie)

J'ouvre les yeux au moins vingt secondes avant que le réveil ne sonne. Je m'appelle Henri et j'ai cinquante ans. J'ai trois enfants, Marie, Mathieu et Quentin, des enfants bien intelligents et dont je suis fier. Les deux aînés sont partis continuer leurs études universitaires à l'étranger. Marie est en Allemagne et Mathieu en France. Pour ce qui est de Quentin, le petit dernier, nous ne savons pas ce qu'il projette de faire, mais pour le moment il est parti vivre en colocation avec un de ses amis et nous le voyons encore pendant les weekends, ou quand il n'a pas cours. C'est fou ce que les enfants grandissent vite, le temps file à toute allure.

Ma femme Zoé dort encore. Sans trop tarder, je me lève et je vais dans la salle de bain me laver le visage pour effacer les traces de l'oreiller. Je porte un débardeur et un short, il est six heures du matin. Je prends la serviette suspendue sous le miroir et je m'essuie le visage avec elle.

Je me change avant de me diriger vers la cuisine pour prendre mon petit déjeuner. J'entends Zoé se lever.

« Tu es bien matinal aujourd'hui.

– Oh, je n'avais plus sommeil, dis-je en ouvrant le frigo.

– Il y a des céréales aux fruits rouges si ça te dis, chéri.

– Mhhh, non c'est bon, je vais juste manger des biscottes. Fais-nous du café plutôt.

– Oui, chef, dit-elle en sautillant.

– Tu n'as toujours pas de nouvelles des enfants ?

– Non.

– Marie ? Mathieu ? Et Quentin ?

– Ils sont sûrement occupés. Quentin a appelé hier soir quand tu étais encore au travail. Il passera dimanche, il veut nous présenter sa petite copine, Clémence.

– Eh bien, comme je le pensais, le temps passe vite. Et dire qu'il y a un an, on déposait Mathieu à l'aéroport et voilà que Quentin a une petite copine ! dis-je en riant.

– Nous avons bien fait de prendre cet appartement. A nous deux, la maison était bien trop grande. En plus, notre portier Marcello est extrêmement sympathique.

– Oui, c'est sûr. Mais il se fait vieux, il devrait partir à la retraite pour enfin pouvoir se reposer.

– Il n'a pas de famille apparemment. Et puis son travail ne le fatigue pas tant que ça je pense. »

Le téléphone sonne. Zoé s'empresse de regarder le nom affiché sur l'écran. Déçue, elle le tend à Henri : c'est un de ses amis qui l'appelle.

« Bon, je vais faire une tarte, je sors faire quelques emplettes pour acheter les ingrédients.

– Moi aussi je veux sortir faire un tour.

– Allons-y ensemble alors.

– D'accord. Préparons-nous alors », dis-je.

Nous avons eu un déjeuner calme. C'était délicieux, j'adore les lasagnes, surtout avec des champignons. En début d'après-midi, on a regardé quelques feuilletons. Puis j'ai enfilé mes lunettes pour lire les journaux pendant qu'elle continuait à regarder ses séries.

« Bon, je vais aller faire ma tarte. Je n'ai pas envie de commencer trop tard, je serai fatiguée ensuite et je n'aime pas remettre à demain, dit-elle en se levant.

– Moi je pense faire une petite sieste.

– Est-ce que tu ne serais pas mieux dans le lit ?

– Oh que non, le canapé est bien meilleur, crois-moi.

– Si tu le dis. »

Je ne sais plus quelle heure il est quand j'ouvre les yeux. Il commence à faire nuit. Je me lève et vais vers la cuisine. Ça sent le gâteau. Zoé est justement en train de sortir la tarte du four. Elle en profite pour humer la douce odeur de tarte sortant du four.

« Et voilà, je n'ai pas perdu la main ! dit-elle en souriant comme une enfant.

– Ça a l'air bon.

– C'est l'odeur qui t'a réveillé ? Tu semblais dormir tellement bien que je n'ai pas osé te réveiller.

– Je me suis assoupi un instant et puis hop ! »

Je m'assieds et la regarde découper deux morceaux de la tarte.

« Tu veux qu'on l'appelle ?

– Qui donc ?

– Mathieu voyons. Je sais que c'est son anniversaire et que c'est pour ça que tu as fais cette tarte. Une tarte aux pommes, hein ? C'est ce qui m'a mis la puce à l'oreille.

– C'est sa préférée... Il doit être occupé, je ne veux pas le déranger.

– Mais non, c'est vendredi, il doit sûrement avoir un peu de temps. Et puis on ne le dérangera pas longtemps. On va juste lui souhaiter un joyeux anniversaire ! dis-je en déverrouillant mon smartphone. En plus il est connecté ! ajoutais-je.

– Vraiment ? Appelle-le alors ! », dit-elle en se rapprochant de moi.

Ça bipe un moment, il ne décroche pas. On essaye une seconde fois, rien.

On attend cinq minutes avant de retenter, au cas où il serait sorti un instant, et on rappelle. Cette fois, il décroche.

« Allô ? Bonjour papa.

– Bonjour fiston, ça va ? On t'appelle juste pour...

– Joyeux anniversaire chéééérii ! », s'empresse Zoé par-dessus mon épaule gauche.

J'entends Mathieu rire, je ris à mon tour.

« Oui, voilà, joyeux anniversaire fiston, c'est pour te dire que nous t'aimons et que nous pensons à toi.

– Tu nous manques !

– Vous me manquez aussi... Et merci de ne pas avoir oublié. Et désolé de ne pas vous avoir appelé souvent.

– Ce n'est rien, tu dois être occupé.

– Appelle-nous quand tu as le temps, OK ?

– Ça marche !

– On a fait une tarte aux pommes, tu t'en rappelles ? C'est ta préférée.

– Mhhhh, oui oui. Ça fait longtemps que je n'en ai pas mangé. Tiens je vais m'en acheter après.

– Sinon, ça va ?

– Oui, mais je dois vous laisser. Je vais sortir avec des amis.

– Pas de souci, vas-y. Nous sommes heureux de t'avoir eu au téléphone aujourd'hui ! dis-je.

– Moi aussi mes parents chéris ! Ah, et Marie m'a appelé, elle m'a dit qu'elle pourrait sûrement venir me voir d'ici peu. Elle n'a encore rien dit, mais vous la connaissez avec ses mystères.

– Quelle bonne nouvelle, appelez-nous quand vous serez ensemble, lança Zoé.

– Oui, maman ! Promis ! Bises !

– Bisous !

– Au revoir fiston. »

Quand il a raccroché, Zoé a pris un morceau de tarte et me l'a tendu. C'est bon, je suis heureux. On a eu notre fils au téléphone et on a pu lui souhaiter un joyeux anniversaire.

I open my eyes at least 20 seconds before the alarm rings. My name is Henri and I'm 50 years old. I have three children, Marie, Mathieu and Quentin, very intelligent children, of whom I am proud. The two elders left to continue their college studies abroad. Marie is in Germany and Mathieu in France. As for Quentin, the youngest, we do not know what he's planning to do, but for the moment he's gone off to live with a friend of his and we see him on weekends or when he's not at his classes. It's crazy how children grow up fast, time flies.

Zoe still sleeps. Without too much delay I get up and go to the bathroom to wash my face to remove the traces of the pillow. I wear a tank top and a shirt ; it is 6am in the morning. I find the towel under the mirror and I wipe my face with it.

I change before heading to the kitchen for breakfast. I hear Zoé getting up.

'You are early today.'

'Oh, I was no longer sleepy,' I say opening the fridge.

'We have red fruit cereals if you want, darling.'

'Mhhh, no it's good, I'm just going to eat crackers. Make us some coffee instead.'

'Yes, sir.' She said, hopping.

'You still have no news from the children?'

'No.'

'Marie? Mathieu, and Quentin?'

‘They are probably busy. Quentin called last night when you were still at work. He will come on Sunday, he wants to introduce his girlfriend, Clemence.’

‘Well, as I said time flies. Thinking that just a year ago we were dropping off Mathieu at the airport, and now Quentin has a girlfriend!”l I said with a little chuckle.

‘We did well by taking this apartment, the house was way too big just for the two of us. Moreover, we have a friendly doorman.”

Yes, but Marcello is getting old, he has to rest and retire.’

‘But he does not have a family, and it seems like his work is not so much tiring.’

The phone rings. Zoé hastens to see the name displayed on the screen. Disappointed she hands it to me, it is one of my friends calling.

‘Good, I'm going to make a pie. I will go out shopping to buy the ingredients.’

‘I'm going out for a walk.’

‘We will go together then.’

‘Okay. Let’s get ready,’ I said.

We had a quiet lunch, it was delicious, I really like lasagna, especially with mushrooms. In the early afternoon we watched a few soap operas and she continued watching her shows while I put on my glasses to read the newspapers.

‘Good, I'll go make my pie. I do not want to start too late, I will be tired and I do not want to postpone it until tomorrow.’ She said, standing up.

‘Yes, I'm going to take a nap.’

‘Wouldn’t it better to sleep on the bed?’

‘Oh no, the sofa is better, believe me.’

'If you say so.'

I do not know what time it is when I open my eyes ; it is getting dark. I get up and go to the kitchen. It smells like pie, Zoe is just taking out the pie from the oven. She seizes the opportunity to smell the odor that the pie gives off.

'And here, I did not lose the knack!' she said, smiling like a child.

'It looks good.'

'Is it the smell that woke you up? You seemed to sleep so well that I did not dare to wake you up.'

'I fell asleep for a moment and then hop!'

I sat down and watched her cut out two pieces of the pie.

'Do you want to make a call?'

'Who?'

'Mathieu. I know it's his birthday and that's why you made this pie. An apple pie, huh?' That's what set me thinking she would like to call him.

'It's his favorite ... He must be busy, I do not want to disturb him.'

'But no, it's Friday, he must surely have some time. And then we will not disturb him for a long time. We're just going to wish him a happy birthday!' I say unlocking my smartphone.

'In addition he is connected!' I added.

'Really? Call him then!' she said, coming closer to me.

It beeps for a moment, he does not pick up. We try a second time, nothing.

We wait five minutes before retrying in case it takes a moment and we call back. This time he picks up.

'Allo? Hello, Dad.'

'Hello son, how are you? We call you for...'

‘ Happy birthday honeeeeeey.’ says Zoé over my left shoulder. I hear Mathieu laughing, I laugh in turn.

‘Yes, voilà, happy birthday son, we love you.’

‘We miss you!’

‘I miss you too... And thank you for not having forgotten. And sorry for not calling you often.’

‘It's nothing, you must be busy.’

‘Well call us when you have time. OK?’

‘I’ll do it !’

‘We did an apple pie, remember? It's your favorite.’

‘Mhhhh, yes yes. I have not eaten it for a long time. Maybe I'll buy some after.’

‘Then, how are you doing?’

‘Good, but I have to leave. I am going out with friends.’

‘No worries, go ahead. We are happy we could talk to you today !’

‘So did I, my dear parents! Ah, and Marie called me, she told me she could probably come and see me. She has not said anything yet but, you know, her and her mysteries.’

‘That's good news, call us then,’ said Zoé.

‘Yes mom! Promised! Hugs!’

‘Kisses!’

‘-See you, son.’

When he hung up Zoe took a piece of pie and handed it to me. ‘It's good, I'm happy, we had our son on the phone and we could wish him a happy birthday.’

Sommaire

Henri a 50 ans. Il habite avec sa femme Zoé dans un petit appartement après que ses enfants soient tous partis. Ce jour là, il se lève à 6h du matin. C'est un jour comme les autres, il se douche et descend pour prendre son petit déjeuner. Zoé le rejoint, ils passent une journée comme les autres et Zoé décide de faire une tarte aux pommes, ce qui surprend Henri, étant donné qu'elle a arrêté d'en faire depuis trois ans. En effet, Henri se doute qu'elle fait cette tarte à l'occasion de l'anniversaire de leur fils Mathieu. Ils réussissent à l'avoir au téléphone et peuvent lui souhaiter un joyeux anniversaire comme il faut.

Summary

Henri is 50 years old. He lives with his wife, Zoe, in a small apartment after his children are all gone. That day, he gets up at 6 am. It is a day like the others, he showers and goes down to have breakfast. Zoe joins him. They spend an ordinary day and Zoe decides to make an apple pie, which surprises Henri since it has been 3 years that she stopped doing it. Indeed, Henri suspected that the reason she had made this pie was for the occasion of the birthday of their son Mathieu. They get him on the phone and wish him a happy birthday.

Vocabulaire / Vocabulary

Secondes - seconds

Réveil - alarm

Fier - proud

Aînés - elders

Coloc' – shared appartment

C'est fou - it's crazy

Serviette - towel

Miroir - mirror

La cuisine - kitchen

Petit déjeuner - breakfast

Salle de bain - bathroom

Oreiller - pillow

Débardeur - tank top

Short - shorts

Sommeil - sleep

Céréales - cereal

Dimanche - sunday

Sympathique - nice

Retraite - retirement

Écran - screen

Tarte aux pommes - apple pie

Champignons - mushrooms

Une sieste - a nap

Morceau - piece

Canapé - sofa

Joyeux anniversaire – happy birthday

Questions

1 - Comment s'appelle le monsieur de l'histoire ?

a. Henri

b. François

c. Carl

d. Damien

2 - Qui est Zoé ?

a. La mère d'Henri

b. La sœur d'Henri

c. La femme d'Henri

d. La cousine d'Henri

3 - Quel âge a Henri ?

a. Henri a 60 ans.

b. Henri a 45 ans.

c. Henri a 52 ans.

d. Henri a 50 ans.

4 - Combien d'enfants a Henri ?

a. Henri a trois enfants.

b. Henri n'a pas d'enfant.

c. Henri a deux enfants.

d. Henri a six enfants.

5 - Que porte Henri ?

a. Une chemise et un jean

b. Un débardeur et un short

c. Un capuchon et un short

d. Un pyjama satin

6 - Qu'est-ce qu'Henri veut manger au petit déjeuner ?

7 – Quelle tarte veut préparer Zoé ?

8 - Qu'est-ce qu'Henri et Zoé ont mangé pour le déjeuner ?

9 - Qui a appelé sur le portable d'Henri ?

10 - Pourquoi Zoé a-t-elle fait une tarte aux pommes ?

Questions

1-What is the name of the gentleman of the story?

a- Henri

b-Francois

c-Carl

d-Damien

2-Who is Zoe?

a-Henri's mother

b-Henri's sister

c-Henri's wife

d-Henri's cousin

3-How old is Henri?

a-Henri is 60 years old

b-Henri is 45 years old

c-Henri is 52 years old

d-Henri is 50 years old

4-How many children does Henri have?

a-Henri has three children

b-Henri does not have any children

c-Henri has two children

d-Henri has six children

5-What's Henri wearing?

a- a shirt and jeans

b-tank top and shorts

c-a hood and shorts

d-satin pajamas

6-What does Henri want to eat for breakfast?

7-What tart does Zoe want to cook?

8-What did Henri and Zoe eat for lunch?

9-Who called on Messenger on Henri's laptop?

10-Why did Zoé make an apple pie?

Réponses

1 - a

2 - c

3 - d

4 - a

5 - b

6 - Henri veut des biscottes et du café.

7 - Zoé veut faire une tarte aux pommes.

8 - Henri et Zoé ont mangé des lasagnes aux champignons pour le déjeuner.

9 - C'est un ami d'Henri qui l'a appelé.

10 - Zoé a fait une tarte aux pommes parce que c'est l'anniversaire de Mathieu aujourd'hui.

Answers

1-a

2-c

3-d

4-a

5-b

6-Henry wants rusks and coffee.

7-Zoe wants to prepare an apple pie.

8-Henri and Zoé ate mushroom lasagna during lunch.

9-It's a friend of Henri who called on Messenger.

10-Zoe made an apple pie because it's Mathieu's birthday today.

Chapter 3 - Animal de compagnie (Pet)

Pixie est une **chatte** à **rayures**. Son **pelage** est gris, noir et blanc. Pixie a deux ans. Elle est très **douce**. Elle adore les **câlins**. Pixie porte un **joli collier**. Le collier est rouge. Il y a le nom de la **propriétaire** de la chatte sur le collier. Le collier est **vert clair**. Le nom de **la propriétaire** est Jenny. Jenny est une petite fille. Elle a huit ans et elle est **rousse**.

Jenny aime les animaux. Elle est fille unique. Les animaux sont ses amis à la maison. Jenny considère les animaux comme ses **camarades**. Elle ne mange pas la **viande** des animaux. Elle n'aime pas les vêtements en **fourrure**. Jenny est végétarienne.

Pixie aime dormir avec Jenny. Elle dort au **pied** du lit. Mais dormir avec un chat **n'est pas bon pour la santé**. En plus, Pixie a des **puces**. **La mère de Jenny interdit** à sa fille de dormir avec un chat. **Pixie n'a plus le droit de s'introduire** dans la chambre de sa maîtresse. Jenny est triste. Mais **c'est pour son bien**.

Jenny a aussi **un poisson rouge**. Le poisson s'appelle Fishy. Fishy est dans **un bocal**. Un jour, Pixie attrape le poisson et le mange. **Jenny écarquille les yeux**. Elle n'a pas le temps de sauver le poisson. Fishy finit dans le **ventre** de Pixie. Jenny est **peinée**. Elle fait le **deuil** de son ami le poisson. **Jenny vide** le bocal. Elle range le bocal dans le débarras. Les chats adorent manger du poisson. Jenny décide de ne plus élever un poisson avec un chat.

Pixie est un chat très propre. Tous les matins, Pixie fait ses besoins dans sa litière. Sa litière est sous les escaliers. Puis Pixie fait sa toilette. La chatte se lèche les pattes. Puis elle va dans le jardin. Elle va sur la pelouse. Elle se prélasse au soleil. Comme tous les chats, Pixie est paresseuse.

Un autre chat rôde autour de la maison. Il s'appelle Bobby. Bobby est le chat de Martin, le voisin. Bobby est orange, noir et blanc. Il n'a pas de collier. Pixie dort sous le soleil. **La gamelle de**

la chatte est dans la cuisine. Vers midi, **Jenny donne à manger à Pixie**. Jenny met des **croquettes pour chat** dans la gamelle. Elle sort et appelle Pixie. La chatte se réveille et va dans la cuisine. Elle mange.

Quelques jours plus tard, Pixie tombe enceinte. Pendant sa grossesse, elle cherche un endroit douillet. Elle s'isole souvent dans l'armoire de Jenny. Après huit semaines, Pixie met au monde trois petits chatons. Jenny les appelle Blacky, Oreo et Bingo.

Blacky est entièrement noir. Oreo est un chat roux. Bingo est noir et blanc. Ils ont tous les yeux jaunes. Jenny offre Blacky à sa grand-mère. Sa grand-mère a besoin d'un chat pour chasser les souris. Mais **Blacky tente toujours de s'enfuir**. La grand-mère de Jenny attache le chat à une corde.

Martin prend Bingo chez lui. Oreo reste dans la maison de Jenny. Le temps passe et les chatons grandissent. Oreo adore le poisson et la **viande hâchée.**

Oréo déteste être **enfermé dans la maison**. La porte est fermée. Oréo saute sur un meuble près de la fenêtre. Il y a **un vase** sur le meuble. Le vase tombe par terre. Le vase est cassé. **Le chat saute par la fenêtre**.

Oreo aime jouer avec **une pelote de laine. Il griffe** le canapé. La mère de Jenny est **fâchée. Ce canapé coûte une fortune. Elle frappe** Oreo avec **un balai**. Oreo est terrifié. Il s'enfuit. **Jenny s'accroupit** pour **caresser** le chat. Puis elle le prend dans ses bras. **La mère de Jenny la gronde. Jenny pose le chat par terre.** Sa mère lui dit de **se laver les mains** avec du **savon**. Jenny obéit.

Un jour, Jenny ne trouve plus Oreo dans la maison. Elle va dans le jardin et l'appelle. Jenny n'obtient aucune réponse. La nuit tombe. Oreo est introuvable. Jenny est inquiète. Sa mère essaie de la rassurer. Mais Oreo ne rentre pas à la maison. Jenny va chez Martin. Elle demande à Martin si Oreo est chez lui. Mais Oreo n'est pas chez Martin. Jenny remercie Martin et retourne dans le jardin. Martin aide Jenny à chercher le chat.

Jenny vérifie **les buissons** et les arbres. Mais **il n'y a aucun chat** dans le jardin. **Il se fait tard**. Jenny rentre à la maison. **Elle n'arrive pas à manger**. Elle pense à Oreo. Jenny monte dans sa chambre. **Elle se prépare pour aller dormir**. Mais **elle ne trouve pas le sommeil**. Jenny se lève. **Elle regarde par la fenêtre**. Mais elle ne voit pas Oreo **dehors**. **Déçue**, elle retourne dans son lit. **Epuisée**, Jenny s'endort vers minuit.

Le lendemain, Jenny descend impatiemment au **rez-de-chaussée**. Mais Oreo n'est pas dans la maison. Jenny pleure. Oreo est perdu. La mère de Jenny la console et la prend dans ses bras. **Jenny déprime**.

Deux jours plus tard, Oreo rentre à la maison. **Il miaule**. Jenny est folle de joie. **Oreo ronronne**. Il est content de retrouver sa maîtresse. Oreo est affamé. La mère de Jenny lui donne de la sardine.

Deux mois plus tard, Pixie tombe malade. Elle est **affaiblie**. Pixie perd l'appétit. **Elle perd du poids**. Elle perd ses poils. Jenny et sa mère l'emmènent chez le vétérinaire. Mais Pixie meurt après trois jours. Jenny pleure à chaudes larmes. **Pixie est enterrée dans le jardin**. Jenny dépose **une fleur** sur la **tombe** du chat.

Jenny a beaucoup de photos de Pixie sur son **appareil photo**. Elle fait **imprimer les photos**. Elle achète un nouvel album photo. Elle met les photos dans l'album. Elle écrit le nom de Pixie sur l'album. Jenny le garde précieusement.

Jenny a un cousin. Il s'appelle Paul. Paul n'aime pas les chats. Les chats sont prétentieux. Paul préfère les chiens. Paul a un chien. Il s'appelle Diggo. Diggo est un cocker anglais. Il est marron. Tous les dimanches, Paul et son père emmènent Diggo dans le parc. Paul joue avec son chien. Diggo est très affectueux. Il aime beaucoup Paul. Son maître s'occupe bien de lui. Digoo aime manger. Il dort dans la cour dans une niche. Parfois, Diggo dort dans la chambre de son maître. Paul est rassuré quand Diggo est près de lui. Le chien garde bien la maison. Diggo n'aime pas les inconnus. Le chien aboie quand il voit des visiteurs inhabituels dans la maison. Les gens ont peur de Diggo. Il est sévère avec les étrangers. Diggo est vacciné contre la rage.

Paul rentre de l'école. **Le chien remue sa queue**. Il est content de voir son maître. **Diggo lèche la main de Paul**. Le petit garçon lave son chien **deux fois par mois**. Entre-temps, il brosse quotidiennement la fourrure du chien.

Le samedi matin, Jenny va chez Paul pour jouer avec lui. Lorsque les enfants jouent dans la cour, Diggo joue avec eux. Diggo connaît bien Jenny et il l'adore. Jenny lui apporte souvent de la **pâtée pour chien**. Jenny pense à **élever un chien**. Mais elle hésite. **Oreo ne s'entend pas avec les chiens.**

English

Pixie is a striped cat. His coat is gray, black and white. Pixie is two years old. She is very soft. She loves hugs. Pixie wears a pretty necklace. The necklace is red. There is the name of the owner of the cat on the collar. The necklace is light green. The owner's name is Jenny. Jenny is a little girl. She is eight years old and she is redheaded.

Jenny loves animals. She is an only child. Animals are his friends at home. Jenny considers animals as her comrades. She does not eat animal meat. She doesn't like fur clothes. Jenny is a vegetarian.

Pixie likes to sleep with Jenny. She sleeps at the foot of the bed. But sleeping with a cat is not good for your health. In addition, Pixie has chips. Jenny's mother forbids her daughter from sleeping with a cat. Pixie is no longer allowed to enter her mistress's bedroom. Jenny is sad. But it's for his own good.

Jenny also has a goldfish. The fish is called Fishy. Fishy is in a jar. One day Pixie catches the fish and eats it. Jenny's eyes widen. She doesn't have time to save the fish. Fishy ends up in Pixie's womb. Jenny is sad. She mourns for her friend the fish. Jenny empties the jar. She puts the jar back in the storage room. Cats love to eat fish. Jenny decides to no longer raise a fish with a cat.

Pixie is a very clean cat. Every morning, Pixie goes to the toilet in her litter box. His litter box is under the stairs. Then Pixie cleans up. The cat licks its legs. Then she goes into the garden. She goes on the lawn. She basks in the sun. Like all cats, Pixie is lazy.

Another cat prowls around the house. His name is Bobby. Bobby is Martin's neighbor cat. Bobby is orange, black and white. He has no collar. Pixie sleeps under the sun. The cat bowl is in the kitchen. Around noon, Jenny feeds Pixie. Jenny puts cat food in the bowl. She goes out and calls Pixie. The cat wakes up and goes into the kitchen. She eats.

A few days later, Pixie becomes pregnant. During her pregnancy, she looks for a cozy place. She often isolates herself in Jenny's wardrobe. After eight weeks, Pixie gives birth to three little kittens. Jenny calls them Blacky, Oreo and Bingo.

Blacky is completely black. Oreo is a red cat. Bingo is black and white. They all have yellow eyes. Jenny offers Blacky to her grandmother. Her grandmother needs a cat to hunt mice. But Blacky is still trying to escape. Jenny's grandmother ties the cat to a rope.

Martin takes Bingo home. Oreo stays in Jenny's house. Time passes and the kittens grow. Oreo loves fish and minced meat.

Oreo hates being locked up in the house. The door is closed. Oreo jumps on a piece of furniture near the window. There is a vase on the furniture. The vase falls to the ground. The vase is broken. The cat jumps out of the window.

Oreo likes to play with a ball of wool. He claws the sofa. Jenny's mother is angry. This sofa costs a fortune. She hits Oreo with a broom. Oreo is terrified. He runs away. Jenny crouched down to pet the cat. Then she takes him in her arms. Jenny's mother scolds her. Jenny puts the cat on the ground. Her mother tells her to wash her hands with soap. Jenny obeys.

One day, Jenny can no longer find Oreo in the house. She goes into the garden and calls her. Jenny gets no response. Night is falling.

Oreo was not found. Jenny is worried. Her mother tries to reassure her. But Oreo doesn't come home. Jenny goes to Martin's house. She asks Martin if Oreo is at home. But Oreo isn't at Martin's. Jenny thanks Martin and returns to the garden. Martin helps Jenny find the cat.

Jenny checks the bushes and trees. But there are no cats in the garden. It's getting late. Jenny comes home. She can't eat. She thinks of Oreo. Jenny goes up to her room. She is getting ready to go to sleep. But she can't sleep. Jenny stands up. She is looking out the window. But she doesn't see Oreo outside. Disappointed, she goes back to her bed. Exhausted, Jenny falls asleep around midnight.

The next day, Jenny impatiently descends to the ground floor. But Oreo is not in the house. Jenny is crying. Oreo is lost. Jenny's mother consoles her and takes her in her arms. Jenny is depressed.

Two days later, Oreo comes home. He meows. Jenny is overjoyed. Oreo purrs. He is happy to find his mistress. Oreo is hungry. Jenny's mother gives him sardines.

Two months later, Pixie fell ill. She is weakened. Pixie loses his appetite. She is losing weight. She is losing her hair. Jenny and her mother take her to the vet. But Pixie dies after three days. Jenny is crying hot. Pixie is buried in the garden. Jenny places a flower on the cat's grave.

Jenny has a lot of Pixie photos on her camera. She has the photos printed. She buys a new photo album. She puts the photos in the album. She writes Pixie's name on the album. Jenny keeps it preciously.

Jenny has a cousin. His name is Paul. Paul doesn't like cats. Cats are pretentious. Paul prefers dogs. Paul has a dog. His name is Diggo. Diggo is an English cocker spaniel. He's brown. Every Sunday, Paul and his father take Diggo to the park. Paul plays with his dog. Diggo is very affectionate. He really likes Paul. His master takes good care of him. Digoo likes to eat. He sleeps in the yard in a niche. Sometimes Diggo sleeps in his master's bedroom. Paul is reassured when Diggo is near him. The dog keeps the house well. Diggo does not like strangers. The dog barks when he sees unusual visitors in the house. People are afraid of Diggo. He is severe with strangers. Diggo is vaccinated against rabies.

Paul is coming home from school. The dog wags its tail. He is happy to see his master. Diggo licks Paul's hand. The little boy washes his dog twice a month. Meanwhile, he brushes the dog's fur daily.

On Saturday morning, Jenny goes to Paul's house to play with him. When the children play in the yard, Diggo plays with them. Diggo knows Jenny well and loves her. Jenny often brings him dog food. Jenny is thinking of raising a dog. But she hesitates. Oreo does not get along with dogs.

Vocabulary

Animal de compagnie – pet house

Chat/chatte – cat (M/F)

Rayure(s) – stripe(s)

Pelage – fur

Doux/douce – sweet

Câlin(s) – hug(s)

Joli – pretty

Collier – collar

Vert clair – light green

La propriétaire – the owner

Roux/rousse – redhead (M/F)

Camarade(s) – friend(s)

Viande – meat

Fourrure - fur

...n'est pas bon pour la santé – ...is not healthy

Puce(s) – flea(s)

Interdire (La mère de Jenny interdit...) – to forbid (Jenny's mother forbids...)

Pixie n'a plus le droit de... - Pixie is not allowed to...

S'introduire – to slip inside

C'est pour son bien – it's for her sake

Un bocal – a fish bowl

Un poisson rouge – a goldfish

Jenny écarquille les yeux – Jenny opens her eyes wide

Ventre – stomach

Peiné/Peinée – sad (M/F)

Deuil – mourning

Vider (Jenny vide...) – empty (Jenny empties)

Pied - foot

Propre – clean

Pixie fait ses besoins – Pixie does its business

Litière – litter

Sous les escaliers – under the stairs

La chatte se lèche les pattes – the cat is licking its paws

La pelouse – the grass

Elle se prélasse au soleil - The cat was basking in the sun

Comme tous les chats – as all cats

Paresseux/paresseuse – lazy (M/F)

Un autre chat rôde autour de la maison – Another cat is prowling around the house

La gamelle de la chatte – the cat's dish

Jenny donne à manger à Pixie – Jenny is feeding Pixie

Croquettes pour chat – cat food

Grossesse - pregnancy

Douillet – cozy

S'isoler (Elle s'isole) – to shut yourself away (She often shuts himself away)

Chaton(s) – kitten(s)

Blacky tente toujours de s'enfuir – Blacky always tries to escape

Viande hâchée – ground meat

Enfermé dans la maison – cooped up in the house

Le chat saute par la fenêtre – the cat jumps out the window

Une pelote de laine – a ball of wool

Griffer (Il griffe) – to scratch (he scratches)

Fâché/Fâchée – angry (M/F)

Ce canapé coûte une fortune – this couch is really expensive

Frapper (Elle frappe) – hit (she hits)

Un balai – a broom

S'accroupir (Jenny s'accroupit) – squat down (Jenny squats down)

Caresser – stroke

La mère de Jenny la gronde – Jenny's mother tells her off

Jenny pose le chat par terre – Jenny puts the cat down

Se laver les mains – wash hands

Savon - soap

Jenny caresse le chat – Jenny strokes the cat

Les souris - mice

Introuvable – nowhere to be found

Inquiet/Inquiète – uneasy (M/F)

Essayer (Sa mère essaie) – try (her mother tries)

Les buissons – the bushes

Il n'y a aucun chat – there is no cat

Il se fait tard – it's getting late

Elle n'arrive pas à manger – she can't eat anything

Elle se prépare pour aller dormir – she is getting ready for bed

Elle ne trouve pas le sommeil – she can't sleep

Elle regarde par la fenêtre – she is looking through the window

Dehors – outside

Déçu/Déçue – disappointed (M/F)

Epuisé/Epuisée – exhausted

Rez-de-chaussée -first floor

Jenny déprime – Jenny gets depressed

Il miaule – he meows

Oreo ronronne – Oreo is purring

Affaibli/Affaiblie – weakened (M/F)

Elle perd du poids – she loses weight

Pixie est enterrée dans le jardin – Pixie is buried in the garden

Une fleur – a flower

Tombe - grave

Appareil photo - camera

Imprimer les photos – print the photos

Une niche – a doghouse

Le chien aboie – the dog barks

Visiteurs inhabituels – unusual visitors

Contre – against

La rage - rabies

Le chien remue sa queue – the dog wags its tail

Diggo lèche la main de Paul – Diggo licks Paul's hand

Deux fois par mois – twice a month

Pâtée pour chien – dog food

Élever un chien – raise a dog

Oreo ne s'entend pas avec les chiens – Oreo doesn't get along with dogs

Chapter 4 - Une vie mouvementée (An Eventful Life)

Martin Martins est en couple avec Jeanne. Martin a trente ans. Il travaille. Jeanne a vingt-et-un ans. Elle est étudiante à l'université. Elle est en première année. Au cours de l'année universitaire, les parents de Jeanne ne peuvent plus supporter les frais d'études de leur fille. Les parents de Jeanne sont pauvres. Au même moment, Jeanne tombe enceinte de Martin. La vie de Jeanne est bouleversée. Elle arrête ses études. Elle va chez le gynécologue.

Quatre mois plus tard, Martin emmène Jeanne à la mairie. Il l'épouse. Jeanne déménage chez son mari. Jeanne et Martin préparent la venue du bébé. Ils aménagent une pièce de la maison en chambre de bébé. Les futurs parents achètent un berceau, une commode, une poussette, un sac à langer, des bavoirs, un thermomètre de bain, un biberon, des paquets de couche, des lingettes pour bébé, des couvertures, des draps, une table à langer, un babyphone, des jouets, du savon pour bébé, du shampoing pour bébé, une brosse à cheveux pour bébé, une tétine, des capes de bain, et des vêtements pour bébé. Les vêtements pour bébé qu'ils achètent sont des brassières pour bébé, des chaussettes, des bonnets et des bodies. Ils peignent les murs de la chambre en bleu ciel. Ils mettent des autocollants sur les murs. Puis ils mettent des décorations enfantines dans la chambre. Ils nettoient la chambre.

Après quatre mois et quelques semaines, Jeanne perds les eaux. Elle envoie un message urgent à Martin. Jeanne appelle un taxi et va à l'hôpital.

Martin la rejoint rapidement à l'hôpital. Jeanne accouche d'un garçon. Elle le nomme Micha. Micha pèse 3kilos 200 à sa naissance. Il mesure 50 centimètres. Les parents de Jeanne lui rendent visitent à l'hôpital. La mère de Jeanne est sa garde-malade pendant son séjour à l'hôpital.

Trois jours plus tard, Jeanne sort de l'hôpital. Elle rentre avec le bébé.

Le temps passe. Micha a neuf mois. Martin travaille comme cadre d'entreprise depuis quelques années. Il espère bientôt obtenir une promotion. Jeanne est femme au foyer. Jeanne s'occupe de la maison et du bébé. Ces responsabilités occupent tout son temps. Tous les soirs, Jeanne est exténuée.

En plus, Micha est un bébé difficile. Toutes les nuits, Micha se réveille en plein milieu de la nuit. Il pleure bruyamment. Même les voisins entendent les cris du bébé. Les voisins sont indulgents envers la famille Martins. Elever un bébé n'est pas une tâche aisée.

Les pleurs du bébé réveillent Martin et Jeanne. Mais Martin fait la sourde oreille. Jeanne se lève. Jeanne va dans la chambre d'enfant. Elle prend le bébé. Micha cesse de pleurer. Puis Jeanne l'allaite. Micha s'endort dans les bras de sa mère. Jeanne remet Micha dans le berceau. Jeanne retourne dans son lit.

Une heure plus tard, Jeanne est à moitié endormie. Micha se réveille. Il se remet à pleurer.

- S'il te plaît, va voir le bébé, Martin, murmure Jeanne à son mari. Il pleure encore.

- Va le voir, répond Martin. Tu sais t'y prendre avec lui.

- Je l'ai déjà consolé tout à l'heure. Je dors à peine. A ton tour maintenant.

- Chérie, je suis fatigué. Je me réveille très tôt demain matin pour aller au bureau. Micha a peut-être encore faim. Moi, je ne peux pas l'allaiter.

Jeanne soupire. Elle se lève encore une fois. Elle va dans la chambre du bébé. Elle le prend dans ses bras. Micha se rendort. Jeanne s'allonge sur le lit dans la chambre de Micha. Elle met le bébé près d'elle. Jeanne s'endort à son tour.

English

Martin Martins is in a relationship with Jeanne. Martin is thirty years old. He works. Jeanne is twenty-one years old. She is a university student. She is in first year. During the academic year, Jeanne's parents can no longer bear the cost of their daughter's education. Jeanne's parents are poor. At the same time, Jeanne becomes pregnant with Martin. Jeanne's life is turned upside down. She stops her studies. She goes to the gynecologist.

Four months later, Martin takes Jeanne to the town hall. He marries her. Jeanne moves in with her husband. Jeanne and Martin prepare the coming of the baby. They set up a room in the house as a baby room. Prospective parents buy a crib, dresser, stroller, diaper bag, bibs, bath thermometer, baby bottle, diaper packs, baby wipes, blankets, sheets, changing table, baby monitor, toys, baby soap, baby shampoo, baby hair brush, pacifier, bathing capes, and baby clothes. The baby clothes they buy are baby bras, socks, hats and bodysuits. They paint the walls of the room in sky blue. They put stickers on the walls. Then they put childish decorations in the room. They clean the room.

After four months and a few weeks, Jeanne lost the waters. She sends an urgent message to Martin. Jeanne calls a taxi and goes to the hospital.

Martin quickly joins her at the hospital. Jeanne gives birth to a boy. She names him Micha. Micha weighs 3kilos 200 at birth. It measures 50 centimeters. Jeanne's parents visit her at the hospital. Jeanne's mother is her nurse during her hospital stay.

Three days later, Jeanne leaves the hospital. She comes home with the baby.

Time passes. Micha is nine months old. Martin has worked as a business executive for several years. He hopes to get promoted soon. Jeanne is a housewife. Jeanne takes care of the house and the baby. These responsibilities occupy all its time. Jeanne is exhausted every evening.

In addition, Micha is a difficult baby. Micha wakes up in the middle of the night every night. He is crying loudly. Even the neighbors hear the baby's cries. Neighbors are indulgent towards the Martins family. Raising a baby is not an easy task.

The baby's crying awakens Martin and Jeanne. But Martin turns a deaf ear. Jeanne gets up. Jeanne goes to the nursery. She takes the baby. Micha stops crying. Then Jeanne breastfeeds her. Micha falls asleep in his mother's arms. Jeanne puts Micha back in the cradle. Jeanne goes back to her bed.

An hour later, Jeanne is half asleep. Micha wakes up. He starts to cry again.

- Please go see the baby, Martin, Jeanne whispers to her husband. He is still crying.

- Go see him, Martin answers. You know how to do it with him.

- I already comforted him earlier. I hardly sleep. Your turn now.

- Honey, I'm tired. I wake up very early tomorrow morning to go to the office. Micha may still be hungry. I can't breastfeed her.

Jeanne sighs. She gets up again. She goes to the baby's room. She takes him in her arms. Micha goes back to sleep. Jeanne lies on the bed in Micha's room. She puts the baby near her. Jeanne falls asleep in turn.

Vocabulary

Mouvementé – hectic

Martin est en couple avec Jeanne – Martin is in a relationship with Jeanne

Année universitaire – academic year

Supporter les frais d'études – pay the education costs

Pauvre(s) - poor

Au même moment – at the same time

Jeanne tombe enceinte de Martin – Jeanne got pregnant from Martin

La vie de Jeanne est bouleversée – Jeanne's life is totally disrupted

Elle arrête ses études – she drops out college

Mairie – city hall

Il l'épouse – he marries her

Ils aménagent une pièce de la maison en chambre de bébé - they convert a room of the house into a nursery

Un berceau – a cradle

Une commode – a chest of drawers

Une poussette – a stroller

Un sac à langer – a diaper bag

Bavoir(s) – bib(s)

Un thermomètre de bain – a bath thermometer

Un biberon – a baby's bottle

Couche – diaper

Lingettes pour bébé – baby wipes

Une table à langer – a baby-changing table

Un babyphone – a baby monitor

Une brosse à cheveux – a hairbrush

Une tétine – a pacifier

Vêtements pour bébé – baby clothes

Brassière(s) – vest(s)

Chaussette(s) – sock(s)

Ils peignent les murs – they paint the walls

Bleu ciel – sky-blue

Autocollant(s) – sticker(s)

Enfantin(s)/Enfantine(s) – childish (M/F)

Jeanne perd les eaux – her waters break

Jeanne accouche d'un garçon – Jeanne gives birth to a son

Garde-malade – nurse

Séjour à l'hôpital – hospital stay

Micha a neuf mois – Micha is nine months old

Cadre d'entreprise – corporate executive

Obtenir une promotion – get promoted

Femme au foyer - housewife

Jeanne s'occupe de la maison – she looks after the house

Ces responsabilités occupent tout son temps - these responsibilities keep her busy all the time

Tous les soirs – every night

Exténué/Exténuée – exhausted (M/F)

Un bébé difficile – a fussy baby

Il pleure bruyamment – he cries loudly

Même les voisins entendent les cris du bébé – even the neighbors hear the cry of the baby

Les voisins sont indulgents envers la famille Martins - The neighbors are indulgent towards the Martins family

Elever un bébé – raise a baby

Une tâche aisée – an easy task

Martin fait la sourde oreille – Martin turns a deaf ear

Micha cesse de pleurer – Micha stops crying

Jeanne l'allaite – Jeanne nurses him

Jeanne remet Micha dans le berceau - Jeanne puts Micha back in the cradle

Jeanne est à moitié endormie – Jeanne is half asleep

Il se remet à pleurer – he cries again

Tu sais t'y prendre avec lui – you are very good with him

Tout à l'heure – earlier

Je dors à peine – I barely sleep

A ton tour maintenant – now it's your turn

Chérie – honey

Pour aller au bureau – to go to the office

Encore une fois – once again

Micha se rendort – Micha falls asleep again

Chapter 5 - Alimentation

Louis suivait un régime depuis quatre semaines consécutives, et il avait déjà perdu 5 kilogrammes. Son nouveau régime est très strict, mais il le suit consciencieusement.

Au petit-déjeuner, il mange un petit bol de flocons d'avoine préparés au micro-ondes avec de l'eau ou du lait. Il mange également une portion de fruit avec ses flocons d'avoine : une banane, des fraises ou une mangue. Et évidemment, son petit-déjeuner ne pourrait pas être complet sans une tasse de café !

Pour le déjeuner, Louis opte pour un repas léger afin d'optimiser sa perte de poids, donc généralement, il mange une salade d'épinards. Dans sa salade, il ajoute des carottes, des oignons, des concombres, des haricots, des croûtons et des noix. Les sauces sont généralement très caloriques, il en ajoute donc une toute petite goutte. Si la salade ne le rassasie pas, il complète son repas avec de la soupe. Il choisit habituellement une soupe à la tomate car il s'agit de sa soupe préférée.

Pour le dîner, plusieurs options sont disponibles, en fonction de ses préférences pour le soir. Il peut manger des pâtes et des légumes cuisinés à l'huile d'olive et aux épices italiennes. Il peut également opter pour du riz et des haricots avec une sauce à l'ail et à l'oignon. Il peut aussi choisir un plat au curry thaïlandais accompagné de chou kale et de patate douce. Toutes ces options nécessitent une préparation culinaire, mais le résultat en vaut la peine.

Tout se passait très bien pour Louis jusqu'au début de la cinquième semaine. Comme la plupart d'entre nous, il occupe un emploi stressant et contraignant et il n'a donc pas toujours le temps de préparer tous ses repas. Son énergie a commencé à diminuer alors que son appétit et sa faim ont rapidement augmenté.

Le petit bol de flocons d'avoine a rapidement été remplacé par un grand bol de céréales sucrées. Et le café noir était désormais généreusement additionné de crème à café hypercalorique.

La salade du déjeuner s'est transformée en repas de fast-food, puisque Louis était toujours en retard pour les réunions. Au départ, il buvait de l'eau lors du déjeuner et de ses autres repas, mais il optait à présent pour du soda.

Et le dîner, après quelques temps, est devenu catastrophique. Louis rentrait du travail épuisé et il manquait de motivation pour cuisiner. La pizza, la crème glacée, les frites et les en-cas constituaient des options bien plus pratiques et ces aliments l'aidaient à apaiser son anxiété.

Après plusieurs semaines, il avait repris les 5 kilogrammes qu'il avait perdues et pour couronner le tout, il avait même pris 5 kilogrammes supplémentaires ! Cet échec a grandement affecté l'humeur de Louis. Il s'est engagé à suivre un régime encore plus strict et à réduire encore plus ses rations la prochaine fois.

Malheureusement, il ne réalise pas qu'une grande réduction de l'apport calorique provoque une baisse d'énergie tout aussi importante et des envies de malbouffe. Après de nombreuses tentatives, il a finalement compris qu'il était plus judicieux de commencer un régime en consommant de la nourriture saine en grande quantité avant de réduire progressivement son apport calorique.

English

Louis has been on a diet now for four weeks and has already lost five kilos. His new diet is very strict, but he follows it extremely closely.

For breakfast, he eats a small bowl of oatmeal cooked in the microwave with either water or milk. He also has a serving of fruit with his oatmeal, like a banana, strawberries, or a mango. And of course, what breakfast would be complete without a cup of coffee?

For lunch, Louis prefers to eat a light meal to maximize his weight loss, so he usually has a spinach salad. On top of his salad, he puts carrots, onions, cucumbers, beans, croutons, and nuts. Dressing tends to have a lot of calories, so he adds just a small dab. If the salad does not fill him up, he'll also eat some soup. Usually, it's tomato soup, as that is his favorite.

For dinner, there are a few options available, depending on what he wants that night. He can have a pasta and vegetable mix cooked in olive oil and Italian spices. Or he can have rice and beans topped with a garlic and onion sauce. He can also have a Thai curry dish with kale and sweet potato. All choices require some cooking, but it's worth it in the end.

All was going pretty well for Louis until the fifth week started. Like many of us, he works a stressful and demanding job, so there wasn't always enough time to prepare every meal. His energy started dropping, while his appetite and hunger started rising rapidly.

Soon, the small bowl of oatmeal for breakfast became the large bowl of sugary cereal. And the black coffee was now drowned in a high calorie coffee creamer.

The salad for lunch turned into fast food meals, since Louis was always running late for meetings. Originally, he was drinking water with this meal as well as every meal, but now it was soda.

And dinner was just hopeless after a while. Louis would come home exhausted from work and could not bring himself to cook. Pizza, ice cream, french fries, and snacks were much easier choices and helped take his mind off all the anxiety.

Several weeks later, he had regained all five kilos he had lost and even gained an additional five kilos on top of that! The failure made Louis feel even worse. He vowed, for his next diet, that he would be even more strict and eat even less food.

Unfortunately, he doesn't realize that the massive drop in calories is causing an equally massive dip in his energy levels and cravings for junk food. It would take many attempts before he finally learned that starting his diet with lots of healthy foods and slowly cutting down calories would be the wiser move.

Vocabulary

alimentation --- food

régime --- diet

perdre du poids --- to lose weight

kilogrammes --- kilograms

petit-déjeuner --- breakfast

bol --- bowl

flocons d'avoine --- oatmeal

micro-ondes --- microwave

lait --- milk

une portion de --- a serving of

fruit --- fruit

banane --- banana

fraise --- strawberry

mangue --- mango

tasse de café --- cup of coffee

déjeuner --- lunch

repas léger --- light meal

salade d'épinards --- spinach salad

carottes --- carrots

oignons --- onions

concombres --- cucumbers

haricots --- beans

croûtons --- croutons

noix --- nuts

sauce --- dressing

calories --- calories

une toute petite goutte --- a small dab

rassasier --- to fill up

soupe à la tomate --- tomato soup

préférée --- favorite

dîner --- dinner

options --- options, choices

le soir --- evening

des pâtes et des légumes --- pasta and vegetable mix

huile d'olive --- olive oil

épices italiennes --- Italian spices

riz et haricots --- rice and beans

sauce à l'ail et aux oignons --- garlic and onion sauce

plat au curry thaïlandais --- Thai curry dish

chou kale --- kale

patate douce --- sweet potato

préparation culinaire --- cooking

emploi stressant et contraignant --- stressful and demanding job

préparer un repas --- to prepare a meal

énergie --- energy

appétit --- appetite

faim --- hunger

céréales sucrées --- sugary cereal

café noir --- black coffee

crème à café --- coffee creamer

hypercalorique --- high-calorie

repas de fast-food --- fast food meals

pizza --- pizza

crème glacée --- ice cream

frites --- french fries

en-cas --- snacks

anxiété --- anxiety

strict --- strict

envies --- cravings

malbouffe --- junk food

nourriture saine --- healthy food

réduire son apport calorique --- to cut down on calories

Questions

1. Quelle quantité de sauce Louis ajoute-t-il dans sa salade ?

A) Pas de sauce

B) Un grande dose

C) Une toute petite goutte

D) Il la recouvre de sauce

2. Quel est le repas préféré de Louis pour le dîner ?

A) Des pâtes et des légumes cuisinés à l'huile d'olive et aux épices italiennes

B) Du riz et des haricots avec une sauce à l'ail et à l'oignon

C) Un plat au curry thaïlandais accompagné de chou kale et de patate douce

D) Le repas préféré de Louis n'est pas mentionné dans l'histoire.

3. Que s'est-il passé lors de la cinquième semaine du régime de Louis ?

A) Son énergie a commencé à augmenter alors que son appétit et sa faim ont rapidement diminué.

B) Son énergie a commencé à diminuer alors que son appétit et sa faim ont rapidement augmenté.

C) Son énergie est restée stable alors que son appétit et sa faim ont rapidement augmenté.

D) Son énergie a commencé à diminuer alors que son appétit et sa faim sont restés stables.

4. La pizza, la crème glacée, les frites et les en-cas sont généralement considérés comme...

A) des aliments sains.

B) un petit-déjeuner équilibré.

C) de la malbouffe.

D) des aliments hypocaloriques.

5. Si Louis pesait 90 kilos quand il a commencé son régime, combine pèse-t-il à la fin de l'histoire ?

A) 85 kilos

B) 90 kilos

C) 95 kilos

D) 100 kilos

Answers

1) C

2) D

3) B

4) C

5) C

Chapter 6 - Exercice (Exercise)

Louis décide qu'il est grand temps de prendre davantage soin de lui-même, il prend la décision de faire de l'exercice. Cette activité lui permettra de gérer son stress, et même de perdre ses kilos superflus. Dès la semaine prochaine, il débutera un programme de jogging qui lui permettra d'aller courir cinq fois par semaine.

Le premier jour, il se lève très tôt avant le travail, il enfile ses chaussures de sport et il est impatient de commencer. Après quelques étirements simples, la séance de jogging débute et tout se passe tout à fait bien. Mais pourtant, au bout de deux minutes à peine, Louis est essoufflé. Il respire difficilement et sa respiration devient très bruyante. Et après seulement cinq minutes, il cesse de courir et commence à marcher. Il prend conscience de la situation. Il est en mauvaise condition physique.

Le temps passe. Les jours deviennent des semaines. Les semaines deviennent des mois. Louis parvient désormais à courir sans s'arrêter pendant 30 minutes consécutives. Il pense qu'il pourra courir un marathon dans un an ou deux. Il est fier de ses progrès, mais son entraînement uniquement consacré au cardio est devenu extrêmement ennuyeux. L'étape suivante consiste donc à le modifier.

Paul et Julien, les amis de Louis, lui ont proposé de soulever des poids après le travail, ils se sont donc tous retrouvés à la salle de sport et ils étaient impatients de passer du temps ensemble. Ils s'engagent à suivre un programme d'entraînement en s'exerçant cinq fois par semaine, et en musclant une zone de leur corps chaque semaine : torse, dos, épaules, jambes et bras.

Chaque jour nécessitait des efforts intenses, mais l'afflux d'endorphines qu'ils ressentaient à la fin de chaque séance d'exercice les récompensaient amplement. Pour se reposer, les hommes se détendaient en marchant sur les tapis de course ou en transpirant dans le sauna pendant 10 minutes.

Le temps passe, et Louis décide que l'haltérophilie ne lui convient pas. Paul et Julien se montrent trop compétitifs dans ce domaine, et l'intensité des entraînements commence à rendre cette activité bien plus contraignante qu'amusante. Comme des cours de yoga sont proposés par la salle de sport, Louis décide donc de s'inscrire, et il est impatient de débuter cette nouvelle activité.

Le cours permet de découvrir un grand nombre d'étirements et de postures qui sont conçus pour assouplir le corps et apaiser l'esprit. Les cours sont loin d'être faciles et ils font transpirer tous les élèves. Cette activité n'est toutefois pas aussi intense que l'haltérophilie. Et elle est beaucoup plus amusante et relaxante que le jogging. Après chaque séance, Louis se sent revigoré et il est impatient de revenir pour en apprendre davantage. Il commence même à discuter avec plusieurs jolies filles qu'il a hâte de revoir chaque semaine. Il s'agit d'un programme qui inclut un avantage supplémentaire à préserver.

English

Louis decides that he should really start taking better care of himself by exercising. It will help manage his stress and even help him lose the extra weight he put on. Starting next week, he will begin a jogging routine, where he will run five days a week.

On the first day, he wakes up extra early before work and puts on his tennis shoes, eager to get started. After some basic stretches, the jogging starts, and everything seems to go well. Within two minutes, however, Louis is out of breath. He's wheezing, and his breathing becomes super heavy. And after just five minutes, the jogging is replaced by walking. He realizes the truth. He is out of shape.

As time passes, days become weeks. Weeks become months. Louis is now able to run continually for 30 minutes. Within a year or two, he could be running a marathon, he thinks. While he's proud of his improvement, doing nothing but cardio has grown extremely boring, so a change of routine is the next step.

Louis's friends Paul and Julien have invited him to come lift weights after work, so they all meet at the gym, eager to spend some time together. They decide to commit to a workout program five days a week, where they will work one body part per week: chest, back, shoulders, legs, and arms.

Each day requires strenuous effort, but the endorphin rush at the end of each workout makes it all worth it. To cool down, the men relax by walking on the treadmills or sweating it out in the sauna for 10 minutes.

Some time passes, and Louis decides that weightlifting isn't a good fit for him. Paul and Julien get too competitive with it, and the intensity of the workouts has become more painful than fun. At the gym, however, they offer yoga classes, so Louis signs up, eager to start.

The classes teach a variety of stretches and poses designed to loosen the body and calm the mind. The lessons are not easy by any means, and they make all the students sweat. Yet, it's not as intense as weightlifting. And it's much more fun and relaxing than jogging. Louis leaves each class feeling refreshed and excited to come back for more. He even starts chatting with some pretty girls whom he looks forward to seeing every week. It's a routine with an extra incentive to maintain.

Vocabulary

Exercice --- exercise

Stress --- stress

Jogging --- jogging

Programme --- routine

Se lever très tôt --- to wake up extra early

Chaussures de sport --- tennis shoes

Étirements simples --- basic stretches

Être essoufflé --- to be out of breath

Respire difficilement --- wheezing

Respiration --- breathing

Marcher --- to walk

Être en mauvaise condition physique --- to be out of shape

Courir sans s'arrêter --- to continually run

Courir un marathon --- running a marathon

Cardio --- cardio

Soulever des poids --- to lift weights

Salle de sport --- gym

Passer du temps ensemble --- to spend some time together

S'engager --- to commit

Programme d'entraînement --- workout program

Torse --- chest

Dos --- back

Épaules --- shoulders

Jambes --- legs

Bras --- arms

Efforts intenses --- strenuous effort

Afflux d'endorphines --- endorphin rush

Se reposer --- to cool down

Se détendre --- to relax

Tapis de course --- treadmills

Transpirant --- sweating it out

Sauna --- sauna

Haltérophilie --- weightlifting

Trop compétitifs --- too competitive

Intensité --- intensity

Cours de yoga --- yoga classes

S'inscrire --- to sign up, to enroll

Étirements et postures --- stretches and poses

Assouplir le corps --- to loosen the body

Apaiser l'esprit --- to calm the mind

Transpirer --- to sweat

Impatient de revenir --- excited to come back

Apprendre --- to learn

Avantage supplémentaire --- extra incentive

Préserver --- to maintain

Questions

1. Quel type de chaussure Louis portait-il pour courir ?

A) Chaussures à crampons

B) Chaussures de sport

C) Talons hauts

D) Bottes de course

2. Pourquoi Louis-a-t-il cessé de courir ?

A) Il a atteint son objectif.

B) Il en avait assez de se lever tôt.

C) Il s'ennuyait énormément.

D) Il ne voulait pas courir un marathon.

3. Louis, Paul, et Julien se sont engagés à suivre un programme d'entraînement qui était consacré...

A) au torse, au dos, aux épaules, aux jambes et aux bras.

B) au torse, au dos, à la course, aux jambes et au cardio.

C) au torse, à la natation, aux épaules, à la course et aux bras.

D) au yoga, au cardio, au jogging, à l'haltérophilie et aux activités sportives.

4. Que font les trois amis pour se détendre après l'entraînement ?

A) Ils courent sur les tapis de course en écoutant de la musique.

B) Ils s'exercent en faisant une séance de yoga de 10 minutes.

C) Ils nagent dans la piscine ou ils prennent une douche chaude.

D) Ils marchent sur les tapis de course ou ils transpirent dans le sauna pendant 10 minutes.

5. Pourquoi Louis a-t-il cessé de soulever des poids ?

A) Il s'ennuyait énormément.

B) Les entraînements étaient trop intenses et trop compétitifs.

C) Paul et Julien ont arrêté de soulever des poids.

D) Louis s'est blessé.

Answers :

1) B

2) C

3) A

4) D

5) B

Chapter 7 - Paris, la plus belle ville du monde (Paris, the most beautiful city in the world)

Martin est un jeune homme plein d'énergie et d'ambition. Il n'est pas salarié. Il travaille **à son compte**. En fait, Martin a une grande passion : Paris. Martin vit à Paris depuis qu'il est enfant. Il connaît Paris par cœur, toutes les avenues, boulevards, rues, **raccourcis**, **passages** secrets, les monuments, et même les célèbres catacombes. Il aurait pu faire cuisinier comme son amie Amanda, mais il n'aimait pas ça. Il a **failli** faire maître d'hôtel. Mais finalement, quand Martin est sorti de l'école de tourisme, il **s'est lancé** en tant que guide touristique, tout seul, en freelance.

Il possède un site internet sur lequel sont affichées toutes les informations le concernant. Ainsi, les touristes qui désirent avoir un guide privé pour visiter la ville de Paris peuvent le trouver sur internet. Martin propose différentes **formules**. La visite simple, avec promenade parisienne classique sur une journée découverte seulement, ou **éventuellement** plusieurs jours. La visite intermédiaire, qui inclut en plus de la balade, une large **gamme** de restaurants à découvrir, allant du camion-restaurant permettant de **manger sur le pouce** au restaurant de bonne qualité. Il est naturellement inutile de **préciser** que Martin connaît tous les restaurants de Paris. La visite de luxe, sur une semaine minimum, avec restaurants gastronomiques, musées, et aussi **boîte de nuit** ou spectacles vivants dans les différents théâtres de Paris. Il existe une formule de luxe avec bonus, dans laquelle s'ajoute une visite des catacombes et une sélection des magasins les plus **réputés** de la capitale. De plus, Martin propose une formule à la carte, dans laquelle il est possible de faire un mélange de toutes les propositions. On peut aussi bien aller au théâtre que manger sur le pouce. Ou bien visiter les catacombes puis manger au Ritz, le fameux restaurant gastronomique, **à proximité de** l'Élysée, sur la place de la Concorde.

Mais cette année, un problème **de taille** se pose. Une nouvelle agence vient de s'installer dans la ville : TransVoyage. TransVoyage est une agence touristique **gigantesque**. Elle **inonde** le marché du tourisme **à coup de** campagnes de publicité surprenantes et d'offres **défiant toute concurrence**, si bien que tous les entrepreneurs individuels comme Martin se retrouvent en grande difficulté. L'année précédente, Martin a **enregistré un chiffre d'affaires** de près de trente-deux mille euros. Cette année, il a perdu la moitié de ses clients. Martin doute énormément ces derniers temps.

Il ne sait pas s'il va pouvoir continuer comme ça ; les fins de mois sont de plus en plus difficiles. TransVoyage gagne de plus en plus d'affaires et vient de signer un contrat avec tous les Ibis Hôtels de Paris. Martin pourrait se restreindre à la banlieue chic de Paris comme Boulogne, Neuilly-sur-Seine ou même Versailles et son très célèbre château officiel des Rois de France et de Navarre. Mais malheureusement, la banlieue n'attire pas les touristes qui souhaitent le plus souvent visiter le centre-ville, comme Chatelet-les-Halles, Notre-Dame de Paris et le quartier Latin, la fontaine Saint-Michel, le Panthéon...etc.

Tout espoir semble perdu pour Martin. Mais un beau jour d'été, un couple américain s'adresse à lui.

— Messieurs dames, que puis-je faire pour vous ?

Martin a toujours eu le sens de la courtoisie.

— Bonjour monsieur. Nous venons vers vous car nous sommes très déçus, **voire même** en colère !

— Ah oui ?! **Mais voyons**, pourquoi être en colère ? Vous êtes ici dans la plus belle ville du monde !

— Oui, **justement** ! Nous aimerions avoir une visite **digne** de cette ville. TransVoyage a **trahi** notre confiance, leur accueil était **médiocre**, à la limite de l'insulte !

— Ah je vois ! Bien, écoutez, je suis à votre entière disposition, dites-moi ce qui vous ferait plaisir, et je vous proposerai une formule qui vous **conviendra**, soyez-en sûr !

— Vous avez carte blanche ! Nous n'avons aucune limite de budget. Nous avons une semaine à partir d'aujourd'hui.

— Alors c'est parti ! Votre visite commence dès maintenant !

Martin sort à toute allure de son appartement et retrouve ses clients dans le très joli quartier du XVème arrondissement. En avant, toute ! Direction, le métro Parisien, arrêt *La-Motte-Piquet-Grenelle* ! Hors de question de visiter Paris sans prendre le métro si emblématique, au moins une fois ! Il ne sert à rien de louer un véhicule, il y a trop de voitures à Paris, et donc trop d'embouteillages. Donc, métro, ligne 6, premier arrêt, champs de Mars et la Tour Eiffel. Ça commence bien pour les deux Américains. En face de la Tour Eiffel, le somptueux Trocadéro. Ensuite, Martin les fait longer la Seine afin de leur faire découvrir les magnifiques quais de Seine avec leurs célèbres bouquinistes. Visite du musée du quai Branly. Une halte devant le palais des Invalides a été obligatoire. Juste en face se trouve le superbe pont Alexandre III. Juste derrière, l'incroyable dôme de verre du Grand Palais.

Ils ont naturellement rejoint l'avenue des Champs-Élysées qui se trouve dans la continuité. Ils ont **dégusté** des plats surprenants au restaurant Bouddha Bar, derrière le Ritz, place de la concorde. Et cela durant une semaine entière, ils sont allés à la comédie française pour assister à une **pièce** de Molière, ainsi qu'au théâtre de l'Odéon. Une semaine de rêve. Les deux Américains ont été si contents, qu'ils en ont parlé à tous leurs amis. Et aujourd'hui, Martin fait deux fois plus de chiffre d'affaires qu'il n'en avait jamais fait auparavant. TransVoyage a fait **faillite** deux ans plus tard pour cause d'insatisfaction générale de la clientèle. Et les visites étaient trop chères. Moralité, il vaut toujours mieux se **fier** à quelqu'un de passionné.

English

Martin is a young man full of energy and ambition. He is not an employee. He works for himself. In fact, Martin has a great passion: Paris. Martin has lived in Paris since he was a child. He knows Paris by heart, all the avenues, boulevards, streets, shortcuts, secret passages, monuments, and even the famous catacombs. He could have cooked like his friend Amanda, but he didn't like it. He almost made a butler. But ultimately, when Martin graduated from tourism school, he started out as a freelance tour guide on his own.

He has a website on which all information concerning him is posted. Thus, tourists who wish to have a private guide to visit the city of Paris can find it on the internet. Martin offers different formulas. The simple visit, with classic Parisian walk on a discovery day only, or possibly several days. The intermediate visit, which includes in addition to the ride, a wide range of restaurants to discover, ranging from the food truck to eat on the go at the restaurant of good quality. It goes without saying that Martin knows all the restaurants in Paris. The luxury visit, over a week minimum, with gourmet restaurants, museums, and also nightclub or live shows in the various theaters of Paris. There is a luxury formula with bonus, in addition to a visit to the catacombs and a selection of the most famous shops in the capital. In addition, Martin offers an à la carte formula, in which it is possible to make a mixture of all the proposals. You can go to the theater as well as eat on the go. Or visit the catacombs and then eat at the Ritz, the famous gourmet restaurant, near the Élysée, on Place de la Concorde.

But this year, a major problem arises. A new agency has just set up in the city: TransVoyage. TransVoyage is a gigantic tourist agency. It floods the tourism market with surprising advertising campaigns and unbeatable offers, so that all individual entrepreneurs like Martin find themselves in great difficulty. Martin had a turnover of almost thirty-two thousand euros the previous year. This year, it has lost half of its customers. Martin has been doubting a lot lately.

He doesn't know if he's going to be able to continue like this; the end of the month is more and more difficult. TransVoyage is gaining more and more business and has just signed a contract with all of the Ibis Hotels in Paris. Martin could restrict himself to the chic suburbs of Paris like Boulogne, Neuilly-sur-Seine or even Versailles and his very famous official castle of the Kings of France and Navarre. But unfortunately, the suburbs do not attract tourists who most often wish to visit the city center, such as Chatelet-les-Halles, Notre-Dame de Paris and the Latin quarter, the Saint-Michel fountain, the Pantheon ... etc.

All hope seems lost for Martin. But one fine summer day, an American couple addresses him.

- Ladies and Gentlemen, what can I do for you?

Martin has always had a sense of courtesy.

- Hello sir. We come to you because we are very disappointed, even angry!

- Ah yes ?! But let's see, why be angry? You are here in the most beautiful city in the world!

- Yes exactly ! We would like to have a worthy visit to this city. TransVoyage betrayed our trust, their reception was poor, bordering on insulting!

- Oh I see ! Well, listen, I'm at your entire disposal, tell me what would make you happy, and I will suggest a formula that will suit you, be sure!

- You have carte blanche! We have no budget limit. We have a week from today.

- So let's go ! Your visit starts now!

Martin rushes out of his apartment and finds his clients in the very pretty district of the 15th arrondissement. Forward, all! Direction, the Parisian metro, La-Motte-Piquet-Grenelle stop! It is out of the question to visit Paris without taking the iconic metro, at least once! There is no point in renting a vehicle, there are too many cars in Paris, and therefore too many traffic jams. So, metro, line 6, first stop, Champs de Mars and the Eiffel Tower. It starts well for the two

Americans. In front of the Eiffel Tower, the sumptuous Trocadéro. Then Martin takes them along the Seine to introduce them to the magnificent quays of the Seine with their famous secondhand booksellers. Visit the Quai Branly museum. A stop in front of the Palais des Invalides was compulsory. Just opposite is the superb Alexandre III bridge. Just behind, the incredible glass dome of the Grand Palais.

They naturally joined Avenue des Champs-Élysées, which is a continuation. They tasted surprising dishes in the Buddha Bar restaurant, behind the Ritz, place de la concorde. And for a whole week, they went to the French comedy to attend a play by Molière, as well as at the Théâtre de l'Odéon. A dream week. The two Americans were so happy that they told all their friends about it. And today, Martin is making twice as much turnover than he had ever made before. TransVoyage went bankrupt two years later due to general customer dissatisfaction. And the visits were too expensive. Morality, it is always better to trust someone passionate.

Vocabulary

À son compte – self-employed

Raccourci – shortcut

Passage – way

Faillir faire qc. – [participe passé : *failli*] – to fall short of, to almost do (sth)

Se lancer [participe passé : *lancé*] – to start as, to go for (sth)

Formule – concept

Éventuellement – possibly, potentially

Gamme – range

Manger sur le pouce – to eat on the go

Préciser – to specify

Boîte de nuit – nightclub

Réputé – famous

À proximité de – near, close to

De taille – huge, serious, major

Gigantesque – gigantic, huge

Inonder – to flood

À coup de – by way of (sth), by means of (sth), through (sth)

Défiant toute concurrence – that defy all competition

Enregistrer un chiffre d'affaires – to post revenues

Se restreindre – to restrict (oneself), to limit (oneself)

Banlieue – suburb

Attirer – to attract, to allure

Voire même – or even

Mais voyons ! – come on !

Justement – precisely

Digne – worthy

Trahir – to betray

Médiocre – poor, low

Convenir [futur, 3ème personne du singulier : conviendra] – to suit, to fit

En avant toute – full speed ahead

Hors de question – out of question, no way

Embouteillage – traffic jam

Somptueux – magnificent, somptuous

Bouquiniste – bookseller

Déguster – to taste, to savour

Pièce (de théâtre) – play (theatre)

Faillite – bankruptcy

Fier – proud

Résumé

Martin est un passionné. Sa passion ? La ville de Paris. Dès sa sortie de l'école de tourisme, Martin devient guide touristique privé. Il travaille à son compte. Il aurait pu faire cuisinier ou maître d'hôtel, mais Martin aime trop la ville de Paris. Tout va pour le mieux jusqu'au jour où une gigantesque agence de voyages du nom de TransVoyage s'installe à Paris. Il hésite à renoncer au centre-ville pour se concentrer sur la banlieue. Mais un jour, des clients en colère contre TransVoyage s'adressent à Martin. Il leur propose une visite de rêve. Depuis ce jour, tout est rentré dans l'ordre pour Martin, et cela, grâce à sa passion : Paris.

Questions

Répondez aux questions suivantes en choisissant une réponse parmi les quatre proposées. (Answer the following questions by choosing one of the four options.)

1 : Quel est le métier de Martin ?

a. Cuisinier.

b. Maître d'hôtel

c. Guide touristique

d. Loueur de véhicules

2 : Parmi les quatre réponses, qu'est-ce qui est inclus dans la formule « de luxe » que propose Martin ?

a. Visite simple

b. Théâtre

c. Une journée découverte

d. Camion-restaurant

3 : Pourquoi Martin n'a-t-il plus beaucoup de travail ?

a. Parce que ses clients sont insatisfaits

b. Parce que ses visites sont trop chères

c. Parce que la courtoisie n'est pas son fort

d. Parce qu'une agence de tourisme appelée TransVoyage fait des offres défiant toute concurrence

4 : Quel est l'itinéraire choisi par Martin pour la visite du couple d'Américains ?

a. Tour Eiffel, quais de Seine, musée du Quai Branly, Les Invalides, Avenue des Champs-Élysées

b. Tour Eiffel, quais de Seine, Trocadéro, Arc de Triomphe, Avenue des Champs-Élysées

c. Tour Eiffel, Notre-Dame de Paris, fontaine Saint-Michel, Palais du Luxembourg, Panthéon

d. Tour Eiffel, Boulogne, Neuilly-sur-Seine, Versailles

Answers :

1. c

2. b

3. d

4. a

Chapter 8 - Le jour où ma vie a changé (The day my life changed)

Bonjour, je m'appelle Mélodie. J'ai vingt-cinq ans. Je travaille pour le gouvernement Français sur la toute nouvelle plateforme en ligne de l'office de tourisme national. Je réponds aux **internautes par le biais d**'une messagerie en ligne. Je prends aussi les appels téléphoniques et les mails. Je **gère** les **réseaux sociaux** liés à la plateforme. J'ai la chance de pouvoir travailler en télétravail. Cela veut dire que je travaille depuis chez moi. Tous les jours c'est à peu près la même routine. Je me lève un peu tard, vers dix heures du matin. Je déjeune, je prends une douche, et je me mets au travail avec double ration de café. J'arrête vers trois heures de l'après midi, je mange un sandwich que je vais acheter juste en bas de mon immeuble. Parfois, quand l'envie me prend et que je n'ai pas la motivation de descendre de chez moi, je me fais **livrer** une pizza, un plat indien ou des sushis. Je retourne sur mon ordinateur vers quinze heures de l'après-midi, et je travaille jusqu'à vingt et une heures du soir, parfois plus, parfois moins, tout dépend du travail qu'il me reste à faire dans la semaine.

Je ne vais pas vous le cacher, mais en vrai, je n'aime pas trop mon **boulot**. Moi, je suis passionnée par l'histoire de mon pays, la France. J'ai un Master d'histoire-géographie. Mais voilà, je ne suis jamais sortie de mon **quartier**. Ce n'est pas vraiment de ma faute. Je suis en **fauteuil roulant** depuis ma naissance. Oh, ne vous en faites pas pour moi, je ne suis pas malheureuse du tout. Enfin, je devrais dire, je ne suis plus malheureuse depuis que ma vie a changé. Oui, **du jour au lendemain**, j'ai décidé de **tout plaquer**.

J'ai quitté mon travail et j'ai lancé une chaîne YouTube que j'ai appelée : Terres de France. Je voulais parler de ma passion. J'en avais marre de discuter avec des gens sur une messagerie pour leur dire des bêtises. Comme je maîtrise très bien les réseaux sociaux, ça a été très facile pour moi. J'ai monté une page Facebook qui a atteint en un mois presque dix mille abonnés. Les gens ont trouvé le concept de ma chaîne génial. Associés à mes comptes Facebook et YouTube, j'ai lancé un compte Twitter pour l'actualité générale de ma chaîne et un compte Instagram pour les photos. Toute une communauté a rejoint mon réseau, si bien qu'en un an, j'ai atteint presque quatre cent mille vues sur mes vidéos. Et là, j'ai commencé à gagner beaucoup d'argent. Il ne me manquait plus qu'une chose, oser sortir de chez moi, partir en voyage, visiter toutes ces villes magnifiques du patrimoine Français. Je voulais voir les châteaux médiévaux de la Loire, les abbayes du Moyen-Âge où les moines ont brassé de la bière pendant des siècles. Et ce jour est arrivé.

En fait, la chaîne de télévision Arte m'a contactée directement, c'est la chaîne culturelle franco-allemande.

— Madame Mélodie Debray ?

— Oui c'est moi.

— Bonjour, ici la **chargée de production** d'Arte. Écoutez, je suis **épatée** par la communauté d'internautes que vous avez réussi à rassembler sur le Net. La gestion de votre réseau social est surprenante. Vous renouvelez sans cesse votre actualité **à la une**. Vraiment, vous êtes une blogueuse remarquable, et votre contenu est de très bonne qualité. Voilà, nous aimerions vous proposer un partenariat, nous souhaiterions vous financer pour que vous réalisiez une série documentaire sur votre chaîne YouTube sur la France et son patrimoine. Qu'en dites-vous ?!

Évidemment j'ai tout de suite répondu oui ! Quelle chance incroyable ! Le téléphone raccroché, j'ai très vite posté la nouvelle sur mon fil d'actualité Twitter et mon journal Facebook. J'ai optimisé le plus possible la visibilité de cette publication afin que plus de gens encore me rejoignent.

Et le tournage a commencé. J'ai fait mes valises, puis j'ai parcouru la France entière pendant plus d'un an. J'ai visité Saint-Malo, la ville fortifiée de Bretagne. Orléans, Paris, Marseille, les châteaux de la Loire, le magnifique château de la Renaissance de François 1er : Chambord. J'ai filmé des épisodes courts sous la forme de

« brèves ». J'ai créé une série dans le style du storytelling. Le tout relayé sur la toile du Net par tweets, tags, publications...etc.

Ce voyage a changé ma vie. Cela a été pour moi une aventure incroyable. Mon **âme** d'exploratrice s'est révélée à moi et m'a complètement transformée. J'aime le côté nomade de la vie, explorer de nouveaux horizons, découvrir de nouvelles histoires, de nouvelles choses. Et la France, quel magnifique pays ! Maintenant, je veux partir à la conquête du monde ! D'ailleurs, j'ai une grande annonce à vous faire, en exclusivité, je viens de signer un contrat de production avec le CNC, le Centre National Cinématographique, pour **tourner** un film, dont le titre sera : Le Tour de Monde, par Mélodie Debray ! Alors je vous dis à bientôt sur le grand écran ! Suivez toute mon actualité sur Facebook, rejoignez-moi sur Twitter, abonnez-vous à ma chaîne. Si ça vous plaît, mettez un petit pouce bleu, partagez et surtout, commentez !

English

Hello, my name is Mélodie. I'm twenty five. I work for the French government on the brand new online platform of the national tourist office. I respond to Internet users through online messaging. I also take phone calls and emails. I manage the social networks linked to the platform. I am lucky to be able to work in telework. It means that I work from home. It's almost the same routine every day. I get up a little late, around ten in the morning. I eat breakfast, take a shower, and get to work with a double ration of coffee. I stop around three in the afternoon, I eat a sandwich which I will buy right at the bottom of my building. Sometimes when I feel like it and I don't have the motivation to come down from my house, I get a pizza, an Indian dish or sushi delivered. I go back to my computer around 3:00 p.m. and work until 9:00 p.m., sometimes more, sometimes less, it all depends on how much work I have left in the week.

I'm not going to hide it from you, but the truth is, I don't really like my job. I am passionate about the history of my country, France. I have a master's degree in history and geography. But now, I never left my neighborhood. It's not really my fault. I have been in a wheelchair since birth. Oh, don't worry about me, I'm not unhappy at all. Finally, I should say, I have not been unhappy since my life changed. Yes, overnight, I decided to quit everything.

I quit my job and started a YouTube channel that I called: Terres de France. I wanted to talk about my passion. I was tired of chatting with people on a message board to tell them nonsense. As I master social networks very well, it was very easy for me. I set up a Facebook page which reached almost ten thousand subscribers in a month. People have found the concept of my channel great. Linked to my Facebook and YouTube accounts, I launched a Twitter account for general news on my channel and an Instagram account for photos. A whole community joined my network, so that in one year, I reached almost four hundred thousand views on my videos. And there I started to earn a lot of money. I was missing only one thing, daring to go out of my house, to go on a trip, to visit all these magnificent cities of French heritage. I wanted to see the medieval castles of the Loire, the abbeys of the Middle Ages where the monks have brewed beer for centuries. And that day has arrived.

In fact, the Arte television channel contacted me directly, it is the Franco-German cultural channel.

- Mrs. Mélodie Debray?

- Yes it's me.

- Hello, here Arte's production manager. Look, I'm blown away by the community of Internet users you've managed to gather on the Net. Managing your social network is surprising. You keep updating your headlines. Really, you are a remarkable blogger, and your content is very good. Here we are, we would like to offer you a partnership, we would like to finance you to make a documentary series on your YouTube channel on France and its heritage. What do you think ?!

Obviously I immediately answered yes! What incredible luck! With the phone on the hook, I quickly posted the news on my Twitter news feed and my Facebook newspaper. I have optimized the visibility of this publication as much as possible so that more people can join me.

And the shooting started. I packed my bags, then I traveled all over France for over a year. I visited Saint-Malo, the fortified city of Brittany. Orleans, Paris, Marseille, the castles of the Loire, the magnificent Renaissance castle of François 1er: Chambord. I filmed short episodes in the form of "briefs". I created a series in the style of storytelling. All relayed on the web of the Net by tweets, tags, publications ... etc.

This trip changed my life. It was an incredible adventure for me. My explorer soul revealed itself to me and completely transformed me. I love the nomadic side of life, exploring new horizons, discovering new stories, new things. And France, what a magnificent country! Now, I want to conquer the world! Besides, I have a big announcement for you, exclusively, I just signed a production contract with the CNC, the National Cinematographic Center, to shoot a film, whose title will be: Le Tour de Monde, by Mélodie Debray! So see you soon on the big screen! Follow all my news on Facebook, join me on Twitter, subscribe to my channel. If you like it, put a little blue thumb, share and above all, comment!

Vocabulary

Internaute – surfer, web user

Par le biais de – by, through

Gérer – to handle, to manage

Réseau social [plural : réseaux sociaux] – social network

Livrer – to deliver

Boulot – job

Quartier - neighbourhood

Fauteuil roulant – wheelchair

Du jour au lendemain – overnight, from one day to the next

Tout plaquer – to chuck everything

En avoir marre de – to be fed up with, to get tired of

Dire des bêtises – to talk nonsense, rubbish

Maîtriser – to master

Monter – to set up, to organize

Abonné – subscriber

(être) **associé à** – to be linked with

Actualité – news

Si bien que – so much that, so well that

Patrimoine – heritage, patrimony

Médiéval [plural : médiévaux/médiévales] – medieval

Moine – monk

Brasser – to brew

Chargé de production – production manager

Épater – to amaze, impress

À la une – on the front page, in the spotlight

Tournage – filming, shooting (of a movie)

Brève –news flash

Relayer – to relay, to spread

Âme – soul

Tourner (un film) – to shoot (a movie)

Résumé

Mélodie est une passionnée en histoire-géographie dont elle est diplômée. Elle aime tout particulièrement l'histoire de son pays, la France. Malheureusement, Mélodie n'a jamais pu voyager car elle est en fauteuil roulant depuis sa naissance. Elle travaille pour le gouvernement Français sur une nouvelle plateforme en ligne de l'office de tourisme national. Mais elle n'aime pas son travail. Un jour elle décide de tout plaquer pour monter sa chaîne YouTube. Mélodie maîtrise parfaitement les réseaux sociaux, et crée des comptes Facebook, Twitter et Instagram pour augmenter sa visibilité. Tout fonctionne à merveille, si bien qu'une chaîne de télévision la contacte pour créer une série documentaire sur le patrimoine Français. Cela marche si bien, qu'elle finit par signer un contrat pour réaliser un film sur le monde entier !

Questions

Répondez aux questions suivantes en choisissant une réponse parmi les quatre proposées. (Answer the following questions by choosing one of the four options.)

1 : Où travallait Mélodie avant que sa vie ne change ?

a. Sur son blog

b. Sur YouTube

c. Sur une plateforme en ligne d'office de tourisme

d. Sur Twitter

2 : Parmi ces réseaux sociaux, lequel Mélodie n'utilise pas ?

a. Facebook

b. Twitter

c. Instagram

d. Snapchat

3 : À quoi sert le compte Twitter de Mélodie ?

a. Pour son actualité générale ?

b. Pour poster ses photos ?

c. Pour ses publications et ses annonces ?

d. Pour avoir plus de visibilité ?

4 : Quelle annonce en exclusivité fait Mélodie ?

a. Elle signe un contrat pour réaliser un film

b. Elle lance une nouvelle chaîne YouTube

c. Elle décide d'arrêter son activité de blogueuse

d. Elle décide de reprendre son premier boulot avec le gouvernement

Réponses

1. c

2. d

3. a

4. a

Chapter 9 - Le Bûcheron (The Lumberjack)

For the first story, it will be written out for you in English first so that you can get an idea of what to expect from the story. Then, read through it in French to practice your French reading skills. This first story is called The Lumberjack or Le Bûcheron in French.

The Lumberjack

There is a lumberjack who lives in the woods and is cutting a tree near the river one day. While chopping down the tree, he drops his axe into the river.

The river is so deep that he can't see to the bottom, and he cannot see his axe at all. He doesn't know how he will get his axe back, so he sits on the edge of the river and begins to cry.

All of a sudden, a god appears. He says that he is called the god of rivers. The god of rivers asks the lumberjack why he is crying, and the lumberjack tells him that he has lost his axe at the bottom of the river.

The god then dives into the river to get the axe. After a few minutes, the lumberjack starts to get worried because the god is still down there, and the river is so deep. Then, the god surfaces. He has come back with an axe made of gold.

"Thank you, but that's not mine." Says the lumberjack

The god puts the axe down and dives into the river again. After a few minutes, he surfaces, and when he comes up he has an axe made of silver in his hand.

"I'm sorry, but that's not mine either." Says the lumberjack

The god dives in again, and this time, he comes up to the surface and out of the water with an axe made of iron in his hand.

“My axe!” The lumberjack exclaims excitedly.

It turns out that the god of rivers is very impressed with the lumberjack’s honesty. He is happy and proud that the lumberjack did not lie in order to take either of the axes that were of much more value than his own- gold and silver being much more valuable than iron. As a reward, the god of rivers gives the lumberjack the axe made of gold and the axe made of silver as well as his own axe. The lumberjack accepts the reward graciously.

The moral of this story is that when we are honest, despite being in a position where we could easily lie and earn something we may really like to have, the universe rewards us in big ways. Honesty is always the best choice, and it comes back to help you later on in even better ways than if you had lied in the first place. You gain a bigger reward from being honest than from taking what you want with dishonesty. When we are honest, people can see that we are genuine, and they want to be our friends as a result.

Le Bûcheron

Un bûcheron qui vit au foret coupe les arbres chaque jour avec le même axe. Cet axe est son possession le plus précieux car il l’utilise chaque jour pour faire son travaille.

Un jour, son axe tombe dans le rivière quand il est en train de couper un arbre très proche du rivière. Le rivière est très très profond, et il ne peut pas voir son axe du tout! Il ne peut pas voir le fond du rivière, alors il ne sait pas comment le sauver et c’est pour ca qu’il ne peut pas récupérer son axe. Il devient triste et il s'assit au bord du rivière et il commence a pleurer.

Tout à coup, un dieu apparaît. Le dieu dit qu’il est appelé le dieu des rivières. Le dieu demande au bûcheron,

«pourquoi est-ce que vous pleurez?

- J’ai perdu mon axe! Dit le bûcheron. c’est tombé dans la rivière et je ne peux pas le voir.

-attends mon gars.»

Le dieu des rivières saute dans l'eau et il va assez profond que le bûcheron ne peut pas lui voir sous l'eau. Il devient peur. Une minute plus tard, le dieu fait surface. Dans son main, il a une axe fait complètement de l'or.

«Je vous remercie, mais ça ce n'est pas mon axe.»

Le dieu plonge encore dans l'eau, et quand il fait surface ce fois, il a dans son main une axe fait complètement de l'argent.

«Je suis désolé, mais ça ce n'est pas mon axe non plus.»

Encore une fois, le dieu plonge au fond du rivière pour récupérer l'axe du bûcheron. Quelques minutes plus tard, le dieu fait surface et dans son main il tient une axe fait de fer. Ce fois, le bûcheron dit,

«C'est mon axe! Vous avez trouvé mon axe!»

Le dieu est très fier du bûcheron car il n'a pas accepter les axes avec beaucoup plus de valeur que l'axe fait de fer qui appartient vraiment au bûcheron. Pour son honnêteté, le dieu veut lui donner une récompense. Le dieu donne le bûcheron l'axe fait d'or et l'axe fait d'argent comme cadeau.

Le leçon dans cet histoire c'est que quand on est honnête, nous sommes récompensés par l'univers dans des façons gros. Quand on est honnête à propos de quelque chose, même si on peut recevoir quelque chose qu'on veut, on peut recevoir des récompenses très grand pour choisir le bon choix. Quand nous décidons de ne pas mentir, les gens peuvent voir que nous sommes genuine et gentille et ils veulent être nos amies comme résultat.

Chapter 10 - L'Arbre (The Tree)

For this second story, it is written in French first, followed by its English translation. This time, read through the story in French first and try to understand as much as you can. Then, once you have done this, read through the English version and see how close your comprehension was when reading it in French first.

L'Arbre

Il y a des vingtaines d'ans, un garçon qui a été très pauvre. Sa famille n'a pas eu assez d'argent pour acheter les jouets ou les choses pour lui de s'amuser avec. Pendant le majorite de son vie, il a dû lui amuser toute seul. Il avait une soeur, mais elle aimait jouer au rivière et le garçon n'aimait pas devenir mouillé alors il ne voulait pas le joindre jamais. C'est pour ca qu'il passait la plupart de son temps au parc qui a été proche de son appartment. Il a joué des jeux imaginaires dans le gazon, ou il a grimper les arbres pour voir toute ce qui se passait en dessous de lui.

Un jour au milieu de l'été, quand il marchait dans le parc comme d'habitude, il a vu un arbre très grand qu'il n'a pas reconnaît comme un arbre qu'il a déjà vu. Il savait qu'il aurait rappelé cette arbre car il a essayé à grimper toutes les arbres très grandes et s'il a vu cette arbre déjà, il aurait essayé de le grimper. Il savait aussi parce que sur le devant de l'arbre, il y avait une signe de papier sur qui était écrit *Je suis un arbre magique. Si vous disiez le charme, vous allez voir le magique.*

Le garçon est devenu très excité, parce qu'il s'est passé chaque jour au parc et il n'a jamais vu un arbre comme ca. Cette arbre a été beaucoup plus grand que tous les autres arbres en ville et il n'a jamais vu une arbre magique. Il aimait beaucoup les arbres et une arbre magique était une rêve pour lui.

Il pensait de tous les trucs magiques qu'il a déjà entendu parler. Car il n'a pas eu une télévision pour regarder les programmes avec des sorcières, il n'a pas su beaucoups de sorts magiques. Il a essayé a rappelé qu'est ce que ses amies ont dises quand ils ont joués les jeux avec les sorcières ou les magiciens. Qu'est qu'ils disent quand ils jettent les sorts? Pense le garcon.

Le garçon a essayé tous les charmes qu'il a pu pensé. Il a dit *abracadabra, sésame, ouvre-toi* et tous les autres qu'il est entendu dans son vie, mais rien n'a pas marché. Il a essayé pendant toute la journée! Il est devenu très fatigué. Il s'assoit sur le gazon sous l'arbre et il a cri,

«S'il te plait! Cheri arbre!»

Tout à coup, une porte géant est ouvert dans le tronc de l'arbre. Le garçon a été très confus, mais il a été contente que l'arbre est ouvert finalement. Le garçon est entré dans le tronc de l'arbre et tout était noir dedans. La porte d'où il est devenu pour entrer dans le tronc de l'arbre a fermé maintenant et le garçon est devenu un peu peur dans le noir. Il cherche pour une façon de quitter, mais il ne pouvait pas voir rien.

Il n'a pas pu voir rien mais en cherchant, il a vu finalement un signe sur le papier blanche qui disait *continuer avec ton magique.*

Le garçon a lu le signe et il lui a demandé à quoi faire maintenant. Il a essayé encore ses mots magiques comme *abracadabra,* et *sésame, ouvre-toi* et toutes les autres qu'il pouvait rappeler dans ce moment de peur. Car il ne savait pas laquelle a réussi à ouvrir la porte la dernière fois, Il ne savait pas exactement quoi dire et maintenant il ne savait pas quoi d'autre il pouvait faire. Il s'assit sur le plancher et il pense. Il ne sait pas quoi faire, mais le seul chose qu'il sait c'est qu'il a senti très contente que l'arbre a ouvert sa porte le première fois alors il a dit,

«Merci! Cheri arbre! Merci pour ouvrir ton porte pour moi la première fois»

Tout à coup, l'intérieur du tronc à illuminée et le garçon a pu voir encore! Il a souri. Il regardait partout pour voir ou il était et il a vu un chemin rouge qui brillait devant lui. Le garçon a été surpris et très excité qu'il a réussi encore.

Le garçon a suivi le chemin et a la fin du chemin était un tas énorme formée de toutes sorts de chocolats et de jouets!

Car le garçon n'a jamais eu ses propres jouets dans toute son vie et il n'a pas eu assez d'argent pour les chocolats, il a été très excitée par ce récompense.

Au bout de la Tronc, en haut de tous les chocolates et les jouets était un signe dernier qui disait *s'il vous plaît et merci sont les mots magiques.*

Le garçon a été très heureux d'avoir trouvé les mots magiques.

Les jours qui ont suivi, Il a apporté tous ses amis et sa soeur à l'arbre et il les a instruire comment ouvrir l'arbre par dire les mots *s'il vous plaît* et *merci.* Il a voulu que toutes les enfants pouvaient jouer avec des jouets et manger du chocolate alors il a partager tous avec eux. Ils ont eu une gros fête plein de chocolats et de jouets dans l'arbre.

Rappelles-toi, les mots magiques sont toujours *s'il vous plaît* et *merci.*

Fin

Le leçon dans cette histoire, c'est que les mots magiques dans n'importe quel situation sont s'il vous plaît et merci. Comme en anglais, il y a des mots magiques en francais aussi.

L'autre leçon c'est que partager avec les amis est toujours plus amusant que garder tout pour toi. Même si le garçon n'avait pas beaucoup de choses, il a voulu partager avec ses amis et sa soeur pour qu'ils pouvaient les amuser aussi.

Le dernier leçon c'est la persévérance. Le garçon est devenu peur quand il n'y avait pas de lumière et il a ete tres fatiguee apres essayer toutes les mots magiques qu'il savait, mais il a persévéré pendant longtemps et les récompenses ont vaut le coût définitivement!

The Tree

Many many years ago, there was a boy who was very poor. His family didn't have enough money for toys or candy or anything like that. He didn't have much to do at home, so he spent most of his days in the park near his house.

One day while he was walking in the park, he saw a huge tree with a sign on the front of it that read: *say the magic words and you will see the magic.*

As he spent most of his time in the park, he would have noticed this tree before if it had been here, he thought. He decided to try to find out what the magic words were.

The boy tried all of the magic words he could think of like *abracadabra* and *Open Sesame* and all others he could think of. He had been trying all day, and nothing worked yet. By this point, he had become very tired.

He sat on the ground at the base of the tree and yelled, exasperated, "Please! Dear tree!"

Suddenly a giant door opened in the trunk of the tree. The boy entered the tree trunk, and it was completely dark inside except for another sign that read: *Continue with your magic.* The boy wasn't sure which magic word had worked in the end, so he tried them all again. Nothing worked, but he was feeling quite thankful that the tree had opened its trunk in the first place, so he said "Thank you! Dear tree."

All of a sudden, the inside of the trunk illuminated, and a red pathway was shining before him. The boy was very excited!

The boy followed the pathway, and at the end of it was a huge pile of chocolate and toys. At the very end of the trunk, there was one final sign that read. *Please, and Thank you are the magic words.*

The boy was so excited that he had figured out the magic words. He had never had toys or chocolate, so he was over the moon! He went back to the tree the next day, but this time he brought his friends and his sister with him. He taught them tall what the magic words were, and showed them that saying them in the right order opened the tree trunk. He and his friends had a big party in the tree trunk, and everyone had so much fun.

Remember, the magic words are always *please* and *thank you*!

The moral of this story is that The magic words in any situation are always please and thank you. These can be said anytime, anywhere, and you will get positive reactions. These reactions may not be toys and chocolate, but they will be people's happiness and kindness.

The second moral of this story is that everything is better when shared with friends and family. The boy didn't have much, but he still wanted to share the gifts he received with his friends and his sister. He wanted to share the reward because he wanted everyone else to be able to enjoy it, too, and he thought it would be more fun to share this reward with them. Generosity with friends makes the experience that much better.

Chapter 11 - Le Champion (The Champion)

Kevin ne veut pas partir. Il reste près du poulain et de la jument. **Le lendemain**, il est toujours là quand monsieur Petit revient. Mais, debout contre la jument, le petit poulain est sur ses quatre jambes. Il tremble, mais il est debout.

– Monsieur, **vous voyez**, il est debout et il boit. **Il est sauvé**, non ? On peut le **garder**.

– C'est un trop grand **risque**, mon petit.

– Mais, je pourrais le soigner. Rester avec lui **tout le temps**. Il deviendra grand et **fort**, vous verrez.

– Alors, tu es **un expert** en chevaux maintenant ? Monsieur Petit est **surpris parce que Kevin semble très décidé**. **Comme s'il savait quelque chose**. Comme un **secret**. Monsieur Petit sait aussi que Kevin est un jeune garçon sérieux. Il peut lui **faire confiance**. Il y a peu de risque si Kevin s'occupe du poulain. Et qui sait ? Peut-être que **le poulain vivra**. Alors, monsieur Petit décide de lui donner **une chance**.

– Bon, si ton père est d'accord, alors je suis d'accord aussi. Mais, rappelle-toi : ce sera ta **responsabilité**. Tu dois t'en occuper **tout seul**. Si tu veux le faire, c'est bien.

Kevin court à la maison. Son père est dans la cuisine avec sa mère. Ils mangent le repas du soir. Kevin demande l'autorisation à son père de soigner le poulain.

– Papa, maman ! Est-ce que je peux soigner le poulain ?

– Monsieur Petit a dit que le poulain est trop faible, répond son père.

– Mais, monsieur Petit a dit que si je veux m'occuper du poulain, c'est d'accord. Si tu es d'accord aussi, Papa.

Le père et la mère de Kevin **se regardent** tous les deux. Ils comprennent que **Kevin souhaite** s'occuper du poulain. C'est les vacances. Il n'y a pas d'école. Kevin a le temps de s'occuper du poulain. Son père lui dit :

– C'est d'accord, Kevin. Tu peux t'occuper du poulain. Ce sera ta responsabilité. C'est beaucoup de travail, tu sais. Tu dois rester près du poulain et de la jument. Le poulain doit boire. Tu dois soigner aussi la jument. Mettre de la paille fraîche pour la litière. Donner du foin pour **la nourriture**. La jument doit marcher un peu tous les jours. Le poulain doit aussi sortir un peu tous les jours. Tu penses pouvoir faire tout cela ?

– Oh, oui Papa, répond Kevin très **heureux**. Merci Papa.

Sa mère lui donne **une pomme**.

– Une pomme pour la jument. C'est sûr, elle aime les pommes. Tous les chevaux aiment les pommes.

– Merci Maman, dit Kevin, très content d'avoir une pomme pour **sa nouvelle amie**.

Très heureux, Kevin va voir sa sœur Isabelle pour lui dire la bonne nouvelle. Isabelle est dans sa chambre. Elle lit un livre. Kevin entre dans la chambre et lui annonce la bonne nouvelle.

– Papa me donne l'autorisation de m'occuper du poulain.

– **C'est formidable**, dit sa sœur Isabelle. Tu vas t'occuper tout seul du poulain ?

– Oui, et de la jument aussi. Tous les jours, la jument doit sortir pour marcher un peu. Et le poulain doit aussi marcher un peu.

– Mais, le poulain ne peut pas se mettre debout, répond Isabelle.

– Si, maintenant, il peut se mettre debout. **Il fait quelques pas**. Monsieur Petit est content. Il a dit que si Papa est d'accord, alors il est d'accord aussi.

– **Je suis très heureuse pour toi**, dit Isabelle.

Kevin retourne à l'écurie. Le poulain est toujours debout. C'est un très bon signe. Il donne la pomme à la jument Rosa. Le petit poulain est trop jeune pour manger des pommes. Quand il sera grand, lui aussi pourra manger des pommes. Kevin entre dans le box pour **brosser** la jument. La jument est **douce** et elle connaît bien Kevin. Elle reste **tranquille**. Elle aime bien se faire brosser. Son **pelage commence à briller**. Kevin lui parle **doucement** :

– Bien Rosa, bien. Tout doux. Je suis avec toi. Ton poulain est très **beau**. On va en faire un champion.

Comme si Rosa **comprennait les paroles de Kevi**n, elle **hennit** doucement. **Le poulain tète** un peu. **Kevin le caresse**. Il aime **sentir sous ses doigts** le pelage doux du poulain.

Tout le monde est très content à l'écurie. Le petit poulain n'est pas mort. Les jockeys viennent le voir. Le père de Kevin vient aussi. Il est **fier** de **son fils**.

Monsieur Petit vient voir à l'écurie.

– Alors, **mon garçon**, tout va bien ? demande-t-il. La jument se porte bien ? Le poulain aussi ?

– Oh, oui Monsieur, répond Kevin. **Encore mille fois merci**. Regardez comme le poulain est debout maintenant. Il boit et il marche. Rosa est douce et gentille avec lui.

– Tu vas le soigner. Le poulain est à toi maintenant. **Sans toi, il ne vivrait pas**.

Kevin ne sait pas quoi dire. Il est tellement heureux. Monsieur Petit lui dit :

– Tu dois lui donner un nom.

– Je veux l'appeler Champion. Ce sera un champion, j'en suis sûr.

– J'ignore si c'est un champion, mais si tu veux l'appeler Champion, alors ce sera Champion.

Le Champion

Résumé

Quand tout le monde part, Kevin reste près du poulain et de la jument. Il veut les soigner. Monsieur Petit dit que si son père est d'accord, alors lui aussi. Kevin va à la maison et son père lui donne l'autorisation. Kevin est très heureux. Il s'occupe de Rosa et du poulain. Puis, Monsieur Petit lui dit que le poulain est à lui. Il faut lui donner un nom. Kevin l'appelle Champion.

When everybody leaves, Kevin stays with the mare and her foal. He wants to take care for them. Mister Petit says that if his father agrees, he also will agree. Kevin goes back home and his father agrees. Kevin is very happy. He takes care of Rosa and her foal. Then Mister Petit tells him the foal is his. He has to give him a name. Kevin chooses Champion as a name.

Vocabulaire

Le lendemain : the next day

Il tremble : he shivers

Vous voyez : you see

Il est sauvé : he is saved

Garder : to keep

Risque : risk

Tout le temps : all the time

Fort : strong

Un expert : an expert

Surpris : surprised

Parce que : because

Kevin semble très décidé : kevin seems to be

Committed

Comme s'il savait quelque chose : as if he knew

Something

Secret : secret

Sérieux : serious

Faire confiance : to trust

Le poulain vivra : the foal will live

Une chance : a chance

Responsabilité : responsibility

Tout seul : all by yourself

Kevin court : kevin runs

Se regardent : look at each other

Kevin souhaite : kevin wishes

La nourriture : the food

Tu penses pouvoir faire tout cela : you think you can do

All this

Heureux : happy

Une pomme : an apple

Sa nouvelle amie : his new friend

La bonne nouvelle : the good news

C'est formidable : it's great

Il fait quelques pas : he takes few steps

Je suis très heureuse pour toi : i am very happy for you

Kevin retourne : kevin goes back

Brosser : to groom

Douce : gentle

Tranquille : quiet

Pelage : coat

Commence à briller : starts to shine

Doucement : quietly

Beau : beautiful

Comprend : understands

Les paroles de kevin : kevin's words

Elle hennit : she neighs

Le poulain tète : the foal sucks

Kevin le caresse : kevin caresses him

Sentir : to feel

Sous ses doigts : under his fingers

Mort : dead

Fier : proud

Son fils : his son

Mon garçon : my boy

Encore : again

Mille fois merci : thank you so much

Sans toi : without you

Il ne vivrait pas : he would not be alive

Questions

1. Pourquoi Kevin ne veut-il pas partir ?

a. Le poulain est mort.

b. Il veut soigner la jument et le poulain.

c. Il veut dormir.

2. Sa mère lui donne :

a. Du pain.

b. Du lait

c. Une pomme

3. Que fait Kevin à l'écurie ?

a. Il dort.

b. Il brosse le poulain.

c. Il brosse la jument.

4. Que ressent le père de Kevin ?

a. Il est fier de Kevin.

b. Il est très content.

c. Il est malade.

5. Pourquoi Kevin donne-il un nom au poulain ?

a. Parce que Monsieur Petit le demande.

b. Parce que le poulain est à lui.

c. Parce que c'est un jeune cheval.

Réponses

1: b

2: c

3: c

4: a

5: b

Chapter 12 - Short Stories I

1st Story

Croyez-vous en l'amour ? Le vrai. Quand vous sentez que cette personne est la bonne, que vous ne pouvez pas imaginer votre vie **sans** lui ou elle ? **Etes-vous en couple** avec cette personne ? La **cherchez**-vous encore, en croyant que vous la trouverez un jour ?

J'ai toujours aimé les films romantiques et les séries TV où deux personnes se rencontrent et se rendent compte qu'ils sont faits l'un pour l'autre. Chaque femme et probablement la majorité des hommes **rêvent** d'un tel amour. J'ai lu des **centaines** de livres sur l'amour, ceux basés sur une histoire vraie et ceux basés sur de la fiction, et je dois **avouer** que je n'y croyais pas. Je ne pouvais tout simplement pas imaginer qu'un jour j'aurais **suffisamment** de chance pour être avec la personne que j'aime **vraiment**. J'ai eu plusieurs **petits copains**, mais je n'ai jamais eu de **sentiments** spéciaux pour aucun de ces hommes. Ce **fut** probablement la raison pour laquelle toutes mes relations amoureuses ont fini si rapidement. Mais un été, tout a changé.

J'avais toujours eu cette pensée dans ma tête qui me **faisait un peu peur**. Quand j'ai commencé à avoir de sérieux problèmes de **santé**, j'ai décidé que si j'étais de nouveau en bonne santé, j'essaierais de faire les choses différemment.

Je suis une femme de 27 ans et je suis en couple avec... une femme. Elle a également fréquenté de nombreux hommes avant. Nous sommes ensemble depuis maintenant 2 ans. Ma famille ainsi que la sienne le savent et acceptent notre relation. Nous passons beaucoup de temps avec eux. Il en est de même pour mes amis. Ceux qui étaient contre l'homosexualité avant ont changé d'avis. Tu as été ami avec quelqu'un pendant de nombreuses années et tu découvres par hasard qu'elle est en couple avec une femme et tu t'en fiches, car elle est encore la même personne. Cela signifie beaucoup pour nous d'avoir leur approbation. Au début, j'étais effrayée de leurs réactions, mais je n'ai jamais été confronté à quelque chose de négatif à cause de mon orientation sexuelle. Nous ne nous montrons de quelque façon que ce soit. Nous passons notre temps comme les couples hétérosexuels, nous allons au cinéma, au restaurant, au théâtre, aux concerts, etc. Nous ne participons pas aux parades LGBT, nous nous sommes rendues une fois dans un club de strip-tease pour gays et lesbiennes, mais ce n'est pas trop notre truc.

Quand je regarde des séries TV ou des documentaires sur les homosexuels, je ne m'identifie pas avec ces gens, pour moi mon orientation est quelque chose de tellement naturel que je ne me sens pas différente à cause de ça. C'est ma **manière d'être.**

Je suis **sortie avec** une femme seulement une fois, et ce fut la meilleure décision de toute ma vie. J'ai rencontré l'amour de ma vie, et cela pose-t-il un problème **quelconque** qu'elle soit une femme ? Je suis vraiment heureuse et je souhaite à tout le monde de connaître un tel **bonheur** dans la vie. Je sais qu'elle est la bonne pour moi, je ne peux pas imaginer ma vie sans elle. Et vous savez quoi ? J'ai finalement commencé à comprendre tous les films romantiques, les livres, etc. Je sais ce que les **gens** dedans ressentent, parce que je **ressens** exactement la même chose.

English

Do you believe in love? The truth. When you feel that this person is the right one, that you cannot imagine your life without him or her? Are you in a relationship with this person? Are you still looking for it, believing that you will find it one day?

I've always loved romantic movies and TV shows where two people meet and realize they're made for each other. Every woman and probably the majority of men dream of such love. I have read hundreds of books on love, those based on a true story and those based on fiction, and I must admit that I did not believe it. I just couldn't imagine that one day I would be lucky enough to be with the person I really love. I had several boyfriends, but I never had any special feelings for any of these men. This was probably the reason why all of my romantic relationships ended so quickly. But one summer, everything changed.

I always had that thought in my head that scared me a little. When I started having serious health problems, I decided that if I was healthy again, I would try to do things differently.

I am a 27 year old woman and I am in a relationship with ... a woman. She has also dated many men before. We have been together for 2 years now. My family and his family know this and accept our relationship. We spend a lot of time with them. It is the same for my friends. Those who were against homosexuality before changed their minds. You have been friends with someone for many years and you find out by chance that she is in a relationship with a woman and you do not care because she is still the same person. It means a lot to us to have their approval. At first I was scared of their reactions, but I never faced anything negative because of my sexual orientation. We do not show ourselves in any way. We spend our time like heterosexual couples, we go to the movies, restaurants, theaters, concerts, etc. We don't participate in LGBT parades, we went to a strip club for gays and lesbians once, but that's not too much of our thing.

When I watch TV series or documentaries on homosexuals, I don't identify with these people, for me my orientation is something so natural that I don't feel different because of it. It’s my way of being.

I only went out with a woman once, and it was the best decision of my life. I have met the love of my life, and does that pose any problem whether she is a woman? I am really happy and I wish everyone to experience such happiness in life. I know it is the right one for me, I cannot imagine my life without it. And you know what ? I finally started to understand all the romantic movies, books, etc. I know how people in it feel, because I feel exactly the same.

Vocabulary

Croire en - believe in

Être en couple - be in a relationship

Chercher - look for/seek

Rêver - to dream

Centaines - hundreds

Avouer - to admit

Suffisamment - enough

Vraiment - truly

Petit copain - boyfriend

Sentiment - feelings

Fut - simple past of être (to be)

Faire peur - be scary

Santé - health

Fréquenter - frequent/go out with

Sienne - hers

Avis - opinion

Se ficher de - not give a damn about

Approbation - endorsement

Effrayé - frightened

Manière d'être - way to be

Sortir avec - go out with/date

Quelconque - any

Bonheur - joy/happiness

Gens - people

Ressentir - to feel

Questions :

Exercise 1

Underline all the adjectives in this text, and find their feminine forms.

Exercise 2

Underline all the verbs from this text which are in passé simple, passé composé and imparfait.

Exercise 3

Translate the following sentences into your native language : « Quand je regarde des séries TV ou des documentaires sur les homosexuels, je ne m'identifie pas avec ces gens, pour moi mon orientation est quelque chose de tellement naturel que je ne me sens pas différente à cause de ça. C'est ma manière d'être. »

....
....
....
....
....

2nd Story

Je suis un homme de 28 ans et j'ai eu beaucoup de succès dans ma vie **sauf** pour une chose. Je n'ai jamais été amoureux. Il y a environ 5 ans, j'ai rencontré une formidable femme sur un **site de rencontre**. Je suis **tombé amoureux** d'elle avec ses beaux yeux verts. **Malheureusement**, elle vivait très loin de chez moi. Nous avons passé plusieurs journées à **discuter de tout et de n'importe quoi**, et un jour, elle a décidé de venir et de me rendre visite car elle avait une semaine de **congés**. J'étais à la fois heureux et en colère. Pourquoi en colère ? Parce qu'une femme ne devrait pas rendre visite à un homme qu'elle ne connaît pas vraiment de cette manière, mais elle dit qu'elle n'avait rien à perdre et beaucoup à gagner.

Les jours que nous avons passés ensemble furent simplement magiques. Je me rappelle de chaque moment que nous avons passé ensemble. Mais à la fin de son **séjour**, j'ai réalisé que cela ne fonctionnerait pas. Elle s'apprêtait à commencer ses études dans une ville très **éloignée** de la mienne, elle semblait assez irresponsable et j'avais un super travail que je ne pouvais pas perdre.

Nous avons passé plusieurs jours à parler au téléphone et à chatter après son départ. Elle m'a même écrit une longue lettre d'amour, mais j'étais trop **têtu** pour m'avouer ce que je ressentais pour cette fille. Je suis sorti avec de différentes femmes, mais je ne pouvais m'arrêter de penser à Kate. Petit à petit, j'ai commencé à regretter ma décision. Kate a trouvé un copain, et ils sont **ensemble** depuis 3 ans. Son copain était du genre **jaloux** et il lui a interdit d'**entrer en contact** avec moi. Je ne suis pas surpris, je ferais peut-être le même si j'étais avec une femme aussi exceptionnelle. Toutes ces années, j'ai été seul, je n'avais plus envie de **rencontrer une femme.**

Mais ensuite, quelque chose de complètement inattendu arriva. Quelques minutes avant le repas de Noël, j'entendis la sonnette de chez moi. J'ouvris la porte et vis Kate devant ma porte. Elle avait un gâteau dans sa main et un petit sac de voyage. Elle était encore plus belle que quand je l'avais vue pour la dernière fois.

« Je ne pouvais pas vivre sans toi plus longtemps », dit-elle.

Ma mère vint entre nous et embrassa Kate sur la joue pour lui dire bonjour.

« On a planifié tout ça ensemble, me dit ma mère. Kate m'a appelé il y a quelques jours après qu'elle ait trouvé mon numéro sur facebook et nous avons tout planifié. »

C'était une soirée très spéciale et le début de quelque chose de nouveau. Nous avons passé les quelques jours suivant à discuter pendant des heures et cela m'**assura** du fait qu'elle était la bonne. Elle n'est pas parfaite, elle est très **étourdie**, elle est toujours **en retard**, mais je l'aime tellement. Après le Nouvel An, Kate a déménagé dans ma ville et je l'ai convaincue de venir vivre avec moi.

Je suis l'homme le plus heureux au monde et je souhaite à tout le monde de connaître un tel amour.

English

I am a 28 year old male and have had great success in my life except for one thing. I have never been in love. About 5 years ago, I met a great woman on a dating site. I fell in love with her with her beautiful green eyes. Unfortunately, she lived very far from my home. We spent several days discussing everything and anything, and one day she decided to come and visit me because she had a week off. I was both happy and angry. Why angry? Because a woman shouldn't visit a man she doesn't really know that way, but she says she had nothing to lose and a lot to gain.

The days we spent together were simply magical. I remember every moment we spent together. But at the end of his stay, I realized that it would not work. She was about to start studying in a city very far from mine, she seemed pretty irresponsible and I had a great job that I couldn't lose.

We spent several days talking on the phone and chatting after he left. She even wrote me a long love letter, but I was too stubborn to admit how I felt about this girl. I went out with different women, but I couldn't stop thinking about Kate. Little by little, I started to regret my decision. Kate has found a boyfriend, and they've been together for 3 years. Her boyfriend was the jealous type and he forbade her from contacting me. I'm not surprised, I might do the same if I were with such an exceptional woman. All these years, I have been alone, I no longer wanted to meet a woman.

But then something completely unexpected happened. A few minutes before the Christmas meal, I heard the doorbell at home. I opened the door and saw Kate outside my door. She had a cake in her hand and a small travel bag. She was even more beautiful than when I had last seen her.

"I couldn't live without you any longer," she says.

My mother came between us and kissed Kate on the cheek to say hello.

"We planned it all together," said my mother. Kate called me a few days ago after she found my number on facebook and we planned everything. "

It was a very special evening and the beginning of something new. We spent the next few days chatting for hours and that assured me it was the right one. She's not perfect, she's very dizzy, she's always late, but I love her so much. After New Years, Kate moved to my city and I convinced her to come and live with me.

I'm the happiest man in the world and I wish everyone to know such love.

Vocabulary

Sauf - except

Site de rencontre - dating website

Tomber amoureux - fall in love

Malheureusement - unfortunately

Discuter de tout et de n'importe quoi - to talk about everything and nothing

Congés - holidays

Séjour - stay

Éloigné - away

Têtu - stubborn

Ensemble - together

Jaloux - jealous

Entrer en contact - get in touch

Rencontrer - to meet

Rencontrer une femme - meet a woman/date a woman

Ensuite - then

Inattendu - unexpected

Sonnette - doorbell

Porte - door

Gâteau - cake

Sac de voyage - travel bag

Assurer - make sure

Étourdi - absent minded

En retard - late

Questions :

Exercise 1

Change the verbs that are in passé composé into passé simple.

....
....
....
....
....

Exercise 2

Underline all the words in this text which belong to the lexical field of feelings.

Exercise 3

Translate the following sentences into your native language : « Les jours que nous avons passés ensemble furent simplement magiques. Je me rappelle de chaque moment que nous avons passé ensemble. Mais à la fin de son séjour, j'ai réalisé que cela ne fonctionnerait pas. Elle s'apprêtait à commencer ses études dans une ville très éloignée de la mienne, elle semblait assez irresponsable et j'avais un super travail que je ne pouvais pas perdre. »

....
....
....
....
....

Chapter 13 - Short Stories II

3rd Story

Ma femme durant une de nos **engueulades** me dit : « Tu peux **enfin** commencer à faire ce que tu veux et être heureux. »

Je l'ai prise dans mes bras, soulevée, et **amenée** dans notre lit où j'ai commencé à l'embrasser passionnément tout en la **déshabillant**.

C'est ma définition du bonheur.

English

My wife during one of our shouts said to me: "You can finally start doing what you want and be happy. "

I took her in my arms, lifted her, and brought her to our bed where I began to kiss her passionately while undressing her.

This is my definition of happiness.

Vocabulary

engueulade - argument, fight (informal)

enfin - finally

amener - bring

déshabiller - to undress

Questions :

Exercise 1

Take each verb that you find in this short story and write which person and tense they are.

....

....

....

....

....

Exercise 2

Translate the whole story into your native language.

....

....

....

....

....

4th Story

Je ne serai pas à la maison durant la **Toussaint**, donc aujourd'hui, après le travail, je suis allé au **cimetière** pour nettoyer les **pierres tombales** et allumer quelques **bougies**, parce que je ne serai plus **capable** de le faire avant longtemps. Au cimetière, j'ai vu un vieil homme, assis sur un banc devant l'une des **tombes**. Il tenait une **fleur de lis** blanche dans une de ses mains ainsi qu'une petite bougie. Il mit ces choses-là sur la tombe, embrassa la pierre tombale et essuya les **larmes** qui coulaient le long de ses joues d'un revers de main.

Je me suis senti très **triste** pour lui, donc je me suis **approché** et ai **entamé** une conversation. Je lui ai demandé qui était à l'intérieur et il me répondit que c'était sa femme, Petunia. J'ai donc demandé combien de temps avaient-ils été ensemble.

Il me regarda d'un air très triste et me répondit : « 47 ans. Pas assez. »

Je ressens toujours un **pincement** au cœur quand j'y pense... je souhaite à n'importe qui de trouver un tel amour.

English

I will not be at home during All Saints Day, so today after work I went to the cemetery to clean the tombstones and light a few candles, because I will not be able to do this for a long time. At the cemetery, I saw an old man sitting on a bench in front of one of the graves. He was holding a white lily flower in one of his hands and a small candle. He put these things on the grave, kissed the headstone and wiped the tears that ran down his cheeks with the back of his hand.

I felt very sad for him, so I went over and started a conversation. I asked him who was inside and he said it was his wife, Petunia. So I asked how long had they been together.

He looked at me very sadly and replied: "47 years old. Not enough. "

I always feel a pinch in my heart when I think about it ... I wish anyone to find such love.

Vocabulary

Toussaint - all saints day

Cimetière - cemetery

Pierre tombale - tombstone

Bougie - candle

Capable de - able to

Tombe - grave

Fleur de lis - lily

Larme - tear

Triste - sad

Approcher - come closer

Entamer - start

Pincement - pinching

Questions :

Exercise 1

Underline all the words in this text which belong to the lexical field of the cemetery.

Exercise 2

Translate the following sentences into your native language : « Je ne serai pas à la maison durant la Toussaint, donc aujourd'hui, après le travail, je suis allé au cimetière pour nettoyer les pierres tombales et allumer quelques bougies, parce que je ne serai plus capable de le faire avant longtemps. »

....
....
....
....
....

5th Story

J'ai le meilleur **mari** au monde!

J'ai toujours aimé **me maquiller**, j'aimais être belle, même si je ne suis pas **moche** naturellement, je me sentais mieux quand j'avais un petit peu de maquillage, comme la majorité des femmes. J'ai fini des formations spéciales, c'est devenu mon hobby. J'ai 30 **tiroirs remplis** de produits de beauté, et je les utilise tous, selon quel type de maquillage je vais faire. Je porte toujours de faux **cils**.

Maintenant, je suis **enceinte** et c'est vraiment difficile pour moi. Je suis un petit peu **déprimée** et je suis en **congé maternité** donc je ne mets plus de maquillage et porte de vieux **vêtements** moches. Je n'accorde tout simplement aucune importance à mon apparence.

Ces deux dernières semaines, mon mari a commencé à **agir** de manière **étrange** et à passer beaucoup de temps devant son ordinateur. J'ai pensé qu'il avait trouvé un nouveau **jeu** et que c'était sa manière d'avoir un petit peu de temps pour lui.

J'ai réalisé à quel point j'**avais tort** quand il m'appela dans la pièce où je garde tous mes produits de beauté. Il me dit de **m'asseoir**, de fermer mes **yeux** et d'être silencieuse. J'ai fait comme il me dit, sans poser de question.

J'ai senti qu'il me mettait du mascara sur mes cils, de l'eye-liner, il fit mes **ongles** et à la fin je l'entendis sortir mes faux-cils de leur **boîte**. J'ai cru qu'il était devenu **fou**, et j'avais même peur qu'il m'**arrache** les yeux par accident. Mais après plus ou moins une heure, il me demanda d'ouvrir mes yeux et de regarder dans le miroir. Je ne pus pas croire ce que je vis. Je ressemblais à une star au moment d'entrer sur le **tapis** rouge. Je lui demandai alors où avait-il appris tout ça. Il me répondit qu'il aimait me regarder quand je me maquillais et qu'il avait passé des heures à regarder des tutoriels sur Youtube, parce qu'il savait à quel point j'étais triste et qu'il savait que je me sentais mieux quand j'étais maquillée.

Ce fut très dur de ne pas **éclater en sanglot**, mais je ne voulais pas **gâcher** mon maquillage. Je n'aurais jamais pensé que mon mari ferait quelque chose comme ça pour moi. Je sais que j'ai **épousé** la bonne personne.

English

I have the best husband in the world!

I always liked to wear makeup, I liked to be beautiful, even if I am not ugly naturally, I felt better when I had a little bit of makeup, like the majority of women. I finished special training, it became my hobby. I have 30 drawers full of beauty products, and I use them all, depending on what type of makeup I'm going to do. I always wear false eyelashes.

Now I'm pregnant and it's really difficult for me. I'm a little bit depressed and I'm on maternity leave so I don't put on makeup anymore and wear old ugly clothes. I just don't care how I look.

In the past two weeks, my husband has started acting strange and spending a lot of time at his computer. I thought he had found a new game and that was his way of having a little bit of time for him.

I realized how wrong I was when he called me in the room where I keep all my beauty products. He told me to sit down, close my eyes and be quiet. I did as he told me, without asking any questions.

I felt that he was putting mascara on my eyelashes, eyeliner, he made my nails and in the end I heard him take my false eyelashes out of their box. I thought he had gone mad, and I was even afraid that he would accidentally tear my eyes out. But after more or less an hour, he asked me to open my eyes and look in the mirror. I could not believe what I saw. I looked like a star when I stepped onto the red carpet. I then asked him where he had learned all this. He replied that he liked looking at me when I was putting on makeup and that he had spent hours watching tutorials on Youtube, because he knew how sad I was and he knew I felt better when I was wearing makeup.

It was very hard not to burst into tears, but I didn't want to spoil my makeup. I never thought my husband would do something like this for me. I know I married the right person.

Vocabulary

Mari - husband

Au monde - in the world

Maquiller - put makeup on

Moche - ugly

Tiroir - drawer

Rempli - filled/full

Cils - eyelash

Enceinte - pregnant

Déprimé - depressed

Congé maternité - maternity leave

Vêtement - clothe

Agir - to act

Étrange - strange

Jeu - game

Avoir tort - to be wrong

S'asseoir - to sit down

Yeux - eyes

Ongle - nail

Boîte - box

Fou - mad

Arracher - pull something off

Tapis - carpet

Éclater en sanglot - burst into tears

Gâcher - waste

Épouser - to marry

Questions :

Gather all the reflexive verbs from the text and translate them into your native language.

....
....
....
....
....

Chapter 14 - Short Stories III

Notre famille – Our Family

Pierre est un père jeune et très sympa. Il est toujours de bonne humeur et rit beaucoup, mais parfois il est un peu grognon, surtout quand il est fatigué. Il est grand, il a les cheveux bruns et une moustache. Il est cuisinier dans un restaurant au centre de la ville, depuis plusieurs années. Il aime beaucoup son travail, mais à la maison, il ne cuisine pas souvent. Quand il cuisine, c'est délicieux, il a même des recettes secrètes. Il a des horaires irréguliers, et travaille souvent le week-end. Janine est aussi une mère jeune et très sympa . Elle est toujours calme, mais parfois elle se fâche, mais heureusement, ça n'arrive pas souvent. Elle est de taille moyenne et a les cheveux blonds et frisés. Elle travaille à mi-temps, le matin, dans une petite épicerie, depuis quelques années; elle aime son travail, qui est varié. Michel et Martine ont les deux les cheveux bruns et sont de taille moyenne. Ils sont très gentils, mais Michel est un peu paresseux, et Martine est têtue. Michel va au collège. En France, le collège suit l'école primaire. Martine va à l'école primaire. Ils vont les deux à l'école à bicyclette. Ils ont congé le mercredi après-midi. Et moi, ils disent que je suis gentil et mignon, mais un peu trop gourmand. J'aime beaucoup m'amuser et mon travail, c'est de surveiller la maison!

English

Pierre is a young and very friendly father. He's always in a good mood and laughs a lot, but sometimes he's a bit grumpy, especially when he's tired. He is tall, he has brown hair and a mustache. He has been a cook in a restaurant in the center of the city for several years. He enjoys his work very much, but at home he does not cook often. When he cooks, it's delicious, he even has secret recipes. He has irregular schedules, and often works on weekends. Janine is also a young and very nice mother. She is always calm, but sometimes she gets angry, but luckily it doesn't happen often. She is of average height and blond and curly hair. She has worked part-time in the morning in a small grocery store for several years; she loves her work, which is varied. Michel and Martine both have brown hair and are of medium height. They are very nice, but Michel is a little lazy, and Martine is stubborn. Michel goes to college. In France, the college follows primary school. Martine goes to elementary school. They both go to school by bicycle. They leave on Wednesday afternoon. And me, they say that I am kind and cute, but a little too greedy. I really like to have fun and my job is to watch the house!

Vocabulary

Père (m.) /father

Jeune / young

Humeur (f.) / mood

Rire / to laugh

Grognon / grumpy

Surtout / mostly

Fatigué / tired

Grand / tall

Cheveu (m.) / hair

Cuisinier (m.) / cook

ville (f.) / town

Travail (m.) / work

Recette (f.) / recipe

Horaire (m.) / schedule

Travailler / to work

Mère (f.) / mother

Se fâcher / to be angry

Heureusement / fortunately

Arriver / to happen

Souvent / often

Taille (f.) / size

Moyen / average

Frisé / curly

Mi-temps / part-time

Matin (m.) / morning

Épicerie (f.) / grocery store

Varié / varied

Les deux / both

Paresseux / lazy

Têtu / stubborn

Aller / to go

Suivre / to follow

École (f.) / school

Congé / off

Mercredi / Wednesday

Après-midi / afternoon

Dire / to say

Mignon / cute

Aimer / to like

Surveiller / to watch

Exercises

A) Questions about the story

1) Est-ce que Pierre est vieux?

2) Est-ce que Pierre est sympa?

3) Pierre travaille-t-il dans un bureau?

4) Où se trouve le restaurant?

5) Quelle est la profession de Pierre?

6) Pierre est-il un bon cuisinier?

7) Est-ce que Janine est sympa?

8) Est-ce que Janine est blonde?

9) Est-ce que Janine travaille dans un restaurant?

10) Est-ce que Janine aime son travail?

11) Comment Michel est Martine vont-ils à l'école?

12) Quel jour ont-ils congé l'après-midi?

13) Quel est le travail de Médor?

Answers

1) Non, Pierre n'est pas vieux.

2) Oui, il est sympa.

3) Non, il ne travaille pas dans un bureau.

4) Il se trouve au centre de la ville.

5) Il est cuisinier.

6) Oui, il est un bon cuisinier.

7) Oui, elle est sympa.

8) Oui, elle est blonde.

9) Non, elle ne travaille pas dans un restaurant.

10) Oui, elle aime son travail.

11) Ils vont à l'école à bicyclette.

12) Le mercredi.

13) Son travail est de surveiller la maison

B) Trouve l'intrus

1) Sympa – grognon – cuisinier – paresseux – gourmand

2) Le restaurant – la maison – l'épicerie – le travail – l'école

(Answers : 1) cuisinier – 2) le travail)

C) Peux-tu énumérer les jours de la semaine?

(lundi – mardi – mercredi – jeudi – vendredi – samedi – dimanche)

D) Quel est le féminin de:

grand

brun

délicieux

secret

Paresseux

Têtu

Mignon

Gourmand

(grande – brune – délicieuse – secrète – paresseuse – têtue – mignonne – gourmande)

E) Quel est cet endroit?

Il y a un tableau noir, des craies, des pupitres, des élèves.

(Answer : une école)

F) Peux-tu conjuguer le verbe avoir au présent?

(j'ai – tu as – il a – elle a – nous avons – vous avez – ils ont – elles ont)

Notre maison – Our House

Nous habitons dans une petite maison. Au rez-de-chaussée, il y a la cuisine, qui est équipée d'une cuisinière, d'un réfrigérateur, et bien sûr d'un lave-vaisselle, car personne ne veut laver la vaisselle, la salle à manger, avec une grande table, toujours recouverte d'une nappe très colorée et des chaises en bois, et le salon avec un canapé, des fauteuils, une petite table, une télévision, quelques étagères remplies de livres et de toutes sortes de bibelots, un piano et une cheminée. Du salon, nous pouvons aller sur la terrasse. Au premier étage, il y a trois chambres et une salle de bain. Il y a aussi un grenier et un sous-sol. J'ai un panier très confortable, qui se trouve près de la porte-fenêtre, mon endroit préféré. De là, je peux regarder dehors, parfois je vois un oiseau, ou un chat qui se promène. Mais je ne suis pas toujours dans mon panier, je vais dans toute la maison, pour voir ce qu'il se passe, et surtout à la cuisine!

English

We live in a small house. On the ground floor there is the kitchen, which is equipped with a stove, a refrigerator, and of course a dishwasher, since nobody wants to wash the dishes, the dining room, with a large table, always covered with a very colorful tablecloth and wooden chairs, and the living room with a sofa, armchairs, a small table, a television, a few shelves filled with books and all kinds of trinkets, a piano and a chimney. From the living room we can go to the terrace. On the first floor there are three bedrooms and a bathroom. There is also an attic and a basement. I have a very comfortable basket, which is near the patio door, my favorite place. From there, I can look outside, sometimes I see a bird, or a cat walking. But I'm not always in my basket, I go around the house, to see what's going on, and especially in the kitchen!

Vocabulary

Habiter / to live

Maison (f.) / house

Rez-de-chaussée (m.) / first floor

Cuisine (F.) / Kitchen

Cuisinière (F.) / Stove

Réfrigérateur (M.) / Refrigerator

Lave-Vaisselle (M) / Dishwasher

Personne / Nobody

Laver / To Wash

Vaisselle (F.) / Dishes

Salle À Manger (F.) / Dining Room

Toujours / Always

Recouvert / Covered

Nappe (F.) / Tablecloth

Chaise (F.) / Chair

Bois (M.) / Wood

Canapé (M.) / Couch

Fauteuil (M.) / Armchair

Étagère (F.) / Shelf

Rempli / Filled

Livre (M.) / Book

Bibelot (M.) / Knick-Knack

Cheminée (F.) / Fireplace

Pouvoir / Can

Terrasse (F.) / Patio

Étage (M.) / Floor

Salle De Bain (F.) / Bathroom

Grenier (M.) / Attic

Sous-Sol (M.) / Basement

Panier (M.) / Basket

Se Trouver / To Be Located

Porte-Fenêtre (F.) / French Door

Dehors / Outside

Voir / To See

Oiseau (M.) / Bird

Chat (M.) / Cat

Se Promener / To Walk

Aller / To Go

Se Passer / To Happen

Surtout / Mostly

Exercises

A) Questions about the story

1) La maison est-elle petite?

2) Où la cuisine se trouve-t-elle?

3) Y a-t-il un lave-vaisselle dans la cuisine?

4) Pourquoi y a-t-il un lave-vaisselle?

5) Comment est la nappe?

6) Y a-t-il une télévision au salon?

7) De quelle chambre pouvons-nous aller sur la terrasse?

8) Y a-t-il un grenier?

9) Comment est le panier de Médor?

10) Où Médor aime-t-il surtout aller?

Answers

1) Oui, elle est petite.

2) Elle se trouve au rez-de-chaussée.

3) Oui, il y a un lave-vaisselle.

4) Parce que personne ne veut laver la vaisselle.

5) Elle est très colorée.

6) Oui, il y a une télévision au salon.

7) Du salon.

8) Oui, il y a un grenier.

9) Il est confortable.

10) Il aime surtout aller à la cuisine.

B) Trouve l'intrus

1) la cuisinière – le bibelot – le réfrigérateur – le lave-vaisselle

2) le chien – le chat – la cheminée – l'oiseau

3) la chaise – le canapé – le fauteuil – la cuisine -

(Answers : 1) le bibelot - 2) la cheminée - 3) la cuisine)

Notre quartier – Our Neighborhood

Nous habitons dans un quartier juste en dehors du centre de la ville. A proximité se trouvent plusieurs petits commerces, l'épicerie où Janine travaille, une boulangerie-pâtisserie, une boucherie, une quincaillerie, une boutique de vêtements, ainsi que quelques petits cafés. Il y a un arrêt de bus qui se trouve à quelques minutes à pied de notre maison. Nous sommes entourés de maisons anciennes, mais aussi d'immeubles contruits récemment. C'est un quartier tranquille. Nous avons plusieurs voisins, une de nos voisines est une petite dame qui promène son grand chien tous les matins, et un de nos voisins est un homme très grand qui promène son tout petit chien tous les matins. Il y a beaucoup de familles avec des enfants, certains sont amis avec Michel et Martine.

English

We live in a neighborhood just outside the city center. Nearby are several small shops, the grocery store where Janine works, a bakery, a butcher, a hardware store, a clothing store, as well as a few small cafes. There is a bus stop which is a few minutes walk from our house. We are surrounded by old houses, but also recently constructed buildings. It's a quiet neighborhood. We have several neighbors, one of our neighbors is a little lady who walks her big dog every morning, and one of our neighbors is a very tall man who walks her little dog every morning. There are many families with children, some are friends with Michel and Martine.

Vocabulary

Quartier (m.) / neighborhood

En dehors / outwards

Commerce (m.) / shop

Épicerie (f.) / grocery store

Boulangerie-pâtisserie (f.) / bakery

Boucherie (f.) / butcher's shop

Quincaillerie (f.) / hardware store

Vêtement (m.) / clothing

Arrêt (m.) / stop

À pied / on foot

Entouré / surrounded

Immeuble (m.) / building

Construit / built

Voisin (m.) / neighbor

Dame (f.) / lady

Promener / to take for a walk

Matin (m.) / morning

Grand / large/tall

Homme (m.) / man

Certain / some

Ami (m.) / friend

Exercises

A) Questions about the story

1) Est-ce que nous habitons dans le centre de la ville?

2) Y a-t-il une boulangerie-pâtisserie dans notre quartier?

3) Où l'arrêt de bus se trouve-t-il?

4) Les maisons qui nous entourent sont-elles modernes?

5) Le quartier est-il tranquille ou bruyant?

6) Avons-nous beaucoup de voisins?

7) Peux-tu décrire une de nos voisines?

8) Peux-tu décrire un de nos voisins?

9) Y a-t-il des enfants parmi nos voisins?

Answers

1) Non, nous habitons juste en dehors du centre de la ville.

2) Oui, il y a une boulangerie-pâtisserie.

3) Il se trouve à quelques minutes à pied de notre maison.

4) Non, les maisons sont anciennes.

5) Le quartier est tranquille.

6) Oui, nous avons beaucoup de voisins.

7) Une de nos voisines est un petite dame.

8) Un de nos voisins est un homme très grand.

9) Oui, il y a beaucoup d'enfants.

B) Read the questions and answer in French about you

1) Peux-tu décrire ton quartier?

2) Peux-tu décrire tes voisins?

C) Trouve l'intrus

L'épicerie – la boulangerie – la boucherie – le voisin – la quincaillerie

(Answer : le voisin)

D) Read the questions and answer in French

1) Dans quel magasin peut-on acheter du pain?

2) Dans quel magasin peut-on acheter de la viande?

3) Dans quel magasin peut-on acheter des outils?

4) Dans quel magasin peut-on acheter du sucre?

(Answers : 1) dans une boulangerie – 2) dans une boucherie – 3) dans une quincaillerie 4) dans une épicerie)

Chapter 15 - Short Stories IV

Un matin – One Morning

C'est le mois de janvier. Aujourd'hui les parents travaillent, et les enfants retournent à l'école après les vacances de Noël. Je vais m'ennuyer à la maison tout seul. Vers sept heures du matin, j'entends le réveil sonner. Personne ne bouge....Je crois qu'il faut que je les réveille. Je saute sur les lits et réveille tout le monde. Ils n'ont pas l'air contents, mais ils se lèvent tous vite, ils se lavent, s'habillent, et mangent leur petit-déjeuner. Je m'intéresse toujours aux repas et vais voir ce qu'il y a à manger. Parfois il n'y a rien de bon. Comme ils sont tous pressés, ils mangent des céréales, ils boivent du café et du jus d'orange, rien d'intéressant pour moi, pas de miettes par terre. Et voilà, ils partent tous à peu près en même temps, et me disent à peine au revoir. Je pense que je mérite une petite sièste, vous ne croyez pas, sans moi, ils seraient restés endormis!

English

It's January. Parents are working today, and children are returning to school after the Christmas holidays. I'm going to be bored at home all by myself. Around seven in the morning, I hear the alarm sounding. No one is moving. ... I think I need to wake them up. I jump on the beds and wake everyone up. They don't seem happy, but they all get up quickly, wash, dress, and eat their breakfast. I'm still interested in meals and will see what there is to eat. Sometimes there's nothing good. Since they are all in a hurry, they eat cereals, they drink coffee and orange juice, nothing interesting for me, no crumbs on the floor. Lo and behold, they all leave at about the same time, and barely say goodbye to me. I think I deserve a nap, you don't think, without me, they would have stayed asleep!

Vocabulary

Mois (m.) / month

Janvier / january

Aujourd'hui / today

Travailler / to work

Retourner / to go back

Noël / christmas

S'ennuyer / to be bored

Seul / alone

Matin (m.) / morning

Entendre / to hear

Réveil (m.) / alarm clock

Sonner / to ring

Personne / nobody

Bouger / to move

Croire / to believe

Réveiller / to wake up

Sauter / to jump

Lit (m.) / bed

Avoir l'air / to seem

Se lever / to get up

Se laver / to wash

S'habiller / to get dressed

Manger / to eat

Petit-déjeuner (m.) / breakfast

Repas (m.) / meal

Aller / to go

Voir / to see

Pressé / in a hurry

Boire / to drink

Miette (f.) / crumb

Par terre / on the floor

Partir / to leave

À peu près / about

En même temps / at the same time

Dire / to say

À peine / barely

Penser / to think

Mériter / to deserve

Sièste (f.) / nap

Croire / to believe

Ils seraient restés (rester) / to stay

(conditionnel passé)

Endormi / asleep

Exercises

A) Questions about the story

1) C'est quel mois?

2) Est-ce que les vacances sont finies?

3) A quelle heure le réveil sonne-t-il?

4) Qui réveille tout le monde?

5) Est-ce que Médor s'intéresse aux repas?

6) Est-ce qu'ils ont le temps de manger?

7) Qu'est-ce qu'ils mangent?

8) Qu'est-ce qu'ils boivent?

9) Que mérite Médor?

10) Est-ce grâce à Médor qu'ils ont pu se lever?

Answers

1) C'est le mois de janvier.

2) Oui, les vacances sont finies.

3) Le réveil sonne vers sept heures.

4) Médor réveille tout le monde.

5) Oui, il s'intéresse toujours aux repas.

6) Oui, ils ont le temps de manger.

7) Ils mangent des céréales.

8) Ils boivent du café et du jus d'orange.

9) Il mérite une sièste.

10) Oui, c'est grâce à lui.

B) Peux-tu énumérer les mois de l'année?

(janvier – février – mars – avril – mai – juin – juillet – août – septembre – octobre – novembre – décembre)

C) Read the questions and answer in French about you

1) A quelle heure te lèves-tu le matin?

2) Que manges-tu pour le petit déjeuner?

3) Est-ce que tu bois du café?

4) Est-ce que tu bois du jus d'orange?

L'école - School

Comme je suis un chien, je ne vais pas à l'école, alors je ne peux pas vous raconter une de mes journées à l'école. Mais j'en entends beaucoup parler. Quand les enfants rentrent de l'école, ils parlent de leurs cours, ils parlent des cours de français, des cours de sciences, des cours de math, et d'autres cours, mais je ne comprends pas tellement, et je ne me souviens plus des noms. Ils parlent des examens, des profs, et de leurs devoirs, qu'ils font à la maison. Il y a des cours qui les intéressent beaucoup et d'autres moins. Ils parlent aussi des leurs camarades de classe et de leurs amis qu'ils rencontrent parfois après l'école. Ils ont aussi des cartables, des livres, des cahiers, des crayons et des gommes. J'aimerais tellement aller avec eux à l'école, mais ils disent qu'ils ne peuvent pas me prendre, c'est bien dommage!

English

As I am a dog, I am not going to school, so I cannot tell you about one of my days at school. But I hear a lot about it. When the kids come back from school, they talk about their lessons, they talk about French lessons, science lessons, math lessons, and other lessons, but I don't really understand, and I don't remember more names. They talk about exams, teachers, and homework, which they do at home. There are courses that interest them a lot and others less. They also talk about their classmates and friends they sometimes meet after school. They also have school bags, books, notebooks, pencils and erasers. I would love to go to school with them, but they say they can't take me, it's too bad!

Vocabulary

Comme / since

Aller / to go

Pouvoir / can

Raconter / to tell/to narrate

Journée (f.) / day

Entendre / to hear

Rentrer / to return

Cours (m.) / class

Comprendre / to understand

Tellement / so much

Se souvenir / to remember

Devoir (m.) / homework

Faire / to do

Beaucoup / much

Moins / less

Ami (m.) / friend

Rencontrer / to meet

Parfois / sometimes

Après / after

Cartable (m.) / school bag

Livre (m.) / book

Cahier (m.) / notebook

Crayon (m.) / pencil

Gomme (f.) / eraser

Exercises

A) Questions about the story

1) Est-ce que Médor va à l'école?

2) Qui parle de l'école?

3) De quels cours parlent les enfants?

4) Les enfants parlent-ils des profs?

5) Est-ce que les enfants ont des devoirs?

6) Ont-ils des camarades de classe?

7) Ont-ils des amis?

8) Est-ce que les enfants voient leurs amis après l'école?

Answers

1) Non, Médor ne va pas à l'école.

2) Les enfants parlent de l'école.

3) Ils parlent des cours de français, de sciences et de math.

4) Oui, ils parlent des profs.

5) Oui, ils ont des devoirs.

6) Oui, ils ont des camarades de classe.

7) Oui, ils ont des amis.

8) Oui, parfois ils voient leurs amis après l'école.

B) la journée

B) Read the questions and answer in French about you

1)Peux-tu décrire une école?

2) Aimes-tu apprendre le français?

3) Préfères-tu les sciences ou les math?

4) Quels sont les cours que tu préfères?

C) Trouve l'intrus

La journée - le livre – le cahier – la gomme – le crayon

(Answer : La journée)

En visite chez la grand-mère – Visiting Grandmother

Le dimanche, nous allons parfois en visite chez la mère de Janine. Elle s'appelle Ariane. Les enfants aiment bien aller chez leur grand-mère. Elle habite dans une petite maison à la campagne. Elle aime cuisiner, jardiner et regarder la télévision. Elle aime aussi leur raconter des histoires du temps de sa jeunesse, et ils écoutent avec beaucoup d'intérêt. Quand nous allons en visite chez elle, elle nous invite toujours pour le déjeuner. Elle cuit de délicieux rôtis qu'elle fait mijoter quelques heures. Quand nous arrivons devant sa maison, nous sentons cette bonne odeur. Avec le rôti, elle cuit des pommes de terre et un légume de saison, parfois de son jardin. Ensuite, il y a bien sûr un dessert. Elle met toujours un peu de viande dans mon écuelle, que je mange en vitesse, mais eux, ils mangent pendant des heures. Et ils parlent tous tellement, et souvent ils parlent tous en même temps. En général, je m'endors à moitié. Le moment que j'attends avec impatience, c'est quand nous allons tous dans son jardin, sauf en hiver, quand il fait trop froid. Elle nous montre avec fierté les fruits et légumes de son potager, et aussi de magnifiques fleurs de toutes les couleurs. Parfois elle en cueille, et fait de beaux bouquets pour décorer son salon.

English

On Sundays, we sometimes go to visit Janine's mother. Her name is Ariane. Children like to go to their grandmother's. She lives in a small house in the countryside. She enjoys cooking, gardening and watching TV. She also likes to tell them stories from her youth, and they listen with great interest. When we go to visit her, she always invites us for lunch. She cooks delicious roasts, which she simmers for a few hours. When we arrive in front of his house, we smell that good smell. With the roast, she cooks potatoes and a seasonal vegetable, sometimes from her garden. Then there is of course a dessert. She always puts a little meat in my bowl, which I eat quickly, but they eat for hours. And they all talk so much, and often they all talk at the same time. I usually fall asleep halfway. The moment I look forward to is when we all go to his garden, except in winter, when it's too cold. She proudly shows us the fruits and vegetables from her vegetable patch, and also magnificent flowers of all colors. Sometimes she plucks them, and makes beautiful bouquets to decorate her living room.

Vocabulary

Dimanche (m.) / sunday

Aller / to go

Parfois / sometimes

Grand-mère (f.) / grandmother

Habiter / to live

Maison (f.) / house

Campagne (f.) / country

Cuisiner / to cook

Jardiner / to garden

Regarder / to watch

Raconter / to tell

Histoire (f.) / story

Temps (m.) / time

Jeunesse (f.) / youth

Écouter / to listen

Déjeuner (m.) / lunch

Cuire / to cook

Rôti (m.) / roast

Mijoter / to simmer

Quelques heures / a few hours

Devant / in front of

Sentir / to smell

Odeur (f.) / smell

Pomme de terre (f.) / potato

Légume (m.) / vegetable

Saison (f.) / season

Jardin (m.) / garden

Mettre / to put

Viande (f.) / meat

Écuelle (f.) / bowl

Manger / to eat

En vitesse / quickly

En même temps / at the same time

S'endormir / to fall asleep

Moitié (f.) / half

Attendre / to wait

Sauf / except

Hiver (m.) / winter

Froid / cold

Montrer / to show

Fierté (f.) / pride

Potager (m.) / vegetable garden

Fleur (f.) / flower

Couleur (f.) / color

Cueillir / to pick

Exercises

A) Questions about the story

1) Comment s'appelle la mère de Janine?

2) Où se trouve la maison de la grand-mère?

3) La grand-mère aime-t-elle cuisiner?

4) Est-ce qu'elle ne cuit que des légumes de son jardin?

5) Est-ce que Médor mange pendant des heures?

6) Que fait Médor pendant que la famille mange et parle?

7) Est-ce qu'en hiver ils vont tous dans le jardin?

8) La grand-mère est-elle fière des fruits et des légumes de son potager?

9) Qu'est-ce que la grand-mère fait parfois avec les fleurs de son jardin?

Answers

1) Elle s'appelle Ariane.

2) Elle se trouve à la campagne.

3) Oui, elle aime cuisiner.

4) Non, elle ne cuit pas que des légumes de son jardin.

5) Non, il ne mange pas pendant des heures.

6) Il s'endort à moitié.

7) Non, ils ne vont pas tous dans le jardin.

8) Oui, elle en est fière.

9) Elle fait des bouquets.

B) Read the questions and answer in French about you

1) Aimes-tu la campagne?

2) Aimes-tu cuisiner?

3) Aimes-tu jardiner?

4) Aimes-tu regarder la télévision?

5) Aimes-tu le rôti?

6) Aimes-tu les pommes de terre?

Chapter 16 - Short Stories V

Le Lièvre - Hare

Un lièvre était très populaire parmi les autres bêtes qui prétendaient toutes être son amie, mais un jour elle entendit les chiens approcher et espérait les échapper avec l'aide de ses nombreux amis. «À quoi servent les amis, se demandait-elle, si ce n'est pour aider en cas de besoin?» En outre, la plupart de ses amis étaient grands et courageux, donc au moins un devrait être en mesure d'aider. Première elle est allée à la Cheval et lui demanda de la porter loin des chiens sur son dos. Mais il a refusé, déclarant qu'il avait un travail important à faire pour son maître. Je suis sûr, "at-il dit," que tous vos autres amis viendront à votre aide."Elle s'est alors adressée au taureau et a espéré qu'il abrogerait les chiens avec ses cornes. Le taureau répondit: «je suis très Désolé, mais j'ai un rendez-vous avec une dame. Cependant, je suis sûr que notre ami la chèvre fera ce que vous voulez. La chèvre, cependant, craint que son dos pourrait être blessé s'il l'emmenait sur elle. Le bélier, il se sentait sûr, était le bon ami à appliquer à. Donc elle est allée au bélier et lui a dit le cas. Le bélier répondit: «une autre fois, mon cher ami. Je n'aime pas interférer à l'occasion actuelle, comme les chiens ont été connus pour manger des moutons ainsi que des lièvres. »Le lièvre s'est alors adressé au veau comme dernier espoir. qui regrettait qu'il était incapable de l'aider. Il n'a pas aimé prendre la responsabilité sur lui-même, car tant de personnes âgées avaient décliné la tâche. À cette époque, les chiens étaient tout près, de sorte que le lièvre a dû prendre à ses talons. Heureusement, elle s'est échappée.

Collin l'ours Koala – Collin The Koala Bear

En rant que Colin, Le Koala câlins réveillé. Il renifla dans la fraîcheur de l'arbre en chêne. Il étira ses jambes potelées et ses petits bras poilus et descendit d'où il dormait haut au-dessus de nuire. Comme il a atteint le fond, il reniflait un peu plus. Il a cherché autour et dans la distance quelque chose de bizarre, il a vu. Plus il se rapprochait, plus tout devenait gros. Quels étaient ces objets colorés? Contrairement à lui et pas du tout le même. Il marchait plus loin en se demandant ce qu'il pourrait être. Doit-il être courageux et Explorer, ou retourner à la sécurité? Avant que sa mère soit décédée, étaient-ils ce qu'elle lui avait averti viendrait? Il y avait des grands, les moyens et deux beaucoup plus petit que certains. Colin a fait son chemin vers les couleurs vives qu'il pouvait voir. Il y avait des roses et des verts et des jaunes aussi, aussi un bleu aussi bleu que la mer. Hommes... Il a regardé les se déplacer Avec hâte et le bonheur. Ils jouaient et riaient, alors pourquoi a-t-il été prévenu? Colin regardait derrière un arbre si grand. Et a réalisé qu'il se sentait heureux et n'avait pas peur du tout. Il se souvint qu'il n'avait plus quelqu'un à aimer Lui. Donc, Il s'est faufilé sur un sac rouge et sournoisement grimpé dans. Comme les humains emballés leurs biens de quitter la forêt ombragée. Colin enroulé tranquillement à aller aussi, sachant qu'il ne serait pas manqué. Et donc Les aventures de Colin ont commencé...

Grande course – Great Race

Aujourd'hui, cinq animaux ont eu une grande course. Tous les animaux étaient très excités au sujet de la course à l'exception de la tortue. La tortue court beaucoup plus lentement que les autres animaux. Les autres animaux: le zèbre, l'éléphant, la Gazelle et le lion se réchauffaient et se préparaient pour la course. Les animaux se moquaient de la tortue pour être un coureur lent.

"Ha-ha petite tortue, vous ne gagnerez jamais la course parce que vous courez si lentement, plus lente que toute autre chose." Le lion se mit à rire.

"Oui, vous êtes un coach si lent..." la Gazelle se mit à rire de rejoindre avec le lion.

Tous les quatre animaux riaient et taquinaient la tortue à quel point il court, mais la tortue est restée forte et innocente.

La grande course a commencé. La corneille a commencé une annonce: «OK tout le monde, nous avons une grande course avec cinq animaux en compétition: le zèbre, l'éléphant, la Gazelle, le lion et la tortue. À vos marques, commencez!"

Le zèbre, l'éléphant, la Gazelle et le lion ont commencé à courir aussi vite qu'ils le pouvaient. Mais, la tortue a commencé très lentement. Les autres animaux qui regardaient la course étaient encourageants et acclament pour la tortue.

"Pourquoi ne nous encouragent-ils pas?" L'éléphant murmura avec colère.

"Oui, nous courons dix fois plus vite que cette tortue lente et Tardie." Le zèbre cria de colère.

Les animaux ont constamment couru rapidement devant chaque arbre. Soudain, l'éléphant courut avec plaisir, mais soudainement, il heurta son tronc contre un bananier. Toutes les bananes de l'arbre sont tombées et ont rendu l'éléphant vraiment affamé. Alors il s'est assis et a chopé les bananes au lieu de continuer à courir.. Donc il ne restait plus que le zèbre, la Gazelle et le lion. La tortue a vu l'éléphant chomping banane et son ventre a commencé à obtenir de plus en plus grand qui a fait rire la tortue.

La tortue marchait immédiatement devant l'éléphant et commença à bouger plus vite. Soudain, il entendit un grand gémisse. C'était du Lion.

"Ma patte me fait mal, je ne peux plus courir!" Il gémit. Donc le lion reposé et gémit de plus en plus, mais la tortue a porté sur la course. Le zèbre et la Gazelle étaient encore dans la course et ils étaient miles en avant de la tortue.

La Gazelle a rapidement couru, mais il a trébuché et est tombé et cogné ses cornes sur la piste.

"Mes cornes!" La Gazelle gémit "je ne peux pas courir avec des cornes mal!" Mais il y avait encore la tortue et le zèbre dans la course à gauche.

Le zèbre a couru après une herbe verte. Il a fait mourir de faim, alors il a commencé à grignoter chacune de l'herbe qui était là. Il a continué à grignoter jusqu'à ce qu'il n'y en avait pas. Mais la tortue courait toujours dans la voie et il a presque atteint la ligne d'arrivée.

«Je vais gagner, je vais gagner. " Le coeur de la tortue battait. Il a même obtenu plus excité et son sourire étiré sur les côtés de son visage très rapidement. La tortue était sur le point d'approcher la ligne d'arrivée.

"Voici la tortue!" La foule a crié. Tous ceux qui regardaient la course ont été plus soulagés et ont commencé à applaudir la tortue. Soudain, le reste des quatre animaux dans la course entendu acclamations en cours.

Aors, ils ont immédiatement retrouvé la piste et couru malgré des blessures. Mais il était trop tard; la tortue est déjà allé au-delà de la ligne d'arrivée.

"Le vainqueur est............. la tortue!" La Corneill aboya. Tout le monde applaudi et acclamé pendant que le corbeau donnait à la tortue son trophée de 1ère place.

En regardant en arrière, les autres animaux ont réalisé qu'ils étaient trop rapides et ont quitté la piste et ne serait jamais taquiner la tortue à nouveau.

Le Steven Magique – The Magic Steven

Steve était un jeune magicien qui a joué de la magie lors d'événements dans son voisinage. Les oiseaux chantaient et le soleil brillait dans le ciel bleu alors qu'il rentrait de l'école en chemise verte et pantalon marron, tenant son sac magique dans la main droite il était particulièrement Heureux parce qu'aujourd'hui, c'était vendredi, ce qui signifiait qu'il avait tout le week-end École et son ami Ashleigh avait une fête d'anniversaire le lendemain où il allait effectuer sa routine. Steven marchait avec un grand sourire sur son visage jusqu'à ce qu'il a couru dans les trois intimidateurs de sa classe, David, Damien, et Derek.

"Hey dork, qu'est-ce que tu as là?" Damien Dit.

"Oui, qu'est-ce que tu as là, dork?" David a imité.

"Aucun de vos Entreprise,"Steven a dit de retour.

"Qu'est-ce que vous nous avez dit? Peut-être que nous allons le prendre et de découvrir par nous-mêmes. Le Damien menacé, piétinant ses bottes en avant tandis que les deux autres garçons se tenait derrière lui.

"Non, laisse-moi tranquille!" Steven a crié, et a couru devant eux sur le trottoir. Il n'avait jamais aimé ces intimidateur Une odeur familière a dépassé le nez de Steven quand il est rentré. Il sentait, cheesy, et savoureux, et délicieux. C'était de la pizza. Sa mère avait obtenu un grand double fromage, le préféré de Steven, mais il avait perdu son appétit. Steven n'a même pas pris une bouchée.

"Quelle est la question, Miel? Tu n'as pas faim? J'ai de la pizza, ta préféré." Sa mère a dit.

"Je vais bien maman, je suis juste pas que Faim,"Steven répondit.

Il ne voulait pas parler des intimidateurs, et il ne voulait plus pratiquer sa magie non plus. Il voulait juste aller se coucher.

Steven est allé à l'étage dans sa chambre et a obtenu son pyjama Sur. Il jeta ses vêtements dans le panier à linge et éteint les lumières et sauta dans le lit-mais Steven oubliait une chose importante.

Claire L'escargot – Claire The Snail

Claire l'escargot se demandait souvent à elle-même, «pourrais-je être plus occupés? " C'était un escargot très occupé. Elle n'était pas très rapide, ce qui signifie qu'elle pouvait faire ce qu'elle avait besoin de faire rapidement, comme aller au jardin. Ses amis l'arrêteront toujours et diront: «claire, pourrais-tu faire ma corvée en premier?» Claire, étant le genre d'escargot qu'elle était, ferait leurs corvées en premier. Mais parce qu'elle était toujours lente, elle ne pouvait pas faire ses propres tâches après qu'elle ait fini avec la leur. Elle s'est toujours dit «je pourrais faire leurs corvées d'abord» chaque fois que ses amis lui ont demandé de faire leurs tâches ménagères pour eux. Ses amis ne savent pas que donner leurs corvées à elle la rendait malade. Elle ne se sent pas bien. Ils ne savent pas cela, et toujours pensé, "Claire pourrait faire mes tâches en premier." Un jour, Claire a commencé à pleurer! "Je pensais que

,e pouvais leurs corvées d'abord! Elle pleurait. Ses amis se sont rassemblés autour d'elle dès qu'ils ont vu la première larme. "Claire, qu'est-ce qui ne va pas? Qu'avez-vous dit à propos de penser que vous pourriez faire nos tâches d'abord? "Je ne me sens pas bien" claire a dit avec un SNIFFLE, "je pensais que je pouvais faire toutes nos tâches. Mais je suis trop lente et trop occupée. S'll vous plaît ne me donnez pas vos corvées et demandez-moi t les faire d'abord. Ses amis se sentaient mal. Ils ne savaient pas que demander autant de choses ferait mal à claire. "Nous sommes désolés. Nous ferons nos corvées maintenant. Claire sourit à travers ses larmes. Ses amis pourraient être très gentils. «Je suis désolé, je ne vous ai pas dit que je ne pouvais pas faire vos corvées en premier lieu. " "C'est bon. Dites-nous d'abord à partir de maintenant. Ses amis ont dit. Claire n'était plus stressée. Elle pouvait maintenant faire ses corvées d'abord, et elle se sentait mieux.

Le Petit Géant Vivant Avec Les Grands Géants – The Living Giant with the Big Giants

Dans une grande ville qui a de grandes personnes et des voitures, il y avait un petit dinosaure et un petit géant. Le petit dinosaure et le petit géant se dirigea vers un petit château qui était en face d'un grand château. Le petit géant demanderait: "quelle chambre peut-on rester?" Les grands géants qui vivaient au grand château n'ont pas aimé le petit dinosaure, le petit géant, ou le petit château. Ils diraient: "Tu es trop petit. Nous ne pouvons pas voir de petites choses comme vous. Allez-vous-en,les gens petit. Le petit dinosaure et le petit géant partiraient, cela les rend toujours très tristes. Mais ils retourneraient le lendemain. Les grands géants diraient encore: "Tu es trop petit. Nous ne pouvons pas voir de petites choses comme vous. Allez-vous-en, les gens petit. Chaque jour, qui est très souvent, le petit dinosaure et le petit géant serait de retour. Après si longtemps, la patience des grands géants a commencé à porter un peu mince. Un jour, un grand géant s'est mis en colère et a demandé avec une voix forte "lequel d'entre vous a décidé de revenir ici?" Avec un peu bruyant, le petit géant répondit: «je l'ai fait. Lequel d'entre vous a décidé que nous les petits ne sommes pas assez bons pour être autour de vous à nouveau? Les grands géants regardaient autour, ils étaient confus car ils ne savaient pas qui avait choisi d'être méchant avec les petits. Les grands géants ont dit: "nous ne savons pas. Nous sommes désolés d'être méchant. Quelle chambre du petit château aimeriez-vous voir? Le petit dinosaure et le petit géant ont été autorisés à Explorer tout le château, qui était inouï. Les grands géants se sentaient mal d'être si méchant avec le petit géant et le petit dinosaure. Le petit géant leur a dit que c'était OK, et tout était OK.

Le trajet en train – The Train Ride

C'était l'été, en début d'après-midi. Jim a couru dans la station. Le train 4,30 était sur le départ. Comme il courait le long de la plate-forme, il a vu une fille juste devant lui. Elle était jeune--à peu près son âge. Il la suivit dans une voiture et s'assit en face d'elle. Elle a sorti un magazine et le lisait. Il a sorti un livre et fait semblant de faire la même chose. Après une minute, il leva les regarder et lui sourit. Elle ne souriait pas en arrière mais lui donnait un regard encourageant. Les deux sont retournés à leur lecture, mais cette fois, elle faisait semblant aussi. Il l'a trouvée attirante et voulait la revoir. Mais comment l'organiser? Il avait une idée. Il prit une vieille enveloppe de sa poche et écrivit les mots suivants: «Hallo! Mon numéro est 123-4567 et je m'appelle Jim. J'aimerais beaucoup vous revoir. Sonne-moi à neuf heures. Le train est arrivé au terminal. Sans regarder la fille, il lui a remis le Enveloppe ou plutôt jeté à elle et sauté du train. Quand il est rentré, il se fait une tasse de café et se demandait... peut-être qu'elle a été un of les gens naturellement sympathiques qui sourient à tout le monde. Il écoutait la radio quand le téléphone sonnait... c'était seulement Umaru. Neuf heures, puis 9; 30 et aucun appel téléphonique de la jeune fille. Se sentant malheureux, il est allé se coucher tôt. C'était un matin brumeux. 'Hallo, c'est Jim? C'est Joan. Vous... 'il était deux minutes après neuf.

Le serpent – The Snake

Ses yeux s'élargissaient alors qu'ils tombaient sur quelque chose d'étrange. Quelque chose se déplaçait lentement et prudemment le long de la gouttière. Le jaune pâle et brun du corps du serpent ait comme un flot de métal coulant. Par quelle erreur la créa .e s'est-elle égarée dans cet endroit improbable? Impossible à aire. Pourtant, il était, Et ses mouvements lents trahissaient le malaise et la confusion. Comme il le regardait, son antipathie instinctive fondu loin. Il comprenait si bien ce que le serpent ressentait. Il Entré son intelligence froide et étroite et partagé sa perplexité en colère. Ses mouvements étaient à l'étroit, son avance difficile, et il était en danger constant de glisser sur le bord. Maintenant et puis il gisait encore dans la réflexion terne, les soins infirmiers colère froide qui ne pouvait trouver aucun évent. Pendant ce temps, la petite plante plié vers le bas par chaque bouffée de Vent battait ses brindilles minces contre la gouttière comme un bouleau. Le serpent ne semblait pas voir la plante. Il avançait jusqu'à ce qu'une légère touche des brindilles tombaient sur sa tête. À cela, il s'arrêta et leva le cou. La petite plante ne faisait maintenant plus que balancer et plonger légèrement. Le serpent, sa tête encore élevé, attendit, la langue vacillante. On pouvait sentir le soulèvement en colère et l'effort dans le cerveau atone-la colère terne rouge en attente d'exploser. Puis vint une forte rafale de balayage le long du mur, et à la fois Les branches se posèrent aussitôt sur la tête furieuse et la frappèrent avec un mouvement qui semblait à la fois comique et affreux à Osun: en un éclair, la tête se élevés plus haut, le cou recula , et il y avait une fente aux brindilles et l'air vide. O acte fatal! Pour frapper, le serpent avait été obligé dele serpent avait été obligé de s'enrouler , et son corps enroulé ne pouvait pas se soutenir sur le rebord étroit. Aucune récupération n'a été possible; Il surbalancé et tomba avec un bruit sourd sur petit toit plat 50 pieds Ci-dessous. Là, Osun vit la créa ture commencer à se tord à l'agonie. Il pourrait faire Pas plus de torsion et tourner sur le même endroit. Osun tremblait, mais sous son Agitation, Il y avait une merveille profonde, troublée. Voici la petite plante qui ondule maintenant avec une sorte de cynisme jaunty. Et il y avait le serpent se tord à l'agonie. Le monde, incontestablement, était un lieu de mystère et d'horreur. Cela a été révélé dans le se tordant du serpent paralysé et dans l'ondulation jaunty de la plante innocente dans le vent.

Conclusion

Congratulations! You have just read short stories in French and in the process, you have learned French vocabulary and stored numerous expressions in your brain which you can use in day to day conversations. We hope you enjoyed reading our characters' adventures and taking the quizzes at the end of each section.

After reading through all the stories and doing the researches from the reading comprehension part, you should now have a much wider French vocabulary than when you first started. You have also learned some interesting facts about French culture and expressions along the way.

French is a colorful language, with many interesting expressions you may not be able to translate exactly in English. You have learned a few common ones in this book, and might be surprised to hear how widely used they are by French people.

Do not worry if there are still words or sentences you find difficult to understand. Learning a new language is a journey, and we are glad to accompany you along the way. You can come back to these stories any time you like, and take the quizzes again to see if your skills have improved.

In fact, may we suggest you go back to the first story and answer the questions again? You will be surprised to find out how much you remember and how much you've learned!

Our short stories are ideal to be shared and talked about. Their short format means you can use them in a language class or group. Do not hesitate to talk about the stories with other French learners.

One reading leads to another, and you will quickly realize you can now understand more complex stories and structures, so keep reading, and keep challenging yourself with new stories, and soon you will speak French like a native!

Printed in Great Britain
by Amazon

77552642R00312